How to
Write &
Sell Your
First Novel

REVISED

How to Write & Sell Your First Novel

by Oscar Collier with
Frances Spatz Leighton

WRITER'S DIGEST BOOKS
Cincinnati, Ohio

ISBN 1-56865-677-7

Edited by Jack Heffron and Roseann Biederman
Interior design by Chad Planner
Cover design by Stephanie Redman

PERMISSIONS

Profile of Angie Ray originally appeared in *Romance Writer's Sourcebook*, published by Writer's Digest Books.

Profiles of Jonathan Lethem and Jeff Noon originally appeared in *Science Fiction and Fantasy Writer's Sourcebook*, Second Edition, published by Writer's Digest Books.

Profiles of Kathleen Cambor and Jean Hegland originally appeared in the 1997 edition of *Novel & Short Story Writer's Market*, published by Writer's Digest Books.

ABOUT THE AUTHORS

Oscar Collier:

In his more than five years as senior editor of the trade book division of Prentice-Hall and twenty-five years as a successful literary agent, Oscar Collier has edited or agented such first novels as *Fields of Fire*, by James Webb, *Old House of Fear*, by Russell Kirk, and other books that have been best-sellers, book club selections, excerpted or condensed in magazines, made into movies, published in foreign countries, reprinted in paperback and even translated into Greek. He is also a self-proclaimed compulsive reader, having "read many thousands of novels of all kinds" in his lifetime.

Frances Spatz Leighton:

Frances Spatz Leighton is the coauthor of more than thirty books, including such highly successful memoirs as *My 30 Years Backstairs at the White House*, *My Life with Jacqueline Kennedy* and *Fishbait: The Memoirs of the Congressional Doorkeeper*. Her extensive expertise as a professional writer is evident in the research done for this book and in its many how-to tips.

Contents

Part Two:
How Twenty-three Novelists Broke Into Print

Introduction

During thirty-seven years in book publishing, one of my greatest satisfactions has been helping first novelists on the path to seeing their books in print—and sharing that pleasure with others in publishing who felt the same way. The thought that I was helping these new novelists add to the body of living American literature has been a powerful motivator.

Since writing the first edition of this book in 1985, Frances Spatz Leighton and I have received many letters from readers, reinforcing our feeling that first novelists need and appreciate a book that can be a companion as they do the lonely but psychically rewarding creative work of writing a novel. It gave us particular pleasure when some of the letters thanked me and my coauthor for helping their writers actually write and sell their first novels!

It is amazing how the verities of book publishing remain the same, despite the personnel and ownership changes in publishing houses. It doesn't matter how many mega-mergers create supergiant publishers, because, as always, new small publishers spring up and some grow. Whether the ultimate owners of the publishers are American, British, Australian, Canadian, German or Japanese, whether they are media conglomerates or Wall Street speculators or even liquor companies, they still have to hire the same sorts of editors who will resolve to buy the same kinds of popular books from authors who can tell good stories. And no matter how powerful, coldly businesslike and dominant the bookstore chains seem, to succeed they still have to be run by managers and clerks who love books.

The fact remains that publishers—whether giant, old, tiny or new—and booksellers—whether chain, discount or independent—still need good first novels. There is an excitement and drama about publication of a novel by a brand new author who has never had a failure, or middling sales; it is possible to dream of unlimited success.

Editors at large publishers talk about publishing only category books of proved types. In fact they reluctantly go along with change, and actually buy and publish many works simply because they are too good to ignore, whether they fit into an established category or not. And meanwhile, we have seen the appearance of many small literary publishers—and observed first novels being published by university presses.

A whole new category of fiction has arisen, the New Age novel, and gay and lesbian publishing have achieved powerful recognition, with whole sections devoted to them at bookseller conventions. Some genres of fiction, such as romance and science fiction, now have small presses devoted to them exclusively. Audio publishing of novels, including original novels just written for specialized audio audiences such as truck drivers, also has grown enormously. More graphic novels are being published, and one, *Maus*, by Art Spiegelman, became a best-seller. Many publishers are experimenting with electronic publishing, thus insuring the future of the novel as we move toward a paperless society. Publishing has become a $32 billion industry in the United States, and authors are beginning to appear on annual lists of America's biggest earners.

A less promising development has been the appearance of novels devoted almost entirely to extreme violence with detailed, graphic depictions of sex crimes, cannibalism and other revolting practices. The publication of such works, sometimes by major publishers, has provoked an outcry from feminists, some booksellers and the periodical press.

Writers are continuing to move away from the typewriter toward computers, so we have added a brief section on using the computer and word processing programs in writing and editing your first novel—the advantages, and the hazards to avoid.

The trend toward decentralization, which we first noted in the 1990 edition, has become even more pronounced. There are more good new publishers in the South, Southwest, Midwest, Northeast, Northwest and Far West than ever before. Agents, too, are more likely to be in decentralized locations. I myself, after twenty-seven years as an agent in New York, have moved to Ohio, and the headquarters of the agency is now run by a new manager, Dianna Collier, in West Palm Beach, Florida. With modern communications—the telephone; fax; e-mail; courier services with one-day delivery of letters, contracts and manuscripts; airplane travel; and video presentations of authors promoting their books—the country seems smaller, and these new locations can be as effective as the old centralization in New York City, Chicago, Boston and Philadelphia. So I have learned that a taste for new, creative work is not bound by geography.

I remember when, as an agent, I sent over a promising first-novel manuscript to Donald I. Fine, a publisher with many years' experience. He liked it and published it. "Published it" might seem like a simple phrase until you remember what it really means. It means he read it, had others read it, negotiated a contract for it, paid money for advance royalties, as well as for the services of a typesetter, designer, paper manufacturer, printer and binder, and that he devoted time personally and passionately to editing it, announcing it and advertising it.

Finally, bound copies were available, and he sent me one of the first copies. When I called to thank him, he asked, "How does it look?"

"Great," I replied. "It's a real first novel."

With deep satisfaction in his voice, he said, "That is what publishing is all about."

Why do Don Fine and hundreds of others in book publishing bother to read countless queries, study thousands of sample chapters and outlines and read dozens of complete manuscripts of unpublished novelists each year? Wouldn't it be easier, and more businesslike, to concentrate on the plentiful supply of new works by published, proven writers, as some agents, editors and publishers do?

There are two compelling reasons to pursue new talent. I truly relish the prospect of being the *first* reader to recognize a gifted new writer—whether a genre novelist or a new writer of literary works. Reading a promising new work puts me ahead of all other readers in the world in enjoying it. And in helping get it published, I share with the author something that makes us both feel good—*being first.*

If I can get such a charge from merely *discovering* a new novelist, think how much more you can benefit from *becoming* one. After all, it is you, not the agent or publisher, who is communicating with all those readers out there.

That said, I must immediately add that in this book, my coauthor and I have tried to write about the current realities of the contemporary scene in American publishing. You won't find many references to works of the far past or frequent quotations from *Aspects of the Novel*, by E.M. Forster, or *The Art of the Novel*, by Henry James, useful as those books are. We have tried to assimilate the actual experiences of modern novelists as they worked and fought their separate ways to publication, and winnow down the vast amount of material written about novelists in the popular and trade press to the most helpful and interesting information for fledgling novelists.

I have to admit that I've dredged up a few anecdotes from my experience simply because they entertain, and I wanted to share them. And my coauthor, Fran Leighton, has assembled some facts and numbers about the financial successes of contemporary novelists that will boggle your mind.

The statistics analysing how many and what kinds of books are published in America, which appear annually in *Publishers Weekly*, have consistently shown for the past ten years that around five thousand books of fiction are published every year in the United States. No actual figure I know of tells how many of these are by new novelists, because many mass-market paperbacks are first novels, and their publishers make no fuss over this fact.

Ann Burns, who collects information about first novels for *Library Journal*, learns of "two hundred to three hundred first novels each year" from those publishers who respond to *LJ*'s semi-annual questionnaire. But she says that some don't respond, particularly paperback publishers of genre novels. She only sends the questionnaire to a list of publishers she thinks might publish first novels because she knows they have done so in the past. It was her impression when I reinterviewed her for this new edition that the number of first novels published has not increased in the past ten years.

Disregarding "vanity press" novels (because this is a book on how to write and *sell* your first novel), even if 10 percent of all works of fiction published annually were first novels, only five hundred new novelists would have seen their works in print with commercial publishers, plus a few more who self-publish.

An article in *The New York Times Book Review* estimated that thirty thousand unsolicited novels are submitted annually to book publishers, while *Books: The Culture and Commerce of Publishing* reports that 60 percent of trade book editors receive more than a thousand "over the transom" submissions each year.

This number is consistent with my own experience because my small agency gets, year after year, about a thousand queries from first novelists. Such figures prove there are certainly a lot of novelists out there writing—many more than get published. Taking the thirty thousand figure, and assuming that many of these were multiple submissions, let's say five thousand actual first novels are completed and submitted each year. Then, if my five hundred or so estimate of how many are published is near the mark, you have a one in ten chance of getting published, unless you do it yourself. Clearly, it's a highly competitive field.

Who are these budding first novelists? My experience as agent, editor and publisher tells me that they come from practically every walk of life. They are bookkeepers, full-time homemakers, millionaires, lawyers, screenwriters, reporters, criminals in prison, doctors, professors, students, casually employed drifters, computer programmers, police officers, soldiers and sailors, senators, spies, editors, college presidents and other people with something to say in fictional form. They are people with a drive to communicate. They are men and women, old and young, diverse in every way.

How do you make the transition from aspiring scribbler to published novelist? This book will tell you how writers—both famous and still on their way—did it and offer hints from their histories that may help you. Some of their strategies may be well worth imitating.

One of the lessons my years in book publishing taught me is that good craftsmanship alone won't necessarily get you published. Naturally, you must strive to meet certain requirements: show a storytelling flair; offer a feeling for characterization; have a passable plot; use an interesting and well-detailed setting, time frame and set of circumstances; and display a sense of spoken and written language. But a number of other elements enter the picture also, and we'll try to point them out, offering you all the latest tips as we go along in this book.

How often have I heard the anguished cry, "But my novel is better than ones I see published!" And how often it was true! This truth is illustrated by the fact that first novels with many rejections have been later accepted by publishers and have succeeded with the public—even to selling a million or more copies. If such a novel had had just one less submission and never found the right publisher who needed an additional work of fiction at just that time or an editor who loved it, it would never have seen print. It would have been just as good as before, but who would know?

In the true success stories of this book, you will learn how first novelists evolved work methods that won publication. You will see threads that weave through their success stories: doggedness, the will to succeed, attention to detail, knowledge of subject matter, willingness to solicit the help of friends and professionals and inventiveness in overcoming everyday obstacles, such as finding time to work undisturbed. A subplot in the lives of some of these writers was seeing or creating an opportunity and being bold or bluff enough to grab it.

Through experience, I have learned of many common errors and problems of first novelists. So my coauthor and I will not only suggest things you can do, but also will focus on other things you should avoid doing. It is a sad fact that in book publishing sometimes a new work is published only because the publisher cannot find enough reasons *not* to publish it. When your editor or agent is pushing for you, he must overcome at least one devil's advocate—and sometimes it may be the president or editor in chief, who is trying to preserve the capital resources of the company. This person asks people to *prove* that he needs your manuscript. So every fault you can remove from your first novel brings it one step closer to publication.

There are several ways to define a "first novel." Some would narrowly restrict the term to books from authors who published a novel before they published any other kind of book (such as a biography or textbook). Others think that the first completed manuscript of a novelist is her first novel, regardless of whether it is published or unpublished, or published later in the novelist's career. Then there are those who would stretch the term a little more and define it as the author's first "mainstream" novel, or the author's first book published under his real name, and would overlook earlier "romance books" or other genre titles published, not counting them as real novels.

I regard category or genre novels as novels first and category second. Romances are not just books, they are novels, and so are the pulp books of the past called "penny dreadfuls" and "dime novels," in the days when a dime bought a big meal.

In this book, the term "first novel" simply refers to the first novel an author has had published and offered for sale to the public, even if the author has had other kinds of books published before. Whether it is mainstream, romance or any other genre does not matter, nor does whether an author may have used some pen name on past novels—just using her real name for the first time does not make a writer a first-time novelist. And I do not count any other manuscripts the author may have lying in the drawer or even under contract for publication at the time. The first published is the first novel.

The reason I have used this definition is that this is a book about *breaking into print as a novelist.* For me, your first novel will be the first one that actually makes it to a bookstore.

So be warned that what you are about to read is not a guideline on how to write "the great American novel." My coauthor and I take the most unpretentious romance novel as seriously as a work of great literary ambition. This is not a work of criticism, but one on how to write and sell your first novel. Good luck!

February 26, 1997
Oscar Collier
Seaman, Ohio

Part One

HOW TO WRITE AND SELL YOUR FIRST NOVEL

1.

The Heart of It

You couldn't get more obscure than John Wessel who worked in a bookstore. He was surrounded by books—none with his byline. He finally threw up his hands and said, "I'd rather write, even badly, than stack other people's books for a living."

He banged out a mystery, *This Far, No Further*, tucked it under his arm and attended a writer's conference. He didn't realize that already his life was changing. Mystery writer Sue Grafton read his manuscript, told him what was wrong with it and how to fix it.

Grafton promised that if he rewrote it according to her suggestions, she would show it to literary agent Molly Friedrich. He did. She did. And voilà, Friedrich not only placed it with Simon and Schuster but worked out a two-book deal for $900,000—even as Wessel was wringing his hands and fretting, "What if no one bids?"

Asked about it later, Molly Friedrich told *Publishers Weekly*, "It was an obvious standout from the first page." And what does his first page say? The opening line of the book speaks of violence quite casually: "He hits you? I didn't know he hits you." As the blurb inside his book says, "Wessel has fixed upon the cruelty in our lives and conjured up a nightmare."

It doesn't matter what your career was or is. You're a writer now. Barbara Mikulski was a U.S. Senator. She's also a novelist now. She had this idea for a mystery story. She didn't trust herself to write it alone. She worked with a coauthor, a former reporter for the *Los Angeles Times*, Marylouise Oates, and the result is *Capitol Offense*, published by Dutton. And what was this idea that dogged her until she wrote it? Well, it's about a male senator who drops dead while dancing the polka and the female senator who replaces him and is determined to solve the crime.

Janet Leigh was a movie star, wife of a movie star, the mother of a movie star. She is now an author of three books—two nonfiction and her first novel, *House of Destiny*, published by Harlequin.

But you say, "I'm not a celebrity, and I've never met Sue Grafton. I haven't even worked in a bookstore. I'm just an ordinary person. I could never write something publishers would want, let alone fight over."

How do you know? If you don't write it, you can't get it published. Simple truth. And it's the simple truth that ordinary people like you join the ranks of authors every year.

Now let's talk about a man whose name is a household word in every family that reads books, sees movies or has a special interest in the military—Tom Clancy. The year was 1975 and he was twenty-eight. He had never been on a submarine. He had never been in the Navy, or any other branch of the service, because of poor eyesight. He was an insurance salesman, and a good one. Today he is the darling of the military and a best-selling author with *The Hunt for Red October* and a string of best-sellers that followed.

What happened?

What happened is that Clancy, back in 1975, became fascinated by newspaper reports of a Russian destroyer whose crew attempted to defect to Sweden. The ship was the *Storozhevoy*, and the defection attempt was led by the ship's political officer, Valery Sablin. Unfortunately Sablin failed, was captured by the Soviets and executed.

Clancy couldn't get the case out of his mind. It struck him that if the ship had been a nuclear-powered sub, it would be harder to find. He thought of writing a book. He had thought of writing a book before but hadn't gotten far before giving up. This time he meant business. He started researching for the thousands of things he would need to know to make such a book sound authentic. Books such as *Guide to the Soviet Navy* and *Combat Fleets of the World* became his favorite reading. Before he was finished, he had read or skimmed some three hundred books and had dared to call numerous naval brass hats and civilian experts on submarines and missiles for answers to questions that stumped him.

Along the way he learned the naval jargon—both American and Russian—that he would need for authentic dialogue. By 1982, he was ready to write. By 1985, he finished his manuscript and had turned it over to the Naval Institute Press, which had helped him a great deal with his research and was interested in publishing it as their first work of fiction.

In Clancy's high-tech international thriller, the captain of the Soviet Union's most advanced ballistic missile submarine tries to defect to the United States and the White House learns of it. The race is on between the Russians trying to find and destroy their own sub before it can get to American waters and the Americans who are trying to save it.

"I never considered giving it to any other publisher," Clancy told my coauthor, Fran Leighton. "They had been very good to me, and besides, I wasn't sure that any other publisher would be interested. But I did make a mild protest when they offered me a $3,000 advance. I said, 'I have to have at least $5,000.' They agreed immediately, and I didn't try to get any more."

But all's well that ends well. The paperback rights to what became a great best-seller were sold for $49,500 and Clancy started sifting through movie offers. Then he was escorted through his first submarine with VIP treatment. And in 1989, his novel, *Clear and Present Danger*, became a number one best-seller the first week of its publication; and his previous book *The Cardinal of the Kremlin* was at the same time number one on the paperback best-seller list in its reprint edition.

Novels continued to explode out of Clancy. It had taken two years to write his first book after he had done his research. It also took two years to write his second book, *Red Storm Rising*, published in 1986, which again featured U.S.-Soviet cold war. This time his publisher was G.P. Putnam's Sons, which remained his publisher through eight subsequent books, from *Patriot Games*, 1987, to *Executive Orders*, 1996.

As he approached his half-century mark in 1997, it was clear to all that books and movies had given Tom Clancy more money than he can possibly spend in a lifetime—*Clear and Present Danger*, for example, got a $4 million advance. He has everything anyone can want including a large estate. And yet, even so, he is not quite satisfied. He has told friends many times, "I would trade what I do to be a commanding officer of a ship." He told Walter Shapiro of *Time*, ". . . command of a ship is probably the best job in the world."

Though his terrible eyesight kept him from the military career he dreamed of, the irony is that the military has come to admire and envy *him*. If fact, Ross Thomas in the *Washington Post Bookworld* gave him the ultimate epithet when he called Clancy "The Novelist Laureate of the military-industrial complex."

The books of Tom Clancy particularly appeal to men. Now let's look at a writer whose books particularly appeal to women. Olivia Goldsmith was a management consultant in Manhattan, but an unhappy one. She worked with CEOs of important companies and saw the inner working of corporations. By lucky chance, she received some stock options. She cashed them in immediately, quit her job and made a deal with herself.

It was this: She would try to write a novel before her money ran out or, failing that, give up the dream of being a writer and get another job.

Goldsmith looks back at that decision as "the bravest thing I've ever done. I wasn't sure I could finish a whole book." The first thing she did was settle on her title, *The First Wives Club*. Only then did she work on the plot that she was determined would make use of what she had learned in ten years of on-the-job training, so to speak. To wit: (1) Men still rule the world and (2) they then go to trade in their wives for younger, blonder, thinner models who will look good on their arms as they enter famous restaurants. "Trophy wives," she calls them.

Olivia Goldsmith did finish the manuscript, and it was translated into twenty-two languages around the world and has sold over a million copies in the United States alone since its first Pocket Books printing in 1993. But not until she sold the movie rights did her career go into high gear, and now she signs seven-figure book contracts with HarperCollins.

Goldsmith's greatest triumph came in 1996 when the Paramount movie starring Bette Midler, Diane Keaton and Goldie Hawn was released in theaters and became the top moneymaker of all movies playing in theaters in competition with it.

Having found her niche, Goldsmith continued turning out amusing and slightly satirical novels with a woman's slant on life.

And how does she, personally, feel about men? She says, "Girls grow up with the warped belief that there's a Prince Charming out there. Don't get me wrong. I like guys. I even love a few, but romance? Nothing but trouble."

The wonderful thing about writing a novel is that your age and sex have nothing to do with your chances when your manuscript gets to the publisher. Helen Hooven Santmyer was eighty-eight years old and in a nursing home when fame finally caught up with her in January 1984. She was unable to go on a promotion tour around the country, but Putnam's was not worried about the lack of a promotional tour when they grabbed the book and put a $250,000 floor on what they would accept for the paperback rights for her novel . . . *And Ladies of the Club.*

It took Santmyer fifty years to finish her book. We'll talk more about her later, but the point I want to make now is that you won't have to wait that long if you follow a few simple suggestions I've culled from my years as a literary agent dealing with authors, other agents and book publishers. I was, at various times, an agent, an editor and senior editor myself in one publishing house, and president of another. I have seen the problems of writing and getting a book published from all angles. So maybe I can give you some new perspectives on your situation.

Let's consider the question of what it takes to become a novelist—the question uppermost in the minds of beginners: "Do I have the right stuff?"

John Gardner, winner of the National Book Critics Circle Award for *October Light* and a well-known teacher of writing, said it best: You need "an almost demonic compulsiveness." He added that it also helped if a person was suffering a bit from some psychological wound or was driven to try to change the world or himself.

That takes in about all of us. And so, now let's see how *you* are going to change the world or your life, not by grabbing a gun or going on a wild shopping spree, but by building your own little world—on paper.

Don't panic. I don't expect the impossible. You are going to get all set. You don't just sit down at the typewriter and say, "Here we go. Page one," though if you want to try that plan, I have nothing against it. But if you follow my plan instead, by the time you do sit down to write page one, you will feel right at home; you will almost feel that it's *not* your first novel.

First, let's walk around the problem and get a view of it. A few questions are in order.

WHAT DOES THE READER WANT FROM ME?

A story. A reader wants you to tell him a story. He's saying, "Let me have a new adventure! Let me escape from danger." Or, "Give me a new, sexy life. Make me rich." Or, "I'm feeling hemmed in with all this city life. Take me out west and let me see blue skies, high mountains, and let me be on the side of the good guys." Or, "Let me escape to another century (backward or forward), I'm tired of this one."

Your reader is going to identify with someone in your book. And it doesn't have to be someone exemplary. He may, for a brief moment in time—the length of time it takes to read your book—become a master computer bank criminal or head of a crime syndicate. Or he may become a child again, but this time joining a gang that is planning to knock off the local video games arcade.

Whatever you choose to write about, you have to assure the reader in the first sentence that you are going to introduce him to his new identity. Take Somerset Maugham's opening line in *The Moon and Sixpence*: "I confess that when first I made acquaintance with Charles Strickland I never for a moment discerned that there was in him anything out of the ordinary."

Aha, the reader knows he is going to delve into someone else's life, through the narrator telling the story in first person, and he's going to be witness to something strange. Curiosity turns pages, and your opening is there to arouse curiosity.

But that's only the opening line, you say. That's not scary. It's the thought of tackling a whole novel that's terrifying.

It shouldn't be.

WHAT IS A NOVEL?

A novel is a story. It's just a story. It has a beginning, a middle and an end. That's all there is and you can handle it.

A short story has the same things, you say. Right. And sometimes a group of short stories centering around the same locale or people are strung together in a book and then you have something like James Michener's *Tales of the South Pacific* or Sherwood Anderson's *Winesburg, Ohio*.

Short stories are making a comeback and are being collected in book form again after a long period of unpopularity with publishers. One memorable collection, which could be worth your examining, is *Burning Your Boats, the Collected Short Stories*, by Angela Carter, published posthumously in 1996 by Henry Holt. If that is your bent, try a short story. Or a novella, which is longer than a short story but shorter than a novel. It's harder to get a novella published and harder to get it reviewed, but writing one may have its rewards. Tobias Wolff managed to get his 101-page book, *The Barracks Thief*, published by Ecco Press, and though it was not reviewed by a single book reviewer, its quality was such that he received the PEN/Faulkner Award for Fiction, and the $5,000 that goes with it.

What makes a novel different from a short story is its length and plot complexity. A short story usually centers around a single incident that shows the character of the hero or villain or that changes that person's life.

A novel, on the other hand, is a string of incidents that builds to a climax and at the end also shows the true character of the heroes and their antagonists—the villains, opponents or spoilers—or changes their lives. A novel can, but doesn't need to, have many more characters than a short story. A novel can span any amount of time. Tom Clancy, in his *The Hunt for Red October*, covers just eighteen days. James Michener, in his sagas like *Poland* or *Hawaii*, spans many generations.

And there is one more difference: A short story often makes just one point. A novel may, but doesn't need to, have one or more subplots if it has a lot of characters. The main character is working toward her goal, and the minor character or secondary character is working toward his own goal. But the secondary character must have some reason to be in the novel, some connection with the main character even if he or the main character is not aware of it. If he's not needed in that story, sweep him out or cut him out and give him his own story in another book.

My personal definition of a novel is that it is a long work of fiction that transports you into a particular culture, or "world." The culture may be the narrow, exotic world of New Orleans medical examiner Andy Broussard in D.J. Donaldson's detective stories, or the vast panorama of Tolstoy's *War and Peace*, which tells you everything about Napoleon's invasion of Russia.

It can be the world of bohemians, as in *South Wind*, by Norman Douglas, or an examination of a group of people on a trip, as in Thornton Wilder's *The Bridge of San Luis Rey*.

It can be everything connected with a particular problem, such as the shipwreck in *Robinson Crusoe*. It can be all the ramifications of a particular imaginary world, as in Niel Hancock's *Circle of Light*.

But in each novel that's been successful with me—that is, one I enjoyed reading—the novelist has decided exactly what and how she will tell you about a particular set of characters in a particular place or set of places, who live in a particular span of time, and to do this efficiently has created a set of rules and limitations within which the characters must live.

That's it. She has told you no more—not one word or sentence more. A good novel is exactly long enough to tell you everything you need to know to understand the story the writer wants to communicate. When the reader finishes a good novel, he sighs, says, "That was good, but I wish there was a little more of it," and regretfully closes the book.

It is the telling-you-everything part that makes it a novel, rather than a short story or novella.

To illustrate further the important point that you must create a set of rules and limitations within which to depict the world of your novel, think of an artist preparing to paint. He chooses a canvas of a certain size to suit his subject or idea, say, two feet by four feet. He decides what colors to use, maybe only green and brown. He decides whether to paint with brushes, a palette knife, or to drip the paint. He elects to use fine lines or coarse ones, or perhaps just blocks of color. These and other decisions set the rules and limitations within which he must create his painting. If his first choices of size, technique and color prove inadequate for his subject, he might come to regard his first effort as a study and start over with a new set of dimensions, colors and painting techniques for his final version.

So you must decide what elements to use to build the world of your novel, and stick with them, or start over with a new set of rules and limitations.

Ernest Hemingway built a world in which people had to survive in spite of hostility and brutality around them, had to kill sometimes, had to be as brutal as their environment. And even when they won, sometimes they still lost. For example, in *The Old Man and the Sea*, the old man finally succeeds in his exhausting, fanatical struggle with the great fish, and it is the triumph of his life. And then what happens? The sharks get it.

What is the world you like to think about? Faulkner thought about the world of the South, of its post-Civil War sadness, of its old families still trying to dig out from the ash heap of war and slavery and guilt and fortunes lost. He built it—someone said he "rebuilt" it—and he gave it a sardonic yet poetic quality.

Hemingway liked to think about safaris in Africa, bullfight rings in Spain and battlefields where brave men died, and he wrote about all these things with starkness.

Some science fiction writers like to think about the world of the future, and that's why they write about it. They are surely not writing about the world they know. And when a writing teacher or writer-friend tells you you *must* write about what you know, you can either reply that, like Faulkner, that is exactly what you are doing—"rebuilding" what you know into a novel—or you can say that, like Hemingway, you prefer to create a world in your own image.

Writing about what you know is fine, and writing what you only dream about in your mind is fine, too. If you choose the winged horse of your imagination, you can take your readers for as fine a ride as Louis L'Amour did in his westerns—and maybe, like him, you can ride right up the best-seller list.

RESEARCH

It took seven years for Tom Clancy to research his first novel. It took less than a week for him to research his fifth one, *Clear and Present Danger*, including a trip to Fort Ord in California to learn about the Army's light fighters.

All the research he had done for his first book—the total immersion in the military world, from military jargon to mind-set to planes, ships, submarines, missiles and covert actions—served him through his whole progression of books, including *Danger*, with its covert war on Colombian drug lords and its unleashing of foot soldiers and fighter planes.

Talking about his lack of long research for *Danger*, Clancy said he felt no need to see the Colombian jungle because if you've seen one jungle, you've seen them all. As for players, "A warrior is a warrior whether they're light infantrymen, submariners, fighter pilots or whatever . . . the personality types are pretty much the same."

The important point here is that if you specialize in a particular subject, the research you do for one novel spills over into the next and next.

Lola Smith, who writes Regency romances under the name Cleo Chadwick, also reaped the benefit of doing intense research up front. It took five years before she felt perfectly at home in the Regency period of English history. Looking back at that ordeal of study, she says, "One becomes an anthropologist in what someone has said will always be a foreign country—the past."

What she told my coauthor about researching the Cleo Chadwick books could be of immense help to any of you who are interested in writing your first historical novel: "For background, historical novels require not only research into the events of the time, but also the clothes worn, artifacts, words in use, social habits and much more.

"I use a number of specialized works, such as *Life in the English Country House*, dictionaries of slang and English etymology, descriptive works about the area where the novel will be set, guidebooks and cookbooks. I read histories of the period as well as biographies and collected letters of people living during the period. I also read novels, poetry, and magazines and journals that people in that era would have read. They reveal how people thought and how they talked, as well as all kinds of fascinating tidbits of private lives."

You can *learn* what you need to know. There are books to read, places to travel to, people to interview—specialists of every kind, from convicts, junkies and pregnant teenagers to priests, judges and bankers, who have actually lived through the kinds of experience you want to novelize. Your own life can be the background that helps you know what they must think and feel. However, beware of too much research!

Nancy Hale, author of such books as *The Empress's Ring, The Young Die Good* and *Dear Beast*, was lucky enough to have Maxwell Perkins as her editor at Scribners and told him she needed to go to Paris to research a book she planned. To her surprise, Perkins was not enthusiastic.

"You don't want to know too much about it," the legendary editor told her. Writing about the incident in her own book on writing, *The Realities of Fiction*, Nancy Hale adds, "The dead hand of research lies heavy on too many novels." She says she learned that Perkins was right when he told her that what a writer must do is "make it up out of your head."

While I think Perkins put it too strongly, it is possible for too much knowledge of a subject to inhibit your imagination. Remember, you can "rebuild" the world you know into a new one in your novel if you want to.

SHOULD YOU WRITE FOR MONEY?

Without exception, the writers I have represented as agent, or whose books I have edited or published, have been writing to express themselves. They wanted to get paid, of course, because their royalties were tangible proof that the public valued their message. As "Adam Smith" says in *The Money Game*, money is a way of keeping score. But money is second, not first.

Let me give you a striking example. When Norman Mailer completed *The Deer Park*, my favorite of his novels, the publisher that had it under contract required that he change six lines that it considered salacious. He refused and kept refusing even though his refusal threatened publication of his novel. The publisher *did* cancel the contract, and it was not easy to get another publisher. Bennett Cerf, for example, is quoted as having commented, when his firm, Random House, turned it down, "This novel will set publishing back twenty-five years."

At that time in book publishing history, the freedom of authors to express their observations about sexual reality was the cutting edge of liberty.

Eventually Mailer was able to make a publishing agreement with G.P. Putnam's Sons, the novel was published and he experienced the triumph of having his integrity vindicated.

This example is inspiring, but it wasn't Mailer's first book. With his first book, *The Naked and the Dead*, he debated with his advisers and publisher how to treat a certain well-known expletive often used by soldiers. It came out in that book of World War II as "fug." So on a first novel, you may have to make some compromises of a practical nature.

Though the issues are rarely as explicit as the one Mailer faced with *The Deer Park*, you may have to listen to your editor's suggestions and make some changes. Just remember the publisher wants a best-seller as much as you and has guided many books to success.

Publishers make mistakes, of course, turning down books they bitterly wish they hadn't, or censoring books that later are published unexpurgated. So it doesn't hurt to argue a little with your editor!

But certainly until the book is done, you are boss. Now, following some general guidelines from me, write it *your* way.

SHOULD YOU TALK ABOUT YOUR WORK?

Some beginning novelists do better if no one knows what they are writing or even that they are writing at all. In my experience with writers, almost all are better off if they do not tell their plots or ask advice of friends and relatives.

Here is a true story. While working on a manuscript, an editor would ask a writer to rewrite a scene, and having done so, the author would invariably show it to his wife. He would then report to the editor, "She said it was awful!" The editor noticed that consistently the better a scene was, the less the wife liked it. So the editor got smart. He would say, "What does your wife think of *this* scene?" and if the wife liked it, he would ask for a rewrite.

The anecdote serves as a good commentary on the value of an outsider's or amateur's advice. Other writers find that if they tell their stories to friends, writing them down becomes boring, so they don't. My advice to you is to be mysterious.

DO YOU HAVE THE TIME TO WRITE A NOVEL?
THE FAVORITE DODGE ...

Don't tell me you wish you could but you just don't have the time. You may even have a great plot you've been toying around with, or an "idea for a novel" in some incident you saw, or a main character—what a story you could build around him! But you guess you'll never get it done. "No time," you say.

That's nonsense, and the experiences of busy careerists who also write books proves it.

I'm going to tell you in a later chapter a sane and sensible way you can write your novel in the course of three months—ninety days!—without having to do anything dramatic like giving up your job, driving your family crazy or going through the agony of loneliness.

But first, let me tell you that Voltaire is said to have written *Candide* in three days. Ken Kesey supposedly wrote *One Flew Over the Cuckoo's Nest* in four. It doesn't really matter—except to the *Guinness Book of Records*. When a book is great, nobody cares how long it took to write.

It is unnecessary to follow the example of these two writers, although maybe you could. I only tell you all this to spur you on, to give you confidence, to show that you *do* have time.

If you are still not convinced that you have time enough to write a novel, read some of the interviews with first novelists that are in part two of this book. Steven Linakis worked full time as a bookkeeper, commuted long hours on the Long Island Railroad and still managed to write a first novel that earned him more than $200,000.

Okay, we have faced your doubts and gained some new perspectives on your situation, answering some preliminary questions. It's time to become more specific.

2.

Mainstream? Crime? Literary? Science Fiction? What Kind of Novel Do *You* Want to Write?

Many would-be writers are put off by the often-repeated advice I mentioned earlier: "Write about what you know." This hoary dictum can be a killjoy for an imaginative person.

As Matt Hughes says in his 1997 suspense novel, *Downshift*, published by Doubleday Canada, "Truth may be stranger than fiction, but you can't rewrite."

So should only murderers write about murder? Women write about women only? Only men write about men? Should we wait for extraterrestrials to come down to Earth before writing about them? Whatever you write about, the real problem is to make it believable—and you can do that through research and imagination as well as through living.

I'm reminded of the science fiction editor's story: A Martian youngster got tired of living underground on Mars and crashed the spaceship he had stolen to joyride. He landed on Earth. He hadn't the faintest idea of how to fix the ship or how to build a device to communicate with Mars—he had been studying ancient literature in his Martian school. Wandering around New York City, after stealing some clothes off a clothesline, he spotted some books in a drugstore with pictures of all sorts of strange and fascinating creatures on them. Making himself temporarily invisible, he grabbed several, went to a quiet park and decoded the language. With his Martian intellect, he quickly read them. "Ah!" he cried. "I know how I'll be able to make a living on this queer planet. I'll write the history of Mars and sell it as science fiction!"

Easily solving the problems of getting a typewriter and paper, he wrote his first story and sent it in to a science fiction book editor. Right away it came back with a letter. "This is the most unbelievable stuff I've ever read," the editor wrote.

The Martian was outraged. He rushed to the editor's office, pushed aside the receptionist and secretary, and in the editor's office, tore off his shirt and brandished all four of his arms.

"How can you say this is unbelievable! I really am a Martian. This is the true history of Mars!"

The editor replied, "You writers are all alike. You always offer the same tired excuses. When somebody criticizes your work, you claim it really happened!"

The editor's point is a good one. It's not what you know that counts—it's whether *the reader believes* you know something. This effect is also called "suspension of disbelief." You achieve this by being so convincing in your details and surprising as a storyteller, by evoking such strong emotion or by making your characters so fascinating that the reader is hooked and wants to read on and learn more. But your fiction must be largely as plausible as what the ordinary reader regards as fact, or accepts as a convention of your genre.

So widen your horizons. Find out what you need to know to convince a reader in any field that turns you on. And you don't always find the information you need in books. Author Kelly Cherry solved her problem with great aplomb when her publisher, Viking, liked her first novel, *Sick and Full of Burning*, but said she needed to flesh out the character and life of the medical student in it. She walked right up to a medical student at Mt. Sinai Hospital's library in New York.

As Cherry tells the story in *The Writer*, she said, "I'll buy you a cup of coffee if you'll tell me what it's like to be a med student."

What he told her extended the book by fifty pages. It was as though Cherry's fictional medical student got a transfusion of living blood from a real medical student. These pages must have helped round out the book, as it was highly acclaimed.

Whether you want to write a story about what you already know or invent a story based on your imagination or research—and often you will do both—you will still have to examine your potential material and think further about what *kind* of novel you want to write to express your story. So let's examine some familiar types of novels.

MAINSTREAM NOVELS

Is your life a shambles in your well-tended suburban house? Do the neighbors think you have the perfect marriage while your wife is packing your clothes and demanding a divorce? Maybe at least a novel can be salvaged from the situation.

This kind of book, about marriage problems, falls into the very broad classification called "mainstream," or general interest, by publishers. Mainstream novels aim at the wide audience—men, women and young adults. They tell us about problems many people can identify with. In the list of labels publishers use to identify different kinds of novels, given at the end of this chapter, I'll define this category further. But first let's look at some examples.

To see how a famous writer handled marriage problems, read Philip Roth's *When She Was Good*. In an article in *Book Week*, Josh Greenfield said that Roth's engrossing themes of family life were "essentially devastating renderings of the eternal bitch coupled with classic castration candidates—sensitive, well-intentioned, weak men."

The mainstream theme of family or ethnic background has absorbed many writers. The same Philip Roth attacked it with bitter humor in *The Ghost Writer*. Mario Puzo capitalized on the myths and facts about being Italian in America and wrote *The Godfather*. Terry McMillan turned the problems of a modern black woman into *How Stella Got Her Groove Back*.

Other mainstream writers look at the world about them, ponder man's journey through life and ask the question: Can we be happy?

John Updike, who published his first novel in 1959—*The Poorhouse Fair*—wrote of life in a home for the elderly. The book has a message in it, an ominous hint that this is life in the world of the future. Loneliness, the emptiness men feel inside, the search for fulfillment continue in his later and more famous books: *Rabbit, Run*; *The Centaur*; *Rabbit Redux*.

Carson McCullers was dealing with a mainstream theme—the problems of a person who is different from others—when she wrote the book that made her an immediate celebrity, *The Heart Is a Lonely Hunter*. It is about a deaf-mute who eventually commits suicide. She had a particular sympathy for those who could not help their handicaps. Crossed eyes in one novel, a hunchback in another. Even in her best-known book, *Member of the Wedding*, pathos is always present and the emphasis is on the pain of childhood and not the happiness—a familiar mainstream subject.

Grace Metalious picked another kind of subject that has a broad appeal—the outrageous goings-on in a small town. What if someone assembled the secrets of a town and a cast of town leaders—a schoolteacher; a beautiful, sensitive young girl; her beautiful, ambitious mother? . . . *She* did and became a household word with that first book, *Peyton Place*. The book became a movie and then a long-running TV series.

Though the book was clearly about a mainstream subject, Metalious stretched the definition of acceptable subject matter, and *Peyton Place* found its publisher almost by accident. Editor Leona Nevler mentioned the manuscript when she went job hunting at the Messner publishing house. She had seen it at Lippincott, where it had received several readings and been rejected. Nevler had read it and liked it, and she urged Kitty Messner to get hold of it. Though Nevler did not end up working at Messner, she did get the assignment of editing the best-seller after Messner contracted for it through its agent, Jacques Chambrun.

Leona Nevler, who became an editor at Fawcett and rose to the top of that company, told me that in the original manuscript, the stepfather who raped the heroine was really the girl's father. But incest was a taboo subject of that period, and so she persuaded Metalious to make the change. This is the sort of decision a mainstream author often faces: How much can the broad audience take and remain fascinated, rather than be repelled?

So you can see that in writing for the mainstream novel's very broad audience, you will have to pick a subject vital enough to be of wide interest—but keep society's conventions and taboos in mind in deciding how much to reveal about it. Probably like Grace

Metalious, you will want to tell it your way and not worry about whether you have gone too far.

GENRE NOVELS

In choosing what kind of novel you want to write, don't feel shy if you want to aim at a narrower audience. "Genre" novels appeal to readers interested in a particular subject, and often follow a success-ful formula that is pleasing to that audience.

So if you have a favorite kind of novel, say, you buy every new historical novel about kings and queens, then you have a good starting point. In choosing what kind of novel you want to write, remember that other novelists' books can be your textbooks, though of course you won't want to copy them too closely.

One thing you will want particularly to pay attention to is the *length* of your first effort, whether it is a genre novel or not. To have a maximum chance of a sale, your first novel should be approxi-mately the same length, measured in number of words, as successful published works of the same type—certainly no longer, and not a great deal shorter.

You probably have unconsciously studied many techniques of fiction writing, and know many formulas used in genre writing, just by the normal reading you have done in school and for pleasure. And if you haven't done much reading, you'd better start now. One of the questions I ask people who tell me they want to write a novel is, "What are some of the recent novels you liked?" If they can't think of any, I stop taking them seriously as potential clients for my literary agency.

Genre novels can be a good place to get your feet wet as a writer. "Vanessa James," who got her start writing romances, was revealed to be the same person as Sally Beauman, who received a million dollars from Bantam for hard- and softcover rights to her "first" mainstream novel, *Destiny*. Stephen Rubin, then editorial director of adult books at Bantam, called it, in *The New York Times*, "a mainstream commercial novel written at a high level," a good example of editors' jargon.

Let's look at some of the better-known genres in detail, before tackling a whole list of them.

Crime, Suspense and Intrigue Novels

Are you engrossed in the crime news in your newspaper? So was Lawrence Sanders, who worked for *Popular Mechanics* and wrote pulp magazine stories on the side for $75 apiece. Bugging devices were much in the news. He played the "What if?" game. What if there were a robbery and for some reason someone had a tape recorder under a bench and happened to record two men talking about it? What if . . . He toyed with the idea and started writing official-sounding reports and memos. The result was *The Anderson Tapes*, a book that gave him a new career, led him to wealth and allowed him to live where he pleased—in Florida, overlooking the water.

Many new mystery novels are published every year. In my own small agency, we have introduced the Brandstetter series by Joseph Hansen, the Kit Franklyn and Andy Broussard series by D.J. Donaldson and the paperback mysteries of Margot Arnold. My former associate Oliver Swan sold more than a dozen "Apple" mysteries by Marc Lovell to Doubleday, among others—and all this because we like to read mysteries.

Mystery stories take the fear out of death by turning it into a problem of *who* done it. We get acclimated to dead bodies by shifting attention to the search for the criminal.

In building a mystery, some writers start with locale. Patricia Moyes used a ski slope and came up with *Dead Men Don't Ski*, with the current theme of drug smuggling. She turned to Paris and its fashion industry and wrote *Murder à la Mode*.

Readers are interested in the thrill of danger they can identify with. Read the opening of Graham Greene's *Brighton Rock*: "Hale knew before he had been in Brighton three hours that they intended to murder him." Now who could put *that* down? How are they planning to murder him? The reader feels a little chill, a little fear . . . and, important in selling books, an instant identification and sympathy for the intended victim.

Do you devour the international news and every spy story you can find? Maybe it's time for you to work out your own cloak-and-dagger plot. However, in this highly competitive field, just remember you will be competing with professionals, past and present, who used to be in the intelligence world—Ian Fleming, John Le Carré, Howard Hunt and many more—so do your homework carefully.

I am one who enjoys novels that give an insider's view of a particular field and have handled some good first novels of this kind—ex-FBI agent Bernard F. Conners's story about the FBI, *Don't Embarrass the Bureau,* and ex-CIA intelligence officer George O'Toole's novel about the CIA, *An Agent on the Other Side.*

But even these two experts in their fields wanted to try other subjects, too. Conners's second novel was *Dancehall,* a suspense novel about a long-forgotten murder that suddenly surfaces, while George O'Toole's second book was a historical novel about the assassination of President Lincoln—*The Cosgrove Report.*

So if you love a mystery and can see something sinister in what is going on next door, or on the boat where you are vacationing, or in a hotel, on a bus, a train, a subway, you may have your career laid out for you. Though this is a specialized kind of fiction, it has a wide audience of devoted fans.

The new trend in crime writing is the use of a female sleuth rather than the traditional male. Sometimes she's a private eye. Sometimes she's with the police department and doubles as a detective if the presence of a male investigator would be too conspicuous. Sometimes she's just an amateur gumshoe from any walk of life who stumbles into a crime situation.

For example, Carolyn Heilbrun, writing under the pseudonym Amanda Cross, used a witty college professor, Kate Fansley, as the sleuth in her first mystery, *In the Last Analysis.*

Carolyn Wheat, who in real life was a Legal Aid attorney, came up with a female lawyer-detective named Cass Jameson to sleuth her way through such books as *Where Nobody Dies.*

And P.D. James invented not one but two female detectives— Kate Miskin, a policewoman sleuth, as well as your more standard gumshoe, Cordelia Gray, PI.

The message to you is that the whodunit field is wide open. A Gallup poll taken a few years back proved it when it found that six of every ten adult readers read mysteries.

Adventure Novels

Would you choose a life of adventure—at least in your mind? Several hundred pages from now, your daydream could end up as a book that goes on to be filmed for TV or the big screen. The adventure story involves the hero proving himself, proving his manhood or his cleverness or superiority in some way. He must overcome a great obstacle to gain his prize. And he must best a clever, mean, cunning villain.

The action usually takes place in some far-off or exotic place—at the bottom of the sea, the North Pole, in the desert or the mountains.

The prize (which the villain is also after) can be gold, a lost treasure, national secrets. The hero has to get there first and then maybe still have to fight for it. Not till the end is it clear that the hero will make it. Maybe when the hero gets to the treasure, the villain is already hovering over it. Or has hidden it.

The reward for winning does not have to be personal wealth, but it can be. The search may be undertaken to help some good guy, or a woman, or somebody's victimized mother. But the reader wants the good guy to win. And in this day of "upward mobility," the hero may win the reader's sympathy by just being the kind of man who refuses to be tied down to a 9-to-5 job. He can be the kind who cares nothing for money and just asks enough of a fee to get along. He simply happens to live for adventure and challenge. Or he is adventure prone: Someone is always seeking him out for help.

To write your adventure story, it is wise to have reference books around with the proper terminology for authenticity of dialogue, description of action and locale. The public library is the best place to start your quest, unless you want to undertake an adventure yourself!

A book that analyzes heroes of adventure stories from the beginning of history is *The Hero With a Thousand Faces*, by mythologist Joseph Campbell. Campbell shows that the mythic hero receives a summons to adventure, which often he initially resists, just as Odysseus did not want to go conquer Troy. Someone, a god, or father or mother figure, urges him on and gives him aid. He is beset by trials and temptations and has setbacks. Like Christian in *Pilgrim's Progress*, he may become bogged in the "Slough of Despond." But he overcomes knotty problems—just as Alexander cut the Gordian Knot—with wit, ingenuity, trickery and bravery. He is often aided by a woman. He achieves his objective, such as killing the life-destroying Minotaur, and gets his reward, such as the Golden Fleece, and thus aids the world and becomes a larger man.

The James Bond novels of Ian Fleming closely follow this mythic formula. The hero, Agent 007—a symbol the psychoanalyst might see as standing for Everyman, because the lucky number seven stands for the seven openings of the human body, and the "00" adds the eyes James Bond uses so well—usually is called away from a life of childish pleasure. His "father and mother," the characters "M" and Moneypenny, must urge him on and practically force him to accept better weapons (symbols of sexual maturity) in preparation for his mission. He confronts, in exotic places, an organization with monstrous forces, headed by a figure with mythic powers engaged in life-destroying evil. Bond (representing the cement that holds civilization together) must face trials and obstacles. Some he wins easily, but he usually suffers at least one terrible setback. Through wit, trickery and life-enhancing sexual vigor, he wins over his opponent, often with the help of a woman, and in the end destroys the evil monster and saves the world. And the reader is satisfyingly entertained by an ancient story in modern dress.

Westerns

A western is a special kind of adventure story that often is a historical novel as well. One of literary agent Lisa Collier Cool's clients who wrote westerns was in a penitentiary. He could write about tough hombres with real authority. To see mean characters, he had only to look around. Dalton Loyd Williams, author of *Bullet for Gold*, may have been in prison, but he had a pleasure only a few modern American authors have experienced: His novel was translated into Greek and published in Greece, where few modern American novels are welcome.

The western formula has many variations. A cowboy story might center around cattle rustling, or rancher vs. farmer. Fred Grove's westerns, published by Doubleday and Bantam, and winner of Spur and Golden Saddle Awards, often center around quarter-horse racing, as in his *Deception Trail*.

King of the westerns, whom I mentioned earlier, was Louis L'Amour. The number of his titles passed the ninety mark, with many becoming best-sellers. It doesn't hurt that a president reads your books: Former President Reagan let it be known that L'Amour was one of his favorite authors.

Science Fiction Novels

If you daydream of other worlds, have an interest in space travel, space medicine, astronomy, terrestrial navigation, and are fascinated by the mysteries of time and space, you have a pseudopod up on science fiction writing.

Science fiction often deals with aliens from other worlds, or humans on other worlds, in the near or distant future. But it doesn't have to. The key word is "science," and the effect of science on people.

Books published in this field can vary from modestly distributed mass-market paperbacks to super best-sellers in hardcover and paperback alike.

The past masters of this genre, such as Ray Bradbury, Kurt Vonnegut, Isaac Asimov and Robert A. Heinlein, have largely been replaced by *Star Wars* novels and future techno-war stories, but more ambitious new works get published, too. This is a fascinating, but rather specialized, genre, and you might want to join an sf fan club or attend a convention of science fiction fans before going too far in deciding to write in this form. Also, it is one of the few forms left with some good magazines that buy stories. If you want to start out with shorter works, a market for them exists.

Horror Novels

Horror stories dwell on people's primitive fears—of being buried alive, of being captured by monsters. Fear of the supernatural. Fear of madness. Coffins. Corpses. The strange powers of ghosts. Supernatural animals. Dr. Frankenstein and Count Dracula live forever to do their work.

If you want to see how a modern horror story is constructed, read one of Stephen King's books, or those of Dean Koontz. Anne Rice has created what might be called comic horror novels with her vampire chronicles.

Horror can be found anywhere; it can come from the reversal of the usual view of life. Ken Greenhall, in *Baxter*, tells of a *very* bad dog, Baxter, and his effect on the lives of his owners and their children. It was made into a French movie and scandalized the pet-loving French. A few years later, Stephen King also tackled the subject of a dog in his horror story *Cujo*.

If you want to try a horror novel, keep in mind that they demand strong, sensitive craftsmanship.

Comic Novels

Humor looks so easy. It isn't. It just reads easy. Actress-writer Elaine May may have said it best, "Never let them catch you trying to be funny." Humor must seem accidental, must catch the reader off guard. Things happen, and somehow the reader finds herself smiling or chuckling. The teller of the story—the author—seems serious, but the situation is so ludicrous or the character so uncomfortable, the reader must laugh, involuntarily.

As someone once said, "One man's misfortune is another man's joke." Humor is perverse. Humans are perverse. Even if they sympathize, they find it funny. Of course, the discomfort must not be too profound or it will no longer seem funny. Most people, though they appreciate the perverse, are not overly sadistic.

Humorous effects are achieved by saying the outrageous. For example, Jean Kerr describes her son in *Please don't eat the daisies*, as "a slightly used eight-year-old."

Unlike Jean Kerr, Herman Wouk, in his very funny novel *Don't Stop the Carnival*, gets his humorous effects, not from clever retorts, but from outrageous situations. A mildly wealthy New Yorker plows all his money into a small Caribbean island resort in order to get away from it all and enjoy life. But everything turns into an emergency followed by a disaster. He must keep the guests from knowing the resort is out of water. He has a handyman who isn't very handy.

Eventually, our suffering hero finds a bright spot, as it appears that he is about to have his sexual fantasies realized. He has enticed the girl who inspires his lust to sail with him on a boat, along with a picnic basket. Before the festivities with her can begin, the heavens begin first. By the time the couple come dragging back to shore, choppy water, searing sun, wind and a boom that keeps hitting her on the head and throwing her to the deck have rendered the would-be playmate, Iris, into a wet, hungry, cursing madwoman.

New Age Novels

This is a new category—fiction in the same spirit as the countless nonfiction "New Age" books that have appeared in the last few years. In the New Age, anyone can become a prophet, through spiritual study, channeling, being visited by aliens, perceiving ghosts, understanding auras, applying astrology, having near-death experiences or a variety of other ways. Using fictional form to pass along wisdom gained by New Age experiences is a natural development of this movement. As with other forms of literary art, the requirements are simple to state but hard to come by: originality, talent and apparent sincerity.

It's All Right to Be Original

You are not locked into writing anyone else's kind of book. Some of the best writers in the world would be lost if they had to turn out a romance novel to earn a living, or if they had to write a detective story. So go along with your own bent of mind. It's easier when you are just beginning to pick the type of book you like and then start with one in that style or category, or as close to it as you can get.

But if you don't know a single book that does what you have in mind, write your book anyway, and you may find you have come up with a new category, or a new variation on one. Just be sure you still give it a beginning, a middle that is moving in some direction and, finally, an ending and resolution that make the reader smile, cry or pause to ponder your message.

Novels may be categorized in many ways. Some entertain, others express a message and still others do both. Some are "women's interest," some "men's interest," and others "juveniles" or "young adult" works.

You will see references to Southern novelists, Jewish novelists, African-American novelists, Irish novelists. Such labels can have meaning to the experienced reader.

Academic commentators and critics might use periods of time for their designations: the early American novel, 1800-1900; the American novel, 1900-1960; the contemporary American novel.

But you wouldn't want to call a publisher and say you have just finished a contemporary American novel. He would laugh and say, "What *kind* of contemporary American novel?"

Publishers and agents have their own shorthand ways of labeling the kind of book you have. Though not everyone uses exactly the same terms, and their jargon is constantly evolving, I have put together below a list of labels and categories that editors, publishers and agents use. If you study and learn these terms, it will help you communicate with members of the publishing industry.

The list is not organized entirely by logic; it also reflects a "feel" for how publishers think. For example, though a war novel is surely a kind of action adventure novel in most cases, so many major works have been war novels that I give them their own separate heading, confident that if I call an editor and say I have a good war novel, she will understand immediately what I mean.

For simplicity, I've kept the list to just twenty main headings. But when you start dealing with publishers and agents, you'll often hear combinations of these terms, such as "medical thriller" or "comic spy caper."

1. MAINSTREAM NOVELS. This large category includes all works with twentieth-century settings that are intended for the general public, rather than some special audience with a particular interest. Subject matter includes coming-of-age, some love stories, initiation into career and the search for professional or business success, family life, problems of ethnic groups, making it socially, coping with milestones of life. Also included are courtroom dramas, dealing with physical and psychological problems, some religious novels, feminist novels and other works that aim at a serious and profound treatment of their subjects for the general audience. Many of these are called *COMMERCIAL NOVELS*, particularly if they aim for very large audiences and deal with "dreams made plausible," with "larger-than-life" characters, as in some of the novels of Harold Robbins, Sidney Sheldon and Jackie Collins.

2. LITERARY NOVELS. Though good literature turns up in every category, editors use this term to describe some novels, so I do too. It includes avant-garde and experimental novels, fiction by writers best known for their styles, re-creations of classic styles and the "magic realism" of works like *The Infinite Plan*, by Isabel Allende. Most of the work of novelists like Philip Roth, Toni Morrison, Saul Bellow, Umberto Eco and Joan Didion I would describe as "mainstream literary novels."

3. WAR NOVELS. Major works like *Fields of Fire*, *The Killer Angels*, *All Quiet on the Western Front*, *From Here to Eternity* and *Catch-22* shape our thought on this subject.

4. COMIC NOVELS. Some of these are *HUMOR*, such as the novels of Peter DeVries; some *SATIRE*, for example, *Changing Places*, by David Lodge; and many simply show wonderful high spirits, such as *Thank You for Smoking*, by Christopher Buckley.

5. PHILOSOPHICAL NOVELS. These are written to make a point about life's meaning. They can be by philosophers, as *The Last Puritan*, by George Santayana; be *UTOPIAN* or *ANTI-UTOPIAN*, like *Animal Farm*, by George Orwell; or

otherwise express political ideas, as in *Maus*, by Art Spiegelman. Allegories fit here also: *The Book of Daniel*, by E.L. Doctorow. Of still another sort is *Siddhartha*, by Hermann Hesse.

6. MESSAGE NOVELS. These deal with pressing social concerns of their period. *The Grapes of Wrath*, by John Steinbeck, is practically a textbook example of the type. Many of the current crop of gay and lesbian novels are really message novels whose message is a cry to be understood and appreciated, such as *Push*, by Sapphire.

7. RELIGIOUS NOVELS. Except for mainstream examples, such as *The Devil's Advocate*, by Morris West, these are mostly brought out by religious publishing houses. Some religious spokespeople, such as C.S. Lewis, prefer fantasy novels to express their views of the universe.

8. EROTIC AND PORNOGRAPHIC NOVELS. These are about sex. They can be divided according to their intended audiences: heterosexual (men, women and both); homosexual (men, women and both); and those with wilder tastes. Erotic novels, sometimes penned by famous authors, have sexual love as their main subject matter and can be quite varied in style. Pornographic novels are usually more programmatic in their treatments of sex acts, and can be divided into hard- or soft-core.

9. ACTION/ADVENTURE/THRILLER NOVELS. These emphasize fast-paced action, often take place in an exotic locale and are usually set in the present or recent past. *SUSPENSE* is another term used for some of them. Other labels that fit into this category are *SEA STORIES, DISASTER NOVELS, MEN'S ACTION ADVENTURE* (including some war stories), some mysteries, some westerns and some horror/occult (where the main emphasis is on action). The word "thriller" is often combined with another label, as in "spy thriller."

10. ROMANCES. The emphasis used to be mainly on courtship, but now courtship often includes sex. These novels, geared primarily to women readers, may be *CONTEMPORARY*, or set in some period of history, such as *REGENCY ROMANCES*. *GOTHICS* follow the formula of a young, inexpe-

rienced girl in an old house or castle, courted or menaced by a sinister man and usually saved by another man. Some are *HISTORICAL ROMANCES*. A subgenre of these is the *BODICE-RIPPER*, in which the courtship gets rough. Many paperback romance lines of books follow strict (but frequently changing) formulas, and other romances, often in hardcover, such as the works of Daphne DuMaurier, are as individual in treatment as mainstream books. The category is elastic and now includes humor, ethnic stories and romances of people with children.

11. HISTORICAL NOVELS. These include some *FAMILY SAGAS* and *FICTIONALIZED BIOGRAPHIES*, such as Ross Leckie's *Hannibal* or Anna Lee Waldo's *Sacajawea*; some picaresque adventure stories set in the past, such as *The Yellow Admiral*, by Patrick O'Brian; and old standbys such as *PIRATE TALES*. Some westerns are really historical novels. Also part of this category are the sweeping panoramas of a great historical period or event, such as *Gone With the Wind* or *War and Peace*.

12. WESTERNS. Most of these are set in the post-Civil War period in the West, Southwest or in northern Mexico, but there are *MODERN WESTERNS*, too. Typically, they involve conflict between ranchers, cowboys, Native-Americans, farmers, outlaws, lawmen, townspeople, the military, prospectors, miners, mine owners and sometimes dude or tenderfoot Easterners, rich or poor. A few are "comic westerns," and lately, some are called "women's westerns."

13. SCIENCE FICTION AND FANTASY. Science fiction is about the effects of science, technology and social and psychological theories on people in the far or near future. A *SPACE OPERA* is an adventure story with science fiction elements. S/f sometimes involves imaginary "aliens" from other worlds. Fantasy is usually about magic or is set in "alternate worlds" with or without dragons and witches. *SWORD AND SORCERY* tales are set in an imaginary Earth past and may have armed conflict as well as witches and warlocks.

14. HORROR/OCCULT NOVELS. These use creepy menaces such as ghosts, witches, Satan worshippers, revived mummies and other cadavers, and monsters like werewolves, vampires and persons with occult powers to scare us.

15. CRIME NOVELS. These include *MYSTERIES, DETEC-TIVE STORIES, CAPER NOVELS* (describing an elaborate crime in detail), *NOVELS WITH A MURDER IN THEM*, and sometimes a novel just mainly about crime. Mysteries and detective stories may be puzzles, hard-boiled action stories or romances with a detective and a crime. But usually the emphasis is on solving a crime, most often murder. Some *SPY STORIES* and novels of *INTRIGUE* are mainly mystery stories.

16. ANIMAL STORIES. One or more of the main characters of these are usually animals. Sheila Burnford's *The Incredible Journey* is a good example. *Tales From Watership Down*, by Richard Adams, is a very different kind of example.

17. MEDICAL AND NURSE NOVELS. *The Clinic*, by Jonathan Kellerman, is an example. Another is *Chromosone 6*, by Robin Cook.

18. NEW AGE NOVELS. *The Celestine Prophesy*, by James Redfield, is a long-running best-seller of this type. Another is *Mutant Message Down Under*, by Marlo Morgan.

19. DIDACTIC NOVELS. Both editors and academics use this label for novels that are mainly intended to teach, or drive home a lesson. *A Piano for Mrs. Cimino*, by Robert Oliphant, for example, teaches the elderly how to deal with their situation.

20. JUVENILE/YOUNG ADULT NOVELS. Virtually any kind of novel except erotic (juveniles seem to prefer adult works in this area) can be written for younger readers, usually featuring a protagonist who is of the age group for whom the novel is intended.

Some books don't fit readily into any category, and publishers call these "offbeat works," which freelance editor Ann Hukill Yeager defines "as practically a genre—it means 'I don't know if I can sell this, but I'm going to try.' " Franz Kafka's *Metamorphosis*, in which a man turns into a giant insect, is an example of a work that defies classification: Is it literary, science fiction, an animal story, black humor or what? Maybe it fits into another informal category, "quirky," or possibly it could be called a fable.

With such an elaborate menu to choose from, surely by now you have found a type of novel that suits your taste—or decided to create your own new kind of novel. Probably you knew in your heart all along what it was. But if this list gives you courage to *announce* to yourself the kind of fiction you like to read and write best, it will have served its purpose.

TIPS

• Decide what type of novel you want to write. Is it a mainstream novel targeting a broad audience or a genre book appealing to a more specific group of readers (mystery, science fiction, etc.)?

• Your novel should be the same length as successful published works of the same type.

• Read other authors' published books for writing techniques and trends.

• Draw readers into your story with a situation that interests or intrigues them.

• Research your topic thoroughly. Read books, visit locales and speak with people like those you are writing about.

• Convince your readers with details and strong characters. It's not just what you know that counts; it's whether the reader believes you know something.

• It's all right to be original—write what you like. Remember, not all books fit neatly into one genre.

3.

Do I Start With the Characters or the Plot?

There is disagreement on which is more important, the plot or the characters of the novel. Ellis Amburn, the former editorial director at Putnam's, says the plot is more important. You have to have plot to make the reader turn pages.

Stephen King would certainly agree with him. In 1991, he was driving cross-country and entered a little town in Nevada. He could see not a single soul walking or sitting around. King says that, "Being who I am," his mind immediately concluded, "They're all dead."

Then his mind asked, "Who killed them?"

And an inner voice said, "The sheriff killed them." Thus was best-seller *Desperation* born.

William Sloane, Holt editor and independent publisher, lectured students at Bread Loaf, Vermont, writers' conferences during his lifetime that it was character. "People," he said, "are the story, and the whole story."

The debate will continue. You would not remember Scarlett O'Hara if she were only beautiful. The action of the novel makes her unforgettable. If someone mentions *Gone With the Wind* by Margaret Mitchell, we think immediately of Scarlett, but we immediately *see* her in the actions that made her so memorable—clawing the bare earth with her hands to find a few stray radishes to keep from starving, driving the team of horses through the burning city of Atlanta.

But where would plot *or* action *or* characters be without dialogue? Who can forget the confrontation on the grand staircase when Scarlett finally insults Rhett Butler to the point where he is walking out on her. She suddenly realizes she *does* love him, realizes the results of her own actions, and wails, "Oh my darling, if you go, what shall I do?" And then comes Rhett's memorable line, by which the novel lives on in the minds of its readers, "My dear, I don't give a damn."

And there at the end of the novel stands Scarlett, alone and still the spoiled child who cannot believe she will not get her own way. Her final words end the book: "I'll think of it all tomorrow at Tara . . . I'll think of some way to get him back. After all, tomorrow is another day."

And so, let's consider all three as you prepare to start your first novel, your characters, your plot and the dialogue your people will use.

Let's take characters and dialogue—how your characters talk— first. Great characters end up as part of the language. We call her a Camille when we speak of a beautiful woman wasting away, full of suffering. We talk of a Captain Queeg to describe an irascible man, abusing his power. We say he's a Sir Galahad to indicate a man so kind to women. And the same for the villain, for example, Dracula, created by Bram Stoker, who is the very epitome of evil.

WHAT MAKES A CHARACTER MEMORABLE?

Character traits make a character interesting and memorable. Traits that reveal themselves. Captain Queeg constantly clicked those little metal balls in his hand in *The Caine Mutiny*, by Herman Wouk. You didn't have to say he was nervous, driven and a little strange. The balls said it.

You didn't have to say Sherlock Holmes was brilliant in Arthur

Conan Doyle's tales about him. It was enough that he was *shown* as being brilliant while at work. What makes him memorable is the fullness of his characterization—his eccentric mode of dress, his violin playing, his use of cocaine when he is bored, his joy when "The game's afoot!", the sort of acquaintances he had, the kind of clients who brought him their problems.

SHOULD YOU WRITE ABOUT THE PEOPLE YOU KNOW?

Chances are, you don't even know yourself fully, so how can you write about what goes on inside another person's mind? If you are talking about physical appearance and things that have happened to another person, be careful about "borrowing" too much from real life. Tell someone's deepest secrets—*she* was a secret alcoholic or *he* swindled his next door neighbor, Mr. Soandso—and you may end up in court.

The rule is you cannot invade someone's privacy or hold her up to ridicule.

So what do you do? You mix up characteristics as you'd shuffle cards. You take a trait you find in one person and a few from another and one from yourself. You change the appearance and make sure the person who once was a swindler looks nothing at all like the man you know. You make it someone other than his neighbor that he cheated. You leave out the real story of how his fiancée found out about it and killed herself on their wedding day because she feared he was marrying her for her money. That has to be shuffled too, and the details removed from your version.

You write fiction, not fact. But even then there is sometimes no way to keep people from seeing themselves.

After the success of her book *Hollywood Wives*, Jackie Collins found that dozens of people in the movie colony identified with one or another of her characters with varying reactions. She had just arrived at a Beverly Hills restaurant with her sister, actress Joan Collins of *Dynasty*, and had ordered a drink. A producer who thought he had been portrayed in the book came storming over and threw a glass of champagne in her face.

Keeping her cool, Jackie Collins said, "Hmm, tastes good. Let's order some more."

William Styron, whose memorable book *Sophie's Choice* also became a memorable movie, admits that his character Sophie was indeed rooted in reality to a certain extent, or at least inspired by a woman he met. As he told students at George Mason University, in Fairfax, Virginia, he was introduced to a "beautiful Polish survivor of Auschwitz. Sophie didn't speak English very well and I was ten years younger than she. . . . Though I was infatuated with her there was clearly no way we could bridge the gap."

But Styron's imagination did bridge the gap, weaving a fictional story of an awful and agonizing secret Sophie was hiding, set against her passionate romance with an emotionally unbalanced biologist.

Judith Krantz, author of *Scruples*, told *Los Angeles Times* reporter Pat Nation, "A novelist has to be schizophrenic without being mentally ill. You draw on a lot of facets of your life for characters and then fictionalize." She added that "a sliver of myself" was in all her characters.

HOW DO YOU BUILD A CHARACTER?

You build a character by asking yourself questions about the person to which only you know the answers.

"Is she tall?" Yes. She's six feet tall. She *hates* it. A little guy is in love with her and keeps following her around. He owns a fabulous resort. She says, "He's taller when he's standing on his money." She can't get rid of him, she says.

Maybe that's the start of a humorous novel about the making of a showgirl who is the top attraction of the nightly show at the short guy's resort. Or maybe she is rich and he is poor and she says, "He's taller when he's standing on *my* money." Maybe she becomes a stand-up comic in nightclubs and this fellow seems to be following her all around the country. At first it seems kind of funny and she starts making quips about size the moment she spots him in the audience. But, eventually, a sinister note creeps in, and she is terrified. It develops into a horror story in which he is a psycho and wants to lock her up and possess her all by himself—no more men looking at her in a nightclub. Or he has been sent to kill her so that someone else will inherit a fortune.

As you see, the plot can grow out of the character, and the character and plot are locked together.

But back to character development. Suppose you're writing a serious novel about a young divorcée involved in a custody fight over a set of twins. Her husband has played Solomon and said,

"Let's separate them, share and share alike." The court case is about to begin.

You will need to know a lot about the husband, the wife, even the judge who handles the case and the wife's best friend, to whom she has confided many things.

Let's take just the wife and write down the answers to all the questions about her so you can read them until you know her inside out and she is alive in your mind:

- How old is she?
- What are her bad habits? Her good ones?
- Is she pretty? Is she conceited?
- What about her disposition?
- Does she really love those children? How do you know? (Maybe she once stood in the rain for an hour to buy them a treat.)
- Does she have a job? Is money a problem?
- What are her hobbies?
- Is she a good housekeeper? Does she have a maid?
- What kind of education did she have? Did she get good grades?
- What was her earliest ambition? Was it achieved?
- Is she artistic in any way?
- How did she happen to marry this man? Did they have an affair or live together first? What irritates her about him?
- What was her background like? Did her parents get along with each other? Did they show her love? Is there some secret in her family? Does she know it?

Start having conversations with her in your mind. What does she say? What is her speech pattern? Suddenly she tells you the twins aren't even his. She doesn't know whether to tell the court. She has never told her husband.

If you are writing the novel from the standpoint of the husband, you might find out different things about her. He says what irritated him most was her attitude toward personal grooming, which he took as a studied insult. "If she had taken a bath now and then, I might have stayed around longer." It galled him that she had only two pairs of panties in spite of all the money he gave her, and wore stockings with snags in them.

It's earthy but we are building real people with real quirks.

Truth within the boundary of the book is what you are looking for. No man is an island but each book *is*. And you are placing every character who lives on that island and will live there forever. When your reader closes the book, she can hop to the next island, but your characters remain on the island to intrigue the next person who picks up the book.

You, as the author, are building a world. *You* make the ground rules. You decide the rewards and punishments of life. Is goodness rewarded? Is goodness even at issue? Does a murderer in some instances deserve to go free, and does the heroine help him escape? Only you have the answer.

To get to the answer, you have to know that heroine by asking all kinds of questions. Is she afraid to open her front door? How does she say hello to people? Is she really evil inside and pretending to be sweet and kind? Or is she so kind that people take advantage of her, saddle her with their dirty work? Is she capable of suicide? Would she slap someone or run to her room and cry and hide her hurt? Would she raise her voice? What *would* make her raise her voice? What do the neighbors say about her? How do they treat her and she, them?

You may not use all these facts in your novel, but you need to know them so *you will know* how she would react when good things and bad happen in your plot.

Your characters have to be compelling and powerful to keep you and the reader interested. But that doesn't mean they are necessarily physically or morally or mentally strong. Walter Mitty, the invention of James Thurber in *The Secret Life of Walter Mitty*, could not stand up to his wife, the parking lot attendant, or even the man selling him dog biscuits. But in his dream world, he was a giant—a bomber pilot, a surgeon, a condemned martyr, among others.

If some character is weak, make him a fascinating case of weakness. If he is evil, let the evil shine through. Let it flow until the reader is filled with it and understands it or accepts the truth of it. Or if the evil man masquerades as virtuous, let there be signs of it so the reader suspects he is a snake. An exception would be if you're writing a murder mystery and the snake is the least likely suspect until the very end. But even there, you still give the reader clues— subtle, hidden ones.

Remember that nobody is all one thing or the other. To be believable, the evil man must have some goodness in him, no matter how slight. Perhaps on the way to kill someone, he stops to feed a hungry alley cat. And the good guy is not all that good. He flirts with another man's wife or borrows money and doesn't care if he pays it back.

The clothes your characters wear are important because they make a statement about their wearers. If the great Gatsby had not worn the clothes he did, he wouldn't have been *The Great Gatsby* who cared so much about his facade that he built his whole life around impressing the girl who got away. F. Scott Fitzgerald's Gatsby, as well as Thurber's Mitty, have become a part of the English language.

HOW DO YOU MAKE A CHARACTER SYMPATHETIC?

Editors frequently tell first-time novelists their characters are not sympathetic enough, giving them the kiss of death with the comment, "Who cares!" Well, the reader had better care or you don't have a sale.

So how do you make characters sympathetic? In many ways. If they're put upon by spouses, salespeople, and other intimidating people like Walter Mitty is, you want them to enjoy their dreams, at least. "Please win," the reader tells them. If the *reader* also feels put upon, the reader becomes the hero in the fantasies as well. The great Gatsby wins your sympathy because you want him to succeed in getting the attention of his love, Daisy. Almost everyone can identify with someone seeking to regain a lost love.

Having a noble goal for which someone scorns him makes a character sympathetic. A young man works hard to perfect himself at his sport instead of going after money and a good job. It is his secret dream to be in the Olympics. Someone important to him and "successful"—maybe a relative—treats him as if he were a bum and says condescendingly, "What do you want to be?"

Eagerly the young man says, "A champion." The smug one looks at him without a flicker of expression and says, "They're a dime a dozen." The young man may not have the sympathy of the successful man, but he has ours.

If the character has a strong goal, the reader will be eager for her to achieve it. If the character is in any kind of danger, the reader is immediately on her side. And the same goes for a character beset by problems, held up to ridicule or scorn or made to look foolish. But you, the author, have to be careful. If the hero goes too far in retaliation by maiming or killing the tormentor, sympathy may turn to contempt or disgust.

YOUR CHARACTER MUST GROW

To be real and interesting, your character must change and advance, or regress, or somehow be different at the end of the novel than he was at the beginning. Characters cannot remain static and neither can real live people unless they are in a catatonic state—and even then they may come out of it!

Think of Scrooge in Dickens's *A Christmas Carol*. He seems so mean and despicable that the reader is almost ready to give up on him, but Dickens makes something happen—a dream—that changes him into a wonderful man at last. You don't have to go that far in your character change—only a Dickens could pull off such a switch— but there can be a less drastic turnabout. Perhaps your character learns a lesson that makes him suffer a bit in silence instead of berating his wife, whose mannerisms annoy him.

Or perhaps he learns that the only way to handle a bullying wife is to confront her right away, not wait and make excuses. Or he makes a decision—to give up his empty dream of starting a new life and settle down to live life now, where he is, with his family.

Whatever he chooses, something vital must hang on it. The decision must matter. And if it matters to your character, it will matter to your reader, and she'll care how it all comes out in the end.

YOUR CHARACTERS CAN GROW
FROM THEME, OR VICE VERSA

Maybe you know what your book is about but have to decide how to make the meaning come alive. Harriet Beecher Stowe had her theme first—slavery and how vicious it was—and her plot in *Uncle Tom's Cabin* arose from her knowledge of slave stories. But until she came up with her characters, Uncle Tom, Little Eva, Topsy and Simon Legree, she could not realize her theme with full force. She wrote a story, not a sermon, and made her characters spring to life so well the resulting novel helped change the history of a nation.

Evan Hunter is a contemporary "thematic" sort of novelist. He started with the theme of fear in the schools—danger resulting from a lack of discipline. How did he know about it? He was a substitute teacher for a short while. He came up with *The Blackboard Jungle*, a novel so successful it not only brought his message to the public as a book, but also again when it was made into a compelling movie. Hunter has said that only after he knew the point he wanted to make did he pick characters and actions to express it. For such a work, a novel is a train of thought pulled by a "theme" engine.

Now let's take a case where the character came first. This legendary story of the book trade tells how Somerset Maugham, the commercially successful British novelist, got the idea for "Rain," a story that became part of his book *The Trembling of a Leaf*, set in the tropical islands of the Pacific.

Maugham was traveling in the Pacific with a male secretary-companion and happened to be in Honolulu when the respectable wives of the community were trying to close down the Iwilei red light district.

Maugham went to see what all the fuss was about and even had an interview with a lady of the night who made him pay double because talk took longer than sex. He also went to court after a police raid to listen to what the judge had to say.

Some of the women opted to leave the island, and it was Maugham's fortune to have a stateroom near one of them who almost drove him crazy by playing her gramophone at all hours of the night and doing a lot of late entertaining with laughter and liquor much in evidence. The woman, whose name was Miss Sadie Thompson, became an object of obsession and fury.

Maugham was much relieved when they docked in Pago Pago because that would be the end of Miss Thompson and her eternal noise machine. His companion, Gerald Haxton, who was not as shy as Maugham, had found out that she planned to get a job in a bar.

Fate stepped in in the form of a quarantine. Maugham found himself in Pago Pago hemmed in by mountains drenched by torrential rains that alternated daily with horrible heat. He quickly developed a fungus on his body and had to spend days in his room, nursing the rash. Fate struck again when Miss Sadie Thompson got a room right across from his in the little *pensione* where he had found pathetic lodging.

Now he had to listen not only to her gramophone but to the squeaking of the bedsprings. Miss Thompson had taken a Samoan lover.

Bored and miserable, Maugham played the game of "What If?"

to while away the time. He had had a single encounter with a missionary's wife before the onset of his affliction. She had bragged about all the souls her husband was saving as he made the rounds by boat from island to island, and how, when they had arrived on the islands, they had found not one single *good* girl, so depraved was the life of the natives.

What if, he wondered, the missionary saved Sadie Thompson's soul? What if he became obsessed with Sadie, persecuted and pursued her, preached at her (the man who raised Maugham was a vicar) offered her pure love instead of the wicked love she was enjoying with the native boy, hammered and hammered at her until she broke down? Then what if, after she is brought to her knees and confesses her sins and seeks repentence, the missionary cannot resist her himself? Well, that's a twist. What happens then?

Maugham had plenty of time to think about it as he listened to the rain and tried not to feel the rash. He made a note about his resolution of the plot: The missionary is found dead—he has slit his own throat. And Sadie? She's the old Sadie again with the gramophone going full blast. Maugham even wrote down the last line. Sadie looks at a passing group of men and spits out the words, "Dirty pigs."

DIALOGUE BRINGS YOUR CHARACTERS TO LIFE

What brings the plot to life is the characters. What brings the characters to life is dialogue—with each character having his own way of talking. Someone once said that if you can't tell which character is talking, if they all sound alike, none of them is talking; it's the author who is talking.

If that happens with your characters, you're in trouble. Try to keep your own speaking pattern out of it. Give each character his pet expressions, even if you hate those expressions yourself. Give each his favorite words and each a different cadence.

Each speaker has his characteristic pattern, his "speech tune." For fun, try imitating someone's speech without using words—just nonsense syllables. Usually you'll find that you can do a good imitation, even get across emotion, without a single recognizable word. Each character will sound a little different from all others. Some will use long words, some short, but usually in a characteristic mixture. Once you have identified the rhythm, the speech tune, of a character, it will be easier to hear this character speak in his own voice in your mind, or when you say his words aloud.

Should You Use Foreign Accents or Dialects?

It's most difficult to copy a foreign accent throughout a novel and very hard to read if you do. You can use just a garbled word now and then to suggest the accent, but better yet, you can show by the speech pattern—the order of the words in the sentence—that a different sound exists.

You can also solve the problem by saying something like, ". . . she said in her thick Irish brogue." Or, "He spoke with a heavy German accent." Or a "slight shadow of a Swedish accent still remained." Or, "She seemed warmer, more approachable than her staid Yankee neighbors, maybe because of the way her voice still reflected the warm sunshine on the vineyards of her native Italy. Her hands, too, conveyed her message of hospitality."

There's always an exception. Black writer Sapphire, who has a single name byline, uses dialect in her first novel, *Push*, and carries it off very well, so well that she received a half-million-dollar advance on a two-book deal from Knopf.

Her book opens with, "I was left back when I was twelve because I had a baby by my fahver. . . . This gonna be my second baby. My daughter got Down Sinder. She's retarded."

Another first novelist, Deborah Iida, employs pidgin English to tell the story of a Japanese-American family in the sugarcane fields of Hawaii. The novel, *Middle Son*, was published in 1996 by Algonquin.

Once in a while there is a book that depends almost totally on a heavy dialect. Such is the case with the hilarious *The One Hundred Dollar Misunderstanding*. It's the story of a white and not too bright adolescent who falls into the hands of a young, streetwise black hooker. The hero has a hundred dollars and is very happy about it. The misunderstanding comes when *she* thinks the money is for her and *he* thinks she likes him for himself. The whole book, by Robert Gover, revolves around the hooker's desperate efforts to separate the money from the teenager.

Much of the humor comes from the difference in their thinking and their speech patterns—his earnest, simple "whitey" speech against her black English gutter talk. Her vocabulary abounds in raunchy insults and endearments that neither he nor the average reader has heard before. Without dialect, without the hooker's unique speech pattern, which gives a glimpse into a strange, colorful subculture, there would be a weak story and no book.

How Do You Make People Sound Natural in a Novel?

How do real people talk? They talk like you. They talk like me. They don't always finish sentences. They speak in fragments of sentences. They seldom make long statements. It's usually short comments with dangling participles and dangling emotions tossed back and forth that is the real stuff of dialogue between two people. And if one seems to be launching into a long speech, the other is apt to say, "Shut up, darling. I've heard that before." That's in a happy kind of conversation. If they are angry, the comments are tossed much faster and collide in midair, overlapping each other.

How your characters talk will also depend on the part of the country or way of life they come from. A western rancher is apt to be taciturn. A Southern girl might be bubbly, a Hollywood matron openly materialistic.

Here's how Joseph Hansen renders light sexual banter between two gay men in his detective novel, *Gravedigger*.

"Look at that," Cecil said, and poked at the omelet with his fork. "What is *in* there, man?"

"Avocado," Dave said, "Cheese."

"Oh, wow." Cecil took a mouthful. His eyes widened. He opened his mouth and panted. "Hot!" he gasped.

"You wouldn't like it cold," Dave said. He pushed the basket of corn bread at him. "You want to play detective with me today? Or have you things to do?"

"Only thing I have to do is you," Cecil said. "Forever. From now on. All right?"

"All right." Dave smiled. "But I won't hold you to it."

"Hold me," Cecil said, "any way you want. Only the last time I played detective with you, you nearly got killed . . ."

Do You Need Much Dialogue?

Yes, you need a lot of dialogue in most novels. It can become dull to read that someone did this and then he did that. It's interesting, on the other hand, to listen in on his conversation, say, one in which he is bragging to a buddy about how he handled that blind date who was trying to wreck his finances at their first dinner together. "I told her, 'Listen, stupid, if you think . . .' "

You don't just *recite* what happened, you show it happening. You talk it through with someone who, in effect, is speaking for the reader by asking the right questions. "But Sam, why did you have to lie to him?" Or, "But Muffie, I thought you hated Jim after the rotten things he said about you to the judge. How come you let him come in the door, let alone stay the night?" The reader's sentiments exactly.

Or this one: "Quick. Behind you!" How much better than: "He shouted to his friend to turn around quickly."

In a normal conversation between two people, it is distracting to read "He said" or "She said" with every line of dialogue. You know who is speaking most of the time, so just an occasional "He said" or "she replied" will keep the reader on track. It is also distracting to read dialogue in which the author has reached for every variation of "said"—asserted, breathed, exclaimed, stated, averred, and on and on. Unless the character really hisses or bellows out the words, don't bother to say so. It's the mark of the amateur to use elaborate variations on "said" just to seem erudite.

You must consider several things in writing dialogue. One is that people talk differently when talking to their peers than when talking to someone who makes them nervous or on guard, such as a boss, parent or social superior. The dialogue must reflect this difference. The vocabulary is different. Sinclair Lewis uses this effect brilliantly in his novel *Babbitt*. When Babbitt visits a pillar of the community, he becomes tongue-tied, embarrassed and overly formal. But when he entertains one of his subordinates, he is jolly, voluble and at ease. As the scenes follow one another, the contrast is easily visible to the reader and reveals much about Babbitt's character and his failure as a social climber.

As part of your building of an adolescent male character in your novel, take a sheet of paper and write down that character's favorite words in talking to his gang members, his father, his mother, his kid sister, his teacher. Maybe with a person he feels safe around— his little sister, perhaps—he rambles on, with "like" and "Right?" thrown in a lot. With a particular teacher, he might be taciturn, sullen, only answering in monosyllables. The reader gets to know that when the boy starts "sir"ing his father, he is going to ask for money or some favor.

Do the same with each of the other major characters. Not only the words but also the tone of voice you choose for your characters convey their emotions—whether love or contempt.

WHAT ARE THE FUNCTIONS OF CHARACTER AND DIALOGUE?

Why have we been discussing the people in your novel and how they talk? Let's go back to the disagreement between the editors at the beginning of this chapter, over whether character or plot was more important to the novel. I'm now ready to take a stand.

I believe the plot is more important, because the plot has the entertainment value that pulls the reader along. The characters are your vehicle, the tools through which you tell your story. If they are strong, they strengthen the plot and the hold on the reader.

But when readers buy a book, they are saying, "Tell me a story."

TIPS

• Character traits make a character interesting and memorable. Build real people who have real quirks.

• Look to others—and to yourself—for characteristics and inspiration. But be sure you are writing fiction, not fact.

• Get to know your characters inside and out. You should be able to answer any questions about your character, whether you actually use that information in your novel or not.

• Balance the good and the evil in each character.

• Clothing can say a lot about the wearer. Your characters' clothing should reveal something about them.

• Make the reader care about your characters. A character with a strong and noble goal, or one who overcomes great obstacles, will have the reader on her side.

• Characters, like people, must grow and change. Don't let your characters remain static throughout the novel.

• Give each character his own speech patterns, pet expressions and favorite words.

- Nationality is an important part of character development, but be cautious when writing in dialect.

- Characters speak just like real people. Use short statements, sentence fragments and interruptions to give dialogue a natural feel.

- Show action through dialogue. The reader wants to hear the character's voice, not the author's.

- Be sparing with the use of "he said" and "she said."

4.

Four Steps Are
All It Takes

By now you are starting to get comfortable with the idea of your own novel. You have some characters, maybe you even have some snatches of dialogue. You may have a message or theme you want to express. But to use these elements, you need to decide how to express your story with action.

WHAT YOUR NOVEL IS ABOUT

Maybe you are worried about finding a good plot. So before getting into a detailed discussion about the structure of your novel, I would like to suggest a plotting aid that arrives fresh every day and costs little to buy—the daily newspaper.

Every issue has material for a dozen plots: A teacher is arrested for sexually abusing a child. The plot thickens: the police raid his home and find pornographic pictures and proof that he belongs to a ring that sells such pictures.

Or, from the same paper: A new journey into space is about to begin. Astronauts are going to have to leave their ship to correct something in another orbiting satellite. What if something were to go wrong, threatening their lives, and another spacecraft must try to save them within a certain length of time?

Or another news story: A sunken treasure is being hauled up from the bottom of the sea. The salvagers must keep the exact location of the sunken ship secret. What if they don't and a modern pirate arrives?

The Ann Landers or Dear Abby columns: Just one week's letters have enough plots to keep writers going for a lifetime. The anguish of a woman who knew of an incestuous relationship between her husband and daughter and said nothing. The secretary who says she is having an affair with her married boss and is not sorry, because, from what he tells her, his wife, the mother of six, has let herself go.

Or, you can reuse one of the oldest, strongest and simplest plots: Boy meets girl, boy loses girl, boy finds girl. That's the plot of *Rebecca*, and every other happy love story. If boy *doesn't* find the girl again, you have *Love Story*, Erich Segal's super best-seller, and hundreds more. But in each story, the characters and details, the opening and ending, are individual inventions of the author.

Let's take a closer look at the structure of a novel. An easy way to think of it is as having three parts: the beginning, the middle and the end.

Suspense writer Graham Greene, speaking at Georgetown University, said, "I generally have a character, a beginning and an end. In between, the middle develops in a way I don't foresee." That's his way. You'll see others. Look at each part of a novel and you'll see what other famous novelists have done with them.

THE JOB OF OPENING LINES

The beginning of your novel must grab the reader and also give a hint of what to expect. If it's a cowboy story, start with your hero moving through the outdoors, or with a confrontation. If it's an adventure or mystery, let a little shadow of danger or some clue appear in the first paragraph—or a suspect or some portent or some concern the main character has about his own safety or the fate or safety of someone he knows or is told about.

If it's the genre of book that publishers call "Romance," let there be assurance right from page one or sentence one that this is going to be about the ins and outs of romance and courtship. Let it be clear that this will be a woman's or girl's mighty struggle to achieve happiness—which in this case translates into finding the right man and falling in love.

Books that cater to females no longer have to be peopled with heroines who only learn about sex on their wedding nights. Look at the opening of a Jackie Collins's book. She has developed a following of millions of women across the country and a good share of men as well. In *The World is Full of Divorced Women*, the first sentence finds the heroine's lover asking her, "Are you bored with sex?" And immediately you learn that she is not bored with sex but bored with him.

In using this first line, Jackie Collins shows she realizes the importance of putting the subject of her novel, sex, right up front. Another writer, Stephen Shadegg, author of a first novel about politics, *The Remnant*, and of a number of nonfiction books, told me how he learned this same lesson early in his career when he was writing for pulp magazines. He sent a story to his editor, and it came back with the notation, "Not enough sex in it."

Shadegg telephoned the editor and said, "What do you mean there's not enough sex in it? There's sex on the first page."

The editor replied, "Yes, but it's near the bottom of the page."

Now let's see how a master of international intrigue, John le Carré, opens his best-seller *The Little Drummer Girl*, how he catches the reader's curiosity in the first sentence while setting the stage in the proper location: "It was the Bodesberg incident that gave the proof, though the German authorities had no earthly means of knowing this." And before you finish the first paragraph, you know a poorly made bomb is involved and that there are clues in the way a bomb is made that give away the identity of the maker, that in effect he leaves his signature on it.

Some editors say that they can almost be sure when they read that opening sentence or paragraph if a book will be well written and exciting enough to publish. Editor Ellis Amburn says, "The beginning novelist is apt to dally around till he gets in gear, or put another way, he meanders until he gets his bearings. In a play it's called 'the horrible scene' where the playwright tries to explain who everyone is and all the relationships. It isn't good in a play and it wrecks a novel." Move quickly into action or conflict.

THE ENDING TELLS YOU WHERE
YOU ARE GOING TO GO

Endings are equally important. Editors prefer a happy ending because readers prefer a happy ending, but happy or not, the ending should tell what happens and *not leave the reader dangling*. Let the reader have the satisfaction that comes with at least knowing the outcome on all the problems and issues that have kept her turning pages all through your book.

Inga Dean couldn't decide how to end her first contracted novel dealing with a woman's unhappy marriage to a Washington, DC, psychiatrist, and so left the ending of *Memory and Desire* hazy, hoping the reader would decide. But Viking insisted Dean make up her mind how her plot was resolved, and she did finally rewrite the ending with what she calls a "semihappy ending."

Happy endings are not necessarily *happy* endings. A happy ending can be justice done. A crime solved. A mean relative finally kicked out of the house. A battle over and done with and the hero still alive. You don't have to look for a dancing-in-the-street kind of happy ending or a kissy-kissy one, though those kinds are good, too, once in a while.

Let's look at the endings of two novels, familiar to everyone. In the first, Charles Dickens's *A Tale of Two Cities*, the "happy" ending is peace of mind, even though the hero, Sydney Carton, gives his life in place of his lookalike, the husband of the woman he loves. His happiness is that he has saved her happiness, and his last words, spoken on the guillotine, are the last lines of the book: "It is a far, far better thing I do, than I have ever done; it is a far, far better rest that I go to, than I have ever known." His words live on forever.

The second ending, that of Charlotte Brontë's *Jane Eyre*, is also one of bittersweet happiness because of Rochester, the strange, brooding, self-indulgent hero who almost made Jane a bigamous wife. At the end, he is laid low, ruined and made blind. But Jane still loves him, and now he can be hers at last—after 403 pages.

The final paragraph shows the new relationship and her quiet joy at being near him and needed: "Then he stretched his hand out to be led. I took that dear hand, held it a moment to my lips, then let it pass round my shoulder . . . I served both for his prop and guide. We . . . wended homeward."

But don't think you have to spell everything out, spend a whole chapter telling what happened to each of the characters for the next thirty years. Rather, you merely have to come to a conclusive stop, with all major action resolved, all loose plot threads tied up neatly. If you have a lot of subplots with threads to keep track of—in a mystery, for instance—you may find you want to knit them up as you go, one by one, along the way, so that only the strongest major strand is left to be knotted at the end.

A conclusion can bog down in a huge mass of exposition—static description—just as a beginning can. Don't let that happen in your book. Say just enough to let the reader know how the major climax was resolved, and then stop before you write another word.

GETTING FROM HERE TO THERE— THE PLOT THAT DOMINATES THE MIDDLE

Your novel is going to tell how you get from *here* to *there*. It's called plotting. The whole trick of the game is that only *you* know where the character is going and how he is going to get there—and *what* waits for him at the end. The reader keeps thinking the character's going one place, but aha, you, the author, know better. *What* you "know better" is the story—the *middle*.

And you, the author, are not telling. If the reader wants to know where the hero is going, let the reader read the book. All the way through. Make her know there's no way of knowing how it comes out for sure until the last page.

Foreshadowing

You may foreshadow and prepare the reader subtly for events still in the distance. But do it lightly, and don't tell very much. If you foreshadow heavily—"but little did he know that later he would marry her"—an editor will write in the margin: "Don't send the reader a telegram." Better to say, if you need to say anything, "He wondered if he dared ask her for a date." Don't close doors until you actually reach them. Show the reader they're temptingly ajar, that there are lots of possibilities, then guide him to that one door and shove him through. When he discovers what's on the other side, he may find another array of doors, all temptingly ajar, until he reaches that last door.

Flashbacks

You may find that your story needs flashbacks to tell the story in a more interesting way. Use them discreetly. Joyce Engelson, now a freelance editor in Manhattan, but formerly editor in chief of E.P. Dutton, and other publishers, says, "Each flashback should result in bringing the reader a little further along in the story." In other words, at the end of a flashback, the reader is wiser, knowing something not known before—a murder hidden for years, the death of a child never talked about.

You can also start your novel with a small flash forward—taken from near a high point of action in the middle of the book. The flash forward grabs your attention, after which the whole book can be told in chronological order. The flash forward tells the reader the essential nature of your story right away; it really is a kind of hook, a variation on strong opening lines.

Flashbacks are one way of giving your reader important information, but you don't have to use them. You can have someone tell the reader what happened. Two people are talking, and one says, "I guess you didn't know her father beat her. I was their neighbor." Or you can have a woman character on trial thinking she knows it would get the jury's sympathy if she told them her mother locked her in the closet as a child but she isn't going to do it. She'll tell them anything but that—she doesn't want to look pitiful. After all, she is a socialite envied by her friends.

Be careful not to use too many flashbacks. The reader can become confused and may finally say, "Who cares?" and close the book. Use them selectively; otherwise, reading your novel may be like watching a Ping-Pong game.

BUILDING YOUR PLOT

However you tell the story, it is the plot, the "how they get from here to there," that is the middle. It's what the reader really wants from the book—experience, entertainment, exercise of her emotions and intellect, vicarious living, enlightenment, edification, a lesson, wit, elegance of language, an adventure, insight—something new that you have created for her, and that she will like enough to tell her friends about.

How do you achieve this?

Plotting is simply playing the game of "What If?"

If you are going to write science fiction, the sky *really* is the limit. What if an ugly/cute creature comes down from another planet and is marooned on earth? And what if a normal family finds him— or, rather, the kids do—and they protect him, afraid of what their parents will do?

Well, you get the picture. You have the plot that captured the imagination of the nation. *E.T.* became a household word for "extraterrestrial."

But plotting is more than simply a premise that sets up what the story is about. You need complications that continue along the way so it isn't too easy for the heroine to reach her goal. In fact, the reader is sometimes in despair, wondering if the hero can overcome all the misfortunes that befall her. Just when she has solved one problem, another, even tougher, comes along. You can approach each of these complications with the "What If?" game. What if, after she escapes from the muggers and runs to the end of the street, she is relieved to see a familiar face? But what if she suddenly realizes that the nice guy she sees is the leader of the gang?

ANOTHER WAY TO PLOT

Say you don't like the "What If?" game. Then look at a plot as a staircase with a chute at the top—like a playground slide.

You have your premise, your opening lines that make an intriguing first step that entices you to want to keep climbing. The reader is curious. What's up there? Now you keep luring him along, adding dangers or complications that threaten the mental or physical well-being of the main character. The reader has to continue climbing to find out what happens. And just as one problem is solved, a worse one pops up on the next step.

Toward the top of the stairs, the reader is almost panting, sharing the character's fear that she'll never escape or reach her goal. It's a fiasco with no way out. Only disaster lies ahead, and the villain will surely win. Maybe he has already won. The reader must find out. He gets up to the climax, the top of the steps, and zoom, down the chute he goes to the fast ending.

In quick succession, all things are revealed, all problems solved or justice is done or undone. Something happens that has its roots back in the plot.

The reader picks himself up and says, "I should have known it all along." He walks away still mulling it over and ready to go to the bookstore to find your next book.

WHAT TURNS PAGES?

Curiosity and suspense turn pages. Until the very end of a book, there must be questions left unanswered. The reader keeps on turning pages to find out what happens. You answer a few questions or solve a few problems along the way, perhaps, and give some true or misleading hints, but the big questions hang there until the end.

Think of *Jurassic Park*, by Michael Crichton. Will the human characters have enough time to repair their technology and survive, or will the preternatural dinosaurs they have created take over? The question was interesting enough to provide material not only for that novel, but also for his sequel best-seller, *The Lost World*.

So pressure of *time* is a great page-turner. Every kind of chase and race. Who will get to the finish line first? To the rescue of anyone anywhere. A boiler is going to explode. The men are locked in. They must either get out or keep the explosion from happening.

Anger over injustice turns pages. The big lie. Someone tells a terrible lie and an innocent man is made to suffer and it takes the whole book to resolve it.

I sometimes think of novel-reading as a sort of addiction. The novelist—the pusher—grabs your attention with line one, hooks you with a little sniff of her product and holds you to the end of the paragraph. But the end of the paragraph makes you want to go on to the next paragraph, eager for more of her stuff, to the end of the page. The end of the page makes you want to turn to the next one. Fascinated, you demand more, and read on to the end of the chapter. But is it enough? No. Now you're addicted. Your attention is so engaged that you have to read to the next chapter, and so on until the end of the book. So each part has a hook that pulls you forward. That's why successful works are sometimes called "page-turners," or, to use the more formal phrase I first heard from publisher Bernard Geis, they have "narrative drive."

A SAMPLE OF A PLOT

Let's take a very simple plot from Rose Wilder Lane's *Young Pioneers*, a short novel published in many editions throughout the world, then made into a TV movie and reprinted in several textbooks.

It opens in the 1850s with the teenage David and Molly marrying and going west in a wagon to find a home. They homestead a claim in the Dakotas and settle in a sod shanty. Molly is just seventeen and David nineteen when their baby, David John, is born. They plant wheat and potatoes on the prairie. Things are going well, when David, anticipating a fine harvest, recklessly buys a load of lumber on credit to start building a house. But calamity strikes—hordes of grasshoppers destroy the growing wheat and potato vines.

They settle on a desperate plan—Molly and the baby will stay and defend the claim, and David will go to Iowa to work and pay their debts. Eventually a neighbor brings a letter—David has a job in a lumbermill. Then another letter—he has had an accident and may not be able to return until winter. Molly tries to get a job in town, but can't find one, and buys barely enough supplies to keep herself and her child alive through the winter on the homestead claim.

A great blizzard comes. Molly copes at first, but the supply of twisted hay she uses as fuel is getting low. The sod shanty is completely covered with snow, except for its smokestack. She realizes she might die and lies in bed with the baby, dreaming.

But David is on his way back. Though left with a limp from the accident, he has recovered and has cash. He sets out through the blizzard and finds the shanty. Molly hears him bump against the smokestack and guides him to safety. The novel ends when the baby says, "Blablub," which Molly translates as "Papa."

That's a plot. It is a simple one, but it makes us cry when the grasshoppers eat the wheat, and laugh at the end when all turns out well. The genius of Rose Wilder Lane and other successful writers is evident in their creation of wonderful details to make the plot pleasurable to follow. You can learn a lot about how to handle such details by studying other novels.

TAKE A CLOSER LOOK AT A NOVEL YOU ADMIRE

The best way to understand the structure of a novel is to take one you have read and liked and make notes as you scan it again. On which page—how far into the action—is each character introduced? How is each introduced? Is something said about one character by another—something derogatory, perhaps?

Note where flashbacks occur and what purposes they serve. How are they introduced? Note any subplot and how it is resolved. Note where the middle crises of the story occur and how the major problem is resolved. How many pages does it take after the main climax for all things to be solved and all things revealed?

Now, go back and study both the opening lines and the final paragraph. How did the author arouse your interest and curiosity, and how does he leave you at the finish?

Don't be afraid that some reviewers may say you're a copy of Clive Cussler or Anne Tyler. The basic methods of storytelling are as old as language itself. Start with whatever style you like. You won't be stuck with it; you can change to another style in your next book if you like. That's what Truman Capote did. His first short stories were heavily influenced by the writing of his fellow Southerner William Faulkner. To me, his first novel, *Breakfast at Tiffany's*, is practically an American version of Christopher Isherwood's *Berlin Stories*. But Capote kept evolving. His *In Cold Blood* was very original, opening a new field, "faction," or the nonfiction novel, which itself influenced other novelists.

Now you are practically ready to plan your first novel, step by step, but you must first make an important preliminary decision.

FROM WHOSE VIEWPOINT ARE YOU TELLING THE STORY?

All stories have to be told from some point of view. Though technicians of fiction can describe many possible points of view, to my mind there are three major ones. The simplest and easiest to understand is the *FIRST PERSON*, using the word "I" as though you were telling a friend something you did yourself, or watched someone else do something and now were describing it. G.J.A. O'Toole, in *The Cosgrove Report*, begins, "I find myself in a strange world." Immediately on reading this, we realize that a character in the story will be its narrator, and the story will be told from this first-person narrator's point of view. We don't yet know whether the narrator is the main character, or a secondary character who somehow learned the story—two different ways of using the first-person point of view.

With that sentence, the author committed himself to the first-person approach and to solving its particular problems—which means he may have to use things like letters, telegrams or documents to get certain information across, or have the narrator eavesdrop on conversations of others to learn certain facts. The narrator is peeping at the world through a peephole we know: our own eyes.

Joyce Engelson, when she was editor in chief of St. Martin's/ Marek, told my coauthor that one of the worst mistakes beginning novelists make is to put a story in the first person when it has too large a cast of characters.

First person looks simple. It isn't. It requires a special light touch, and the "I" must not get in the way of the story. "I" can become boring, and can make it difficult to include things that are far away.

But the most important difficulty—one that beginning novelists often don't take into consideration when they start in the first person—is the difficulty of characterization. If your story is told from a first-person narrator's point of view, all characters are seen through that narrator's eyes only. A male narrator may have a character that makes him oblivious to the thoughts and feelings of women. A female narrator may have some blind spots about men. So it may take a lot of effort to get across the most basic facts about the characters—how they dress (does the narrator see herself in a mirror?), how they feel, their mannerisms.

But that said, I have to admit some great and small novels have been effective in the first-person viewpoint. *Robinson Crusoe,* a pioneer piece of fiction in the modern novel form, was written in 1719 in the first person. Daniel Defoe wanted his readers to think his adventure story of being shipwrecked and marooned for four years on an island really happened. And they did. Even today, it seems very real.

So first person is a good way to tell a relatively simple story. In a detective or police story, it gives greater believability.

If the narrator is not the central character, a slight story can be enhanced by the emotional involvement of the narrator as an interested bystander. Truman Capote, in *Breakfast at Tiffany's,* mentioned earlier, strikes just the right note when he tells the story of Holly Golightly:

> I didn't trust my voice to tell the news . . . I thrust the letter
> at her . . . her eyes squinty with sleep . . .

Or this bit of intimacy when Holly and "I" are wandering about New York arm in arm and pass a Woolworth's:

" 'Let's steal something,' she said, pulling me into the store. . . ."

First-person writing makes it even more of a lark when Holly puts a Halloween mask on her own face and then puts one on "I" and leads him out of the store by the hand. "Outside, we ran a few blocks." And "I" makes the reader feel the exhilaration he discovers in "successful theft."

There are two other main ways to tell a story, each in the *THIRD PERSON*, using the pronouns "he," "she," "they" and "it," rather than "I." First, there is the *OMNISCIENT OBSERVER* who sees and knows all. Using this method, the author can hop, skip and jump from Rome to Berlin to Tucumcari from paragraph to paragraph if he is daring enough. He can have the reader look in and share the feelings, thoughts and actions of opposing generals, as Tolstoy does in *War and Peace*. He can view a battle panoramically, and then swoop down to watch an individual soldier.

This godlike point of view was a favorite of writers of the past, and best-selling authors of today sometimes use it too. It is very tempting when you have a large cast of characters. But this method is probably too permissive for a beginning novelist. It is only successful when the story is told so brilliantly, in such an absorbing manner, or with such storytelling skill that the reader suspends disbelief and comes to accept that the novelist really does know that much about the action and characters. If this technique is poorly done, the reader finds it improbable and cannot buy the idea of the writer knowing the inmost thoughts and most secret actions of his many characters.

Between first person and omniscient observer lies an easier way. It could be called *RESTRICTED THIRD PERSON*. You tell the story in the third person—"he," "she," "they," "it" does this and does that. But instead of having an all-seeing observer, you limit what can be seen to what one person, or two people, or at most, a small group of people, can see.

For example, in the Henry James novel *The Ambassadors*, we follow along behind, and peer over the shoulder of, the main character as he comes to Europe and tries to carry out a mission. As "he" learns and sees things, the reader learns and sees them too. Focusing on one character's actions, the story is unified. But Henry James, the author, is not as limited as the main character—James gets a chance to describe things—his main character, the settings and the other characters—so he is able to include much more detail than if he used first-person narration.

If you wanted to write a story about a group of travelers who are hijacked, you might want to switch to the point of view of each character to tell some part of the story. You will have several points of view—but still not have an omniscient observer. The story can be as credible as you make your characters and their actions. If such shifts make you nervous, you could adopt some unifying device such as having a journalist interview each one.

To avoid confusion, *most writers try not to shift points of view within a chapter*. It is essential to clearly identify which character is viewing what in each part of the book. This is a really important point. Lack of a clear and consistent point of view is one of the most common faults I find in first novels submitted to me.

Critics, writers, editors, even agents, have opinions, often annunciated as divine wisdom, about the best point of view to use in telling a story. My own opinion was expressed by the famous bridge teacher and player Charles Goren: "I never quarrel with success." If it works, use it. And if it doesn't work, even if you have written half your novel, abandon it and switch to a fresh point of view.

So, with preliminaries out of the way, let's go on to a concrete plan.

WRITING YOUR NOVEL

Step One: The Premise

The first step in writing your novel is simply to tell yourself, "I want to write a novel about . . ." and then state the premise in just a paragraph. Or even a sentence. Just for starters, I'll give you one:

> I want to write a story about a man who is planning to kill his wife. She's the obstruction to his happiness.

I see that doesn't explain enough and so I add:

> He has developed a passion for a girl half his age and is afraid he will lose her if he doesn't marry her soon. He's afraid to get a divorce because then he will be penniless. His wife is the fabulously wealthy benefactor who gave him

the money for his business, a business that is now failing.
He has led the girl to believe he is the one with the money.
He must make sure he inherits his wife's fortune.

Now I have a strong premise that can go in many directions. It really could be—and maybe should be—told from the wife's viewpoint. She would get more sympathy. The reader will hope she is somehow saved. Maybe she finds out in some interesting way that he is playing around and slowly she gets the feeling that she is not safe.

It might be more unusual to tell it from the young girl's viewpoint. Marian isn't really an exploitative person. She was just lonely and he was so tender and attentive. She needed comfort. Her boyfriend of three years had sent her a "Dear Marian" letter and she found out he had moved in with her closest girlfriend. So, she did need sympathy and the dependability of an older man.

He has said he's divorcing his wife. Why shouldn't she plan to marry him? She might even invite her ex-boyfriend and her ex-girlfriend to the wedding—let them turn green with jealousy.

In working out the premise and the viewpoint of your novel, it's good to take a look at it from the viewpoint of each of your major characters. Take your time. Just let it percolate in your mind until you suddenly know how you want to handle it, until it feels right to you.

Let's say I have decided to go ahead with my first impulse, which was to tell the story from the man's viewpoint. Now comes the next step.

Step Two: The Opening Line or Lines

I've thought of two. I'll put them both down.

> Greg told himself he would be perfectly justified in bumping off the irritable, tired harridan in his bed. He was sure it would not bother him in the least—it was the best solution.

That gives it the suggestion of a psychological study. Will he have the guts for the evil deed? The second way:

> Kurt looked over the medicines in his wife's flesh-pink bathroom. What combination, he pondered, might be lethal to a 200-pound woman? There was only one problem. It had to look like suicide.

Now we have the start of a detective story. I can almost see the arrival of the detectives at the big mansion to ask a few friendly questions. Will he be able to outwit them?

Step Three: The Ending

If you know where you are going, it's easier to get there. It some-times happens that a writer changes her mind about an ending, or a publisher says a different ending would improve the story, but generally the original ending stays.

For the psychological study, I end on an ironic twist:

> Greg turned and found himself looking into a gun. With a sick feeling, he saw that his wife and Marian were standing together like old friends. Where had Marian come from? And quietly, a policeman opened the door.

For the detective story:

> As they led Kurt away, he turned and saw that Marian's old boyfriend was back, with his arm around her. It was the final blow.

Step Four: The Middle

The middle is simply a matter of getting from here to there—from your opening line, which hints what's going to happen, to the ending, which shows how it turns out.

The middle is the *megillah*, the monster, the whole schmeer. But you can handle it. You take it one incident or action at a time. You talk out loud, or to yourself, and say, What if they do this or that to him, how will he react? And then what happens if he tries to solve his problem this way, but someone turns against him? The false friend gets him in deeper trouble in order to grab the prize himself—the prize being money, a woman or prestige.

Many writers, such as Joyce Carol Oates, say they let a plot simmer for as long as necessary in the mind without writing it down and then sit down and write it fast and furiously. That's fine if that's the way your mind works, but others work better by being methodical and writing it down as it comes to them.

An easy way to start a loose outline of your novel is to take a sheet of paper for each chapter and write the action that takes place there. If you come up with sixteen flows of action, then you have sixteen chapters. Keep each chapter in its own folder—sixteen chapters, sixteen folders. Each chapter can be as long or short as you like, but it has to have a beginning and an end. Or at least a resting place or a new question raised. Though one small crisis is over at the end of the chapter, the reader must never doubt that there will be more trouble ahead. Or perhaps a note of hope ends a chapter and the reader wonders if the fortunes of the hero are indeed going to change.

If your novel is going to be 270 to 300 pages, the average chapter might be 16 to 20 pages, some longer, some shorter.

Don't be afraid to waste paper. Use separate sheets to throw into the appropriate folder anything that helps your plot. Eventually, some folders may grow fat. It's all right to overwrite. Editing will take care of it. But that comes much later.

Just as you now have a basic outline of your novel, you can now, if you wish, write an individual outline of each separate chapter, adding a page or more to the material in each chapter folder. You might want to indicate where major crises will arise, making sure to space them out in the book. You might want to say where each major character will be introduced and note it in the file folder for the right chapter.

If you have a subplot or several subplots, sketch in each chapter folder how that theme or concurrently running story moves along and how it is resolved. The hero's buddy may be feuding with a cattle baron. But this action must have some effect on the novel you are writing, or else the feud is a different story and belongs in some different novel. Everything in your novel must relate somehow and influence the main character or action of your plot. Your main character also may be involved in a subplot in which he has a secondary goal. It, too, must be resolved or explained somehow before the end of the book. The readers may care a lot that the hero is saving a little boy buried in a mine explosion, but they read on to find out what happens in the major plot—the hero's courtship of a girl whose parents have thrown him off the property and even had him arrested.

YOUR CHARACTERS CAN HELP YOU WITH YOUR PLOT: THE FREE-FORM WAY

Many novelists, Graham Greene, for example, object to writing outlines of their novels because of the pleasure they get in letting the characters "take over" and dictate the story.

Joseph Wambaugh, former policeman and author of *Echoes in the*

Darkness and other best-sellers, frankly admits plotting is the hard part for him. He told *Writer's Digest,* "Interaction between characters is what I do best. I have to rewrite, rewrite again and again."

Maybe, like Amelia Walden, author of *To Catch a Spy* and other novels, you'll feel that when you've fleshed out your characters so that they come to life in your mind as real people, they take over and write the novel. Walden says she's found plotting is easy, even effortless, in the hands of the right characters—maybe with an occasional small nudge from the author to keep them headed in the right direction.

If you're that sort of writer, a full-scale outline may be the worst possible way for you to start working on your novel. It may kill all the joy of discovery, even if the lack of a detailed overall plan leads you into a blind alley or two along the way. What you got into, you can get out of. Just go back and take a different turn, once you realize some character, intent on her own troubles, has pulled you off course.

But I still maintain that if you're a beginning writer, you'll find it helpful to outline as much as you can your first time out. It is your security and will keep you from going adrift. Later, you can become more casual about plotting.

So there you have it: The elements you need to consider—and maybe actually write down—in four steps to planning your first novel:

1. You know what your novel is about.

2. You write an opening.

3. You plan and write the ending.

4. *Then*, you devise a plot and characters to take you from here to there. Ideally, you start an outline consisting of pages or folders for each of the flows of action, or chapters.

You have actually started writing!

TIPS

• Look at the daily newspapers for plot ideas.

• Grab the reader's attention at the start of the novel, hinting at events to come.

• Plan what you want your characters to do—your plot. The author should have a clear idea where the plot is heading from the start, but the reader should not.

• Tantalize the reader by foreshadowing the plot. Reveal enough to keep him reading, but don't give the ending away.

• Inform the reader about past events through flashbacks, conversations between characters and conversations a character has with herself.

• Examine novels you like for tips on story structure.

• First-person point of view is useful for novels with a small cast of characters, or a rather simple story. It also conveys a greater sense of believability.

• The third-person omniscient point of view allows the reader a glimpse inside the minds of a large cast of characters.

• Restricted third person allows the action to be viewed through a few characters rather than one omniscient observer. This device gives the author a wider scope and allows for more detailed description.

• For clarity, avoid point-of-view shifts within chapters.

• Make sure every chapter has a clear beginning and end. Chapters should be placed within the book for a reason.

• Be as organized as you feel comfortable being. Many writers outline their entire novels, then outline each individual chapter. Don't be afraid to waste paper during the writing process.

• Everything in your novel must relate to and somehow influence the main character and action in your plot.

• Don't leave the reader hanging. You should tie up all loose plot threads—then promptly end the book. Save your characters' future lives for the sequel.

5.

Profanity, Sex Scenes and Other Puzzlers

We have covered a lot of ground, but I'm sure you have some pressing questions. Here are the ones first-time novelists ask me most frequently.

WHAT'S IN A NAME?

The answer is, in a story, a lot. Dickens's use of "Scrooge" in *A Christmas Carol* is perfect. You can almost see the mean, scrunched-up old fellow. When William Thackeray called one of the characters of *Vanity Fair* "Becky Sharp," it wasn't hard for him to complete her characterization. But you probably will not want to go as far as Emily Post did in her nonfiction book, *Etiquette*, and use names like "Mr. Newly," "Clubwin Doe," and "Mrs. Worldly." Still, the name has to sound and feel right for the character.

Dennis Fawcett, who writes under the pen name "Richard Owen," used to sit in the glass-enclosed office next to mine at his 8:45-4:30 editorial job, and often would be pounding away at the typewriter. From time to time, he would pause and pick my brain, asking "What's a good last name for an elderly Texan?" or, "Give me a first name for the wife of a young New York artist." He must have had his characters clearly in mind—he would look off into space at his mental picture before accepting or rejecting my suggestions.

You will probably want to use dictionaries of names to help you find a name that conveys the right picture of your character if you don't have me around.

You still have a problem, however, and that is picking a name that no actual person in your plot's location has. You don't want someone with the name you use to rise up and claim you are writing about her and that she has been damaged by your characterization. When you have your character's name picked out, consult the phone book of that locale to be sure no one has quite the same name, or even one similar if the name is unusual.

Bonnie Golightly, a New York writer originally from the South, was so annoyed at Truman Capote's use of the name "*Holly* Golightly" for the main character of *Breakfast at Tiffany's* that she started a lawsuit against Capote and his publishers. (No verdict was rendered.) Her name is an unusual one for New York, and she knew socially many of the members of the New York gay community that Capote knew also.

If you think hers was a special case, consider what happened to Carolyn Chute when she was a first-time novelist, writing a completely fictitious book about an incestuous family in Maine. She used the family name "Bean" because it is an interesting name and a very common one in Maine. Everyone knows it's safe to use a name like "John Smith"—there are so many of them no one could say that he was the character intended. So Bean seemed safe. For the town, Chute came up with the name of Egypt. A check of an atlas showed no town in Maine by that name.

The book was published as *The Beans of Egypt, Maine,* and it was a success, but what Chute had not foreseen was the anger of Bean families of Maine and the verbal abuse that would result. Nor did Ticknor & Fields, her publishers who put out 235,000 copies in hardcover and paperback simultaneously. It turned out that though there was no town of Egypt, sections in several towns were called by that name.

It is also a sensible precaution to change the location of your novel. You might try to pick a different state, one with similar physical characteristics to the one of your setting. But you must research the new location to avoid embarrassing mistakes.

HOW MANY CHARACTERS DO YOU NEED?

I would answer: as few as you can get away with to tell your story fully. Be cautious before adding additional characters just because they are colorful or interesting to write about—good characters may require their own subplots and throw your novel off its main course. Each additional character requires the reader to hold more information in her head to understand your story. So the bottom line answer here is "exactly as many as your story needs."

For most plots, you need at the very least a main character, a villain or adversary, and the main character's sidekick, friend or co-conspirator.

It may turn out later that the friend or sidekick is really on the side of the villain, but that's beside the point. The point is that the main character or hero needs the sidekick for dialogue. He just can't keep talking to himself. Everyone tells someone what is on his mind. Someone has to be the sounding board so the main character can voice thoughts in a natural way.

The sidekick is important for another reason. When the main character is acting stupid or irrational, the friend asks the questions the reader wants to know. Or makes the perfectly sensible suggestion that the reader wants to shout at the main character. In other words, the sidekick is standing in for the reader.

Sometimes the sidekick is the one the reader identifies with, as in *The Great Gatsby*, in which the narrator of the story, who is telling what happens in first person, lives next door and sees what goes on. In that case, the narrator gets more and more involved with the characters in the plot because he is invited to the parties and is enlisted by the main character to bring a certain beautiful woman— the object of Gatsby's all-consuming love—to the party.

I have gone on at length about the sidekick in order to make the point that you, the author, must flesh out this person so the reader feels the sidekick has a life of her own. She is not just a limp washcloth to be picked up now and then to wipe the face of the hero.

In the same way, the villain or adversary must be credible and

well developed—and he may have a sidekick too, or at least associates to herald his arrival and to do the less important work.

So, in deciding how many characters to use, keep in mind how
many you need to tell your story.

DO YOU NEED PERMISSION TO QUOTE?

If you quote more than a few words of the works of other authors
in your novel and the material you quote is in copyright, you will
probably have to get permission from the copyright owner, or the
publisher who controls the rights to the work, in order to include it
in your novel. Titles of works are not copyrightable, so merely using
a title of a song or poem or any work within your novel is no problem.
But using songs—even one line—requires permission. That is because a song is such a short work, even quotation of a single line is
appropriating a substantial part of it. The same reasoning applies
to poems. Usually, authors delay seeking permission to quote until
their novels are under contract to publishers, and then inquire of
their editors about the publishers' policies on securing permissions to
quote. Under most publishers' contracts, the author ends up paying
whatever fees are necessary.

An interesting instance of quotation within a novel involved my
agency several years ago, when Little, Brown & Company published
Myra Breckinridge, by Gore Vidal. When I read the book, I noted
that the transsexual hero/heroine, Myron/Myra, was depicted as
fascinated by the works of Parker Tyler, a critic whom I represented
as literary agent. Vidal had quoted extensively from Parker Tyler's
book *Magic and Myth of the Movies*, without having asked or received permission to do so. At Tyler's suggestion, I queried Little,
Brown about this, and suggested that since the quotations made up
about 1 percent of the whole book, Tyler should receive 1 percent
of *Myra*'s earnings.

Little, Brown resisted this suggestion, and Parker Tyler later
learned through an acquaintance that Gore Vidal's view was that
his quotation of this work, which he admired, helped, not hurt, Parker
Tyler. Tyler asked his good friend Charles Boultenhouse, then manager of Brentano's Fifth Avenue bookstore, to check the sales of his
books, comparing their sales before and after publication of *Myra
Breckinridge*. Boultenhouse reported that, indeed, it was true—the
sales of his books in general had picked up after Vidal's novel was

published. Tyler decided to drop the whole matter.

Not many authors would be as rational about such unauthorized quoting of their work as was Parker Tyler. So you would be on much safer ground, regardless of your publisher's advice, to secure permission to quote any copyrighted material used within your novel, even if it is a quotation from your own work—such as a nonfiction piece published by another house.

PROFANITY AND LOVE SCENES— HOW DO YOU HANDLE THEM?

Do you find that every character seems to be rapping out profanity in your novel? If so, it's not realistic. Not *everyone* curses. If one character has to curse, let her. But don't throw in obscenities to sound modern or liberated. This is not a novel about *you*; it's about a bunch of other people.

The same goes with sex scenes. They're not obligatory. But if used, should they be explicit or suggested as going on in some other room, out of sight, out of hearing? You can do either, but it must seem natural. Is explicit sex central to your plot? It could be in the case of a rape or of a seduction scene, but even here, different writers would use different methods. Either way, it's not going to stop the sale of your book to a publisher. If your editor wants a sex scene made more or less explicit, you can talk with him about it and reach some agreement or compromise.

To see how scenes of sexual passion can be handled with skill and feeling and yet not rely on four-letter words, study Vladimir Nabokov's *Lolita*, the story of a middle-aged man who cannot resist his mad passion for a beautiful nymphet and, in order to possess her, runs away with her. Nabokov died in 1977, but the word "Lolita" will be forever in the English language as meaning a child temptress. The scenes are erotic but not obscene, even translating nicely to the movie screen. Yet the pathetic quality of the romance comes about in the book and movie through clever use of contrasts—the girl's petulance set against the aging lover's slavishly eager attempt to please her by putting nail polish on her toes and doing whatever other menial task she assigns him.

By way of contrast, I remember when an editor, after reading a client's work, called me to complain, "I know this is a realistic story about a race riot in a prison. But to use 'motherfucker' eleven times on one page is excessive."

Sex scenes seem to fit very naturally into historical novels. I remember that I learned a lot about sex as a young adolescent from *Anthony Adverse*, by Hervey Allen, and I noticed my twelve- and thirteen-year-old female cousins reading *Gone With the Wind* with avid attention.

As a freshman in college, my more sophisticated taste was satisfied by works such as Henry Miller's *The Tropic of Cancer*, and later, by Edmund Wilson's *Memoirs of Hecate County*. Novels that I remember with affection as part of my education can't be very bad!

However, my advice is don't go overboard with graphic violence and explicit sex scenes. In the mid-1990s there appeared a few novels published by major publishers that contained so much explicit sex, often of a bizarre nature, and so much violence that some bookstores refused to stock and sell them. Though I'm against censorship and agree with George Bernard Shaw's reply to the question, "What should a little girl read?"—"Anything she can get her hands on"— still, I don't want to clutter my mind with the fantasies of the mad Marquis de Sade. But sex and the profane are part of life and have their entertainment value.

Though I don't buy all the novels of Jackie Collins as does my coauthor, Frances Spatz Leighton, we agree about Collins's reasoning that there is life under the covers for women as well as men. As Collins puts it, she wants to show that her women are "not sluts and they're not nymphomaniacs—they're just women who like sex as much as men do."

STREAM OF CONSCIOUSNESS—SHOULD YOU USE IT?

Dialogue may be handled in several ways. One is to say only what the characters speak aloud and let the reader guess at the thought behind the words. Many authors prefer that and so do many readers. In a western, it is assumed the good guy says only what he means and his actions show if he is going to play a trick on the bad guy, or he confides his plan to his sidekick.

In the novels of manners mirroring life in our sophisticated, complex society, the author tells not only what the character is saying, but what she is saying in her thoughts, which is frequently at odds with her spoken words. The reader feels almost like a psychiatrist or a mind reader.

Past masters of characters' stream of consciousness were James Joyce in *Ulysses* and Virginia Woolf in *Mrs. Dalloway*. Both novels are engrossing literary experiments worth great study, but they are unique—solitary monuments on the road not taken by popular literature—and hence not suitable to imitate.

However, after reading them, you will see better how to use characters' thoughts in your own novel, if you are using stream-of-consciousness techniques.

WHERE DO YOU GET YOUR TITLES?

For some writers it's fun to come up with titles, but for others, it's torture. If you find it hard, remember that you don't have to have a title when you begin—or even after you finish your novel. If necessary, you can put a label on it that says something like "Untitled Western." That's better than a title you think might turn an editor or agent off, such as *Here's Mud in Your Eye*. So if you don't have a title yet, don't despair; you can write your novel anyway. Often you will find you have developed what's called a "working title," the name you use for convenience in thinking about your novel, and such a mental label will do until you come up with a better one.

Since the title is the main hook, the very thing that first catches a reader's eye, you will have to think about the problem eventually. But where do you get one? A title can come from anywhere. From the air. From your subconscious. From the name of your main character, or his nickname. That's how John Updike came up with the titles *Rabbit, Run*; *Rabbit Redux*; and *Rabbit Is Rich*. Rabbit is the nickname of his main character. Open the Bible or a volume of Shakespeare and touch a verse with your eyes closed. The Bible gave William Faulkner *Absalom, Absalom!* just as Shakespeare gave him *The Sound and the Fury*. And Hemingway reminds us that according to Ecclesiastes, *The Sun Also Rises* upon the just and the unjust.

Titles come from a line of poetry, nursery rhymes and even from children's stories. One of Agatha Christie's most successful mysteries was entitled *Ten Little Indians*. And Hemingway's *For Whom the Bell Tolls* is from a work by John Donne.

Hemingway spent a great deal of time getting exactly the right title. When he thought of *For Whom the Bell Tolls*, he wrote elatedly to his famous editor, Maxwell Perkins at Scribner's: "I think it has the magic that a title has to have." Hemingway had one reservation about the title, fearing some people might think he was talking about toll charges and the Bell telephone company. "If so, it is out," he wrote Perkins, quite seriously.

Humorous titles are harder to come by, because they require that you give a clue to the light mood of the story. Jean Kerr, whose amusing book about family life was made into a movie, got her title in a perfectly simple way. As she told it, she was having a dinner party and had told her twin sons all the things they were *not* to do, like use the guest towels or leave their bicycles on the front steps—"but I forgot to tell them not to eat the centerpiece on the table." Presto! *Please don't eat the daisies.* To keep it conversational, she capitalized only the first word.

And you know you're going to be getting more than a staid travelog when you pick up a book called *Around the World With Auntie Mame*. Auntie Mame, flitting about the bookstores and movie screens of the world, earned her creator, Patrick Dennis, a fortune. Actually, the fortune was earned by Edward Everett Tanner III, the author's real name. Tanner had the rare pleasure of seeing three of his titles on the best-seller list at the same time.

Since James Clavell's *Tai-Pan* and *Shogun*, novels about the Orient have tended to sport very brief or single-word titles, as does Eric Van Lustbader's *The Ninja*. But don't forget Pearl Buck's best-seller about China, *The Good Earth*.

Titles can come from the names of places—islands, cities, states, countries. Michener used many—from *Tales of the South Pacific* to *Poland*. One new title of Michener's caught a president's eye in 1996. President Bill Clinton took time out from his reelection campaign to read a few chapters of *This Noble Land*. Martha Grimes, an American author of murder mysteries, picks up a new title for a book every time she goes to England for a vacation—which is often. That's because she names all her books for British pubs, such as *The Dirty Duck* and *The Old Silent*.

If you call your local post office, you'll find no mailing address for a place called Lonesome Dove, Texas. But Lonesome Dove is very real to those reading the western epic of Texas native Larry McMurtry, which is set in the area near the Mexican border around the 1800s. And Edna Ferber chose the apt word *Giant* for her blockbuster tale of Texas.

In 1981, Sue Grafton had the quaint idea of using the alphabet to title her mysteries, which star the tough-but-not-heartless private eye Kinsey Millhone. Grafton determined from the start that if her first Kinsey Millhone book, *A Is for Alibi*, brought a demand for more Kinsey books, she would sweep right through the alphabet, and by now, her success is such that one day she may have to go on to *& Is for . . .*

Sometimes a character's wistful yearning makes a title that excites the imagination: *The Magic Mountain*, by Thomas Mann; *Lost Horizon*, by James Hilton, with its dream of wonderful Shangri-La just beyond the map's boundaries; *Like Water for Chocolate*, by Laura Esquivel.

Margaret Mitchell chose the last line in her book about the Civil War to be her title—*Tomorrow Is Another Day*. But the publisher felt it fell flat, and Mitchell chose another quote from the book, *Gone With the Wind*, to be the title.

You may think up a strange and mysterious title that's still dramatic enough to make a reader want to find out what it means—for example, *The Clan of the Cave Bear*, by Jean Auel, about a prehistoric tribe, or *Lord of the Flies*, by William Golding, about a more modern and sinister tribe made up of castaway boys.

Some authors have been known to send a whole list of suggested titles along with their manuscripts, encouraging the publisher or agent to decide which is best. *This isn't a good idea*. It makes the author look wishy-washy and uncertain. The publisher and the agent want to believe the author knows what he is doing—that he has certainty of inspiration. I always prefer to see *one* strong title. It's taken for granted that the title may be changed after your novel interests a publisher willing to pay for the change (and the book). But you can send a title list *after* the book has been accepted.

Publishers—the editor, the sales manager or the president—sometimes come up with good titles, and even agents have made suggestions that eventually were accepted. A few of my title ideas have ended up on books, but I won't mention which ones, to protect the privacy of the authors.

Some book buyers pick novels simply and solely by their titles. One woman told me she buys any book that has a woman's name as a title. And in her hand was Erica Jong's novel *Fanny*. She probably missed that author's earlier *Fear of Flying*.

James M. Cain, author of a string of memorably named best-sellers and movies, such as *The Postman Always Rings Twice* and

Double Indemnity, lived near Washington, DC, before his death, and often told my coauthor, Frances Spatz Leighton, stories about his career.

Cain's early years were a series of failures and career changes, from singer to reporter, would-be young novelist to professor of journalism, editorial writer to initially unsuccessful Hollywood scriptwriter. He couldn't seem to get a script done, and play-doctor Vincent Lawrence gave him many tips. What Lawrence taught him about plotting, plus the terse, blunt style he had developed as a reporter, at last made him sure, in a burst of insight, that he was overripe to write a novel.

He had a theme—murder for profit of a wealthy man by his wife, in league with her lover. But he needed a good title. He consulted Lawrence, his mentor. There followed a conversation Cain firmly believed was most responsible for his whole success. Instead of *giving* him a good title, Lawrence started reminiscing about problems of his own early career. When Lawrence was living in Boston and writing plays, he had been nervous and excited as he awaited an answer through the mail to his submissions to New York producers.

Lawrence described how he had fervently pleaded with the postman to give the doorbell some extra rings as a signal if he had a letter from a producer or any letter from New York. But the mailman would not be swayed, and solemnly said, "No, we always ring twice so you know it is the postman."

And boom, Cain had his title for his first murder novel, a best-seller that found its way eventually to the stage and screen—*The Postman Always Rings Twice*. Suddenly James M. Cain was eating regularly, even growing wealthy, and writers were coming to *him* for advice.

TIPS

• Choose your characters' names carefully. The names should sound and feel right for the characters.

• If your novel is set in a real place, check the phone book to make sure no one by that name lives in the area.

• Employ as many characters as the plot needs—no more, no less. Three popular character types are the hero, the sidekick and the villain.

• Obey all copyright laws when including the works of other authors in your novel. To quote from copyrighted material requires permission by the author or publisher. Book and song titles are not subject to copyright laws.

• Profanity and love scenes should be used if they are appropriate to the character and plot of the novel. Excessive or gratuitous violence should usually be avoided.

• Stream of consciousness is an intriguing dialogue technique but it is not common to popular literature.

• Spend some time deciding on a title for your novel-in-progress. It's better to call your manuscript "untitled" than to give it an inappropriate title.

• Be creative with your title. Titles can come from poems, songs, stories, names, places—the only limit is your imagination.

• Do not send in an entire list of suggested titles to a publisher or agent. One strong title shows certainty of inspiration.

6.

Gearing Up and Writing It

This chapter could also be called "Where to Write, When to Write, and How Much to Write Each Day."

I remember an old print called "The Writer's Inspiration." It shows a man sitting on the edge of a bed writing at a tiny desk in a small room filled with wife and a swarm of children. The man has paused, quill in hand, to look up at his inspiration mounted on the wall—a painting of a balloon. I often think of this heroic hack when I hear of the great efforts writers make to get out their pages, regardless of the problems they face.

But there is no reason to make it harder than you have to. You have choices, and you can make your work much easier by thinking about the work habits you want to establish, then choosing the best one possible for yourself.

The first question you should ask yourself is, "How much am I expected to write each day?"

THE DAILY QUOTA—THREE PAGES

From what I have been told by many writers, three pages a day is a sensible quota. It is an amount that should keep you from panicking, because it is not asking too much. You can sit down and write three double-spaced pages—I know people who write letters longer than that.

It would be foolish to pooh-pooh the small amount and say, "Oh, I can write five pages a day. Or six. *That's* my quota." Writers who set themselves too high a quota have been known to throw up their hands and drop the whole project. They become disappointed in themselves. With three pages you will be proud of your steady progress and work more or less serenely, knowing that in just ninety days—three months—you will have the first draft of an average-sized book.

Of course, if certain days you feel really creative and want to write more pages, go to it. But don't think this lets you off the next day from doing your three solid pages.

WHEN SHOULD YOU WRITE—WHAT TIME OF DAY?

Everyone has a time of day when she feels most alert. That's the time you should write. It doesn't matter when, as long as you go to it every day in the same place and at the same time so that it becomes as routine as getting up and putting on your clothes.

Hemingway wrote every morning, either standing at the type-writer, if he was making clean copy, or sitting at a cigar-maker's table, if he was writing a first draft, which he did in longhand. Then it was off to his boat, *Pilar*, to fish for the afternoon. He chose to stand for two reasons. He liked to pace, and his leg frequently ached from an assortment of wounds. He was apparently accident prone.

James Michener, whom my coauthor met when Michener was a guest at the National Press Club in Washington, confessed that he was a "two-finger typist." But those two fingers had taken him through some twenty-nine manuscripts. He writes every day, seven days a week—just as if he still needs the money.

Michener's routine is simple: up at 7:30 and at the typewriter in something like five minutes, with just a pause to drink a glass of "battery acid"—his name for grapefruit juice. How long does he work? Like Hemingway, Michener almost never writes in the afternoon.

But there the similarity ends. Hemingway wrote only about five hundred words daily when working on his first draft, carefully counting them at the end of the work session and keeping a log of his progress. Michener turns out an average of six pages a day, a good clip. It adds up to forty-plus pages a week.

Another morning worker, my client Niel Hancock, the fantasy novelist, says, "When I get up in the morning, I take my .45 off the bedside table and hold it to my temple, and I say to myself, 'Well, are you going to get right to work?' " Near his bed, he keeps the nonelectronic, old-fashioned machine that has never failed him, and which he has named "Manual, the Talking Typewriter." That way he has no excuse not to sit right down and get to work.

Tom Clancy was so used to working odd hours at the office and at home on his insurance business that he wrote *The Hunt for Red October* in both places—at home, "with the noise of children around me," and at the office on his computer, whenever it wasn't being used for business.

Joseph Wambaugh—*The New Centurions, The Blue Knight* and others—takes the physical approach to gearing up for each day's work session. He runs two miles every morning before attacking the four pages—one thousand words—he forces himself to turn out before he will eat a solid meal.

And he works even while running. Wambaugh carries a little note pad wherever he goes, jotting down any good thought that occurs to him.

William Faulkner, before he was famous, once made a wheelbarrow into a desk. He wrote his novel *Mosquitoes* on the makeshift desk while supervising the shoveling of coal to feed the boilers at the University of Mississippi power plant.

Regardless of *where* you write—and you can do it practically anywhere—the key is to turn out pages of copy *each* day and not deviate from your schedule.

Now you're going to say, "But aren't there exceptions? Does everybody have to write *every* day to keep the flow?" I have to admit that yes, of course, there are some exceptions. And a notable one is Mary Higgins Clark, who has had a hit parade of winners. Her routine, she says, is to write only some days each week. But she is faithful to her time of writing. She begins her sessions at 5 A.M. when she is fresh and has a clear mind.

Even though this works for Mary Higgins Clark, I stand by what I have said and strongly urge you, as a first-time novelist, not to allow yourself the luxury of days off. Develop a writing rhythm to your day and stick to it.

SHOULD YOU WRITE ALONE?

Should you write alone? Not necessarily, though some must, because they cannot stand a whisper of noise. Others get the shakes when faced with isolation while trying to write, even if they live alone. They must seek out a more public place. The New York Public Library has a room for writers. If the library in your town doesn't, you might get one started. Some novelists rent space in other people's offices. Some have a kindly friend who provides space, family sounds and kitchen privileges in a private home.

James T. Farrell wrote his novels in the dead of night when the world was still. A new novelist, David Small, author of *Almost Famous*, found he wrote best after dinner and after the problems of the day had faded away—from 9 to 11 P.M. No matter where he was, even on planes or in a hotel room, wherever his business trips for a Pennsylvania medical society took him, he wrote from 9 to 11.

WHERE IS THE BEST PLACE TO WRITE?

For some it's a matter of getting away from children and noise. But others get claustrophobia trying to write in the same place they live—whether surrounded by people or not. Some feel lonely at their typewriters and need the stimulus of knowing others are working on creative projects all around them. They need the sign of people, the sound of typewriters.

If the loneliness of writing gets to you, you might do what writers have been doing in New York for years to solve this problem. Share the cost. Rent a little cubbyhole of an apartment to as many writers as can comfortably fit in. In Greenwich Village there's one called the Writer's Room.

All that can be heard in the Writer's Room is the clicking of a typewriter here and there. Some authors are writing in longhand. All respect the two taboos, which are not to speak to anyone—even to ask for the use of a pencil—and not to make eye contact. Talking is permitted only in the lounge, where there is a dictionary and a few other reference books, a coffeemaker and a refrigerator stocked with cottage cheese. Exercise pads are on the floor for naps or exercise. Writers slip in and out, keeping their own hours, some leaving to go home and others to go to work in offices.

About seventy writers use the place, paying $100 to $150 a month depending on whether they write in the open or have an entirely enclosed space where they can use a word processor or can telephone without disturbing others.

Judith Rossner of *Looking for Mr. Goodbar* fame came with her sleeping bag and stayed for sixteen-hour stretches at a time, working and napping and sometimes crying over her typewriter as she clicked away. Nobody asked what she was working on.

David Small, mentioned earlier, was unusual in his easy adjustment to different locales for writing, but others have chosen even stranger places to write. A few have written fiction in their parked cars, because they got a feeling of peace and quiet in an enclosed little private world of glass and steel. Marcel Proust used a cork-lined room, a pretty good equivalent to an ivory tower!

When you find the spot where you feel best while writing, the very place will actually help you get in the mood to turn out your daily three pages-plus. One woman wrote at the kitchen pass-through bar. Another writer, after he had earned enough money from writing, thought that he deserved something better than the cramped corner of his house where he had written facing the wall. He built a new room, a lovely study with a view of trees and flowers. But he found he couldn't concentrate when looking at moving objects like leaves blowing in the wind and children and dogs. He had to move his desk to a corner of the room and face the wall.

Are You Ready Now?

Okay, you feel you are ready now. You have your plot, your characters, your ream of paper, your favorite place to work, and you know the time of day or night you feel most alert. That magic moment is now approaching. Now do you sit down and start writing?

No. Not for just another minute or two. Or five, if that's what it takes. Because you still haven't decided exactly what you are going to write that day—what part of your novel.

Sit down with a cup of coffee and your looseleaf notebook, or pace around with it, glancing at it and imagining the scene you are going to jump into, the dialogue the characters are going to have or the description of the place where the murder or love scene or act of heroism is going to happen.

Aha, you've found the segment that fits your mood this day? Good.

PSYCHING UP

Some perfectly normal people exist who can hardly wait to start their writing session each day. They, alas, are the rare lucky ones. Harold Robbins, author of *The Carpetbaggers* and *The Betsy*, likes the daily act of writing so much that he once said, "The only time I'm completely selfish is when I write a book." He explained that it was the only time he felt completely free and was in complete charge, having everything his way and not having to be concerned with "the consideration of other people."

The rest of the first- and even tenth-time novelists say, "Oh God, how did I ever get into this? Who told me I can write—I'll fix him." The good news is that if the book makes the best-seller list eventually and you are making the grand tour to promote it, you will forget the pain and pacing of "book-birth" and be spouting about the joys of writing, like Robbins.

The problem is you can't wait for inspiration. I know people who have waited a lifetime for inspiration.

This might be one of your good days, or a day that is not so good. But *you* are going to write words, paragraphs, scenes, out of your imagination *every* day, rising above your mood, if necessary. And why? Because you have made this commitment. You are going to finish a whole novel. You may write a masterpiece—or at least a book a publisher somewhere will praise and want. No, better than that: It may be the next most-talked-about best-seller. Anna Lee Waldo did it with *Sacajawea*. James M. Cain did it with *The Postman Always Rings Twice*.

So there's your answer—anything can happen. You may write a big one, too. So, what you can do to get started? Plenty. You are going to psych yourself up before each session. If I were doing it, I would tell myself something like this:

I'm going to get just three pages done today. It's not much. Just three pages. I can hardly wait. I love the plot. I know exactly what I'm going to say in my first line today and after that, I'll just get going. Somehow the rest of the three pages will come to me. I'll look at the notebook and I'll just keep writing. All I have to do is expand what it says on that page. I'm going to think like the female character. I'm going to think like that fool she's trying to impress. I'm going to talk. I'm going to put in that great line I thought of last night. Thank goodness I put it down. I'm clever. I can hardly wait to get started. Here we go. . . .

THE MOMENT OF TRUTH—HOW DO YOU WRITE THOSE THREE PAGES A DAY?

You sit down. You don't doodle. You don't dawdle.

You put your fingers on the typewriter or computer keyboard and you go. Or you pick up the pencil or pen if you are writing in longhand, like the old masters, and you write page after page on a yellow legal pad or a spiral-bound notebook or colored paper or white typewriter paper.

You do not stop until you have finished your three pages.

You do not get up to look up a word. Just put a question mark in the margin so you'll know where to find it later.

You don't go to the bathroom unless kidney stones would result.

You don't take phone calls. You can take the phone off the hook and let people get a busy signal. Or you can just let it ring so people think you're not home. Just tell all your friends not to call during this two- or three-hour period in which you are unavailable to the phone. Or get an answering service or an answering machine. You don't have to be as extreme as Carolyn Chute, author of *The Beans of Egypt, Maine*. She could not cope with any of the above, and so simply disconnected her phone—permanently.

You don't jump up and pace around trying to decide whether your character says a thing this way or that or reacts this way or that. You simply put both ways down and put that good old question mark in the margin so you can ponder it and decide later.

You just keep writing in a straight line shot at the plot the way you thought it through. You try to go into a trance in which your characters come to life and take over for you and tell you what they want you to write down.

If they won't speak up, do it for them, muttering aloud if you like, writing the dialogue as best you can. You may later be surprised at how good it is. And write all you want. Don't stint yourself. You can always cut out the redundancies and the maudlin notes later.

You work along a while and suddenly you're out of the mood. You want to quit for the day and make up for it tomorrow. Don't. Keep going. You can do it. It's only *three* pages.

The main thing is to keep the rhythm of work going. You will get used to it in a week or so of starting a novel. You will get keyed up and anxious when your set writing time arrives. You will become like a firehorse of old, ready for the signal to run to the fire. Or like the horse who knows the way home and doesn't have to be told what to do. He takes the wagon there—home—a step at a time, just as you are going to take your characters home to the last page.

But you won't get there unless you condition yourself.

It took John Grisham just one hundred days to write *The Pelican Brief*, just keeping a steady schedule and working two to four hours every morning. He worked through bouts of flu, company coming and everything else.

Every day will be a triumph if you have managed somehow to keep writing and get those three pages done. Give yourself a little treat of some sort, some reward. Your personal carrot. Some writers relax with a drink afterward. Some have a sweet. Some get on the phone and have a talk with a friend—on any subject but the book.

Of course, if you become a big success, you can give yourself a bigger reward. Tom Clancy, after finishing *Clear and Present Danger* on a tight deadline, went on a cross-country train trip (he never flies), taking his wife, four children and two friends, renting a whole parlor car for their exclusive use.

WRITER'S BLOCK

Harold Robbins may say he never has writer's block. But most writers do, and I can't promise you that it will only happen once.

Say it happens again and this time it's worse. Much worse.

You're sailing along but suddenly you can't think of what to say. You reach in the air and it's not there. You start to get panicky. Don't. I guarantee it will pass if you don't waste time struggling with that particular bit now. Just leave some blank lines and keep going with the next person's dialogue.

You're still stuck. You absolutely cannot continue the scene where you are. You are dry. You have nothing more to say anywhere in this scene and you know it's not finished. Okay, no sweat. Look in your notebook quickly and choose a different situation or scene that is more to your liking today. Make a note on the typed or handwritten page where you are leaving off that you are switching to chapter so-and-so "where John is hunting for the body in the woods."

Now take a new sheet of paper, or open a new document on your computer screen. Label the top *Chapter so-and-so. John hunting for body.* And now keep those fingers moving. You may get so involved when you are writing about the body search that you write five pages instead of the three required for the day. Good. But that doesn't mean you only have to write one page tomorrow. Keep the count going. It's three plus any extras. Extra pages will make you *feel great!*

You might even want to have a day-by-day calendar or a chart and on it, at the end of every day's session, write the date, which scenes and the number of pages you did. Example: "April 3, Started argument John with father, Chapter 6. Wrote 1 page. Switched to Chapter 8, Search for body. 2 pages. Total 3 pages."

The accumulation of pages is your reward. The true sign that you are getting there. Progress, like virtue, is its own reward.

Maybe you're stuck because your character isn't motivated strongly enough. Now may be the time for you to reveal why your character's life will be in shambles if he fails to stop the villain. Whatever the individual motivations of your characters are, those motivations must be made very clear. If the reader doesn't know, doesn't *feel*, why the fellow wants to climb the mountain or why the girl has centered her romantic fantasies on this one particular man, the reader will lose interest in a hurry. If the *characters* don't care, your reader surely will not care either.

If your characters have no goals, that's even worse, unless you are writing a book like J.D. Salinger's very touching and effective *The Catcher in the Rye*. Sixteen-year-old Holden Caulfield is simply reacting to life as he wanders around. Oh, he has some vague hope of growing up and watching little kids play in a field, but it is *life* that is in effect the strong character in the story, and *life* is buffeting him about.

Maybe your dissatisfaction is triggered this day by the feeling that not enough is happening in one particular phase of your plot. It's blah. This may be just the time to throw in that extra-awful thing that could happen. Remember, you thought about it on the bus and jotted it in your little notepad? Your heroine makes a sudden, terrible mistake. Novels are like life, and life is like a game of Monopoly where if you land in the wrong square, you are in trouble. But your reader keeps hoping your character will land on the squares marked with the rewards of life. Try tossing your heroine into the wrong square—give her an instant problem. Or, as screenwriter Martin Roth says, chase your hero up a tree and throw rocks at him, to see how he responds.

Dwelling on your mood is a luxury you can't afford. The writing mood will catch up with you once you get absorbed in your plot, action or the dialogue—what the characters are screaming or cooing or conniving about that day. Yes, when you finally are *in the mood*, you won't want to stop. The time will fly and you may find yourself with an extra page or two. Writers have told me that days that started out most poorly have sometimes ended up most productive.

The great American psychologist William James tells, in *The Varieties of Religious Experience*, of days when he woke up and felt so bad he wondered if he could live through the day. Later, in the midst of a lecture to his students, he would suddenly realize he felt wonderful. His own words cheered him up.

YOU'RE HANGING IN THERE

Your novel is moving right along and you're feeling as well as a first-time novelist can, some days elated and some days wondering if simple torture on a medieval rack wouldn't be easier. You've written a little part of this chapter and all of that chapter. And almost all of a couple others.

It's important to keep track of what is written because sometimes you have lived it in your mind so much you think you already wrote it. This is especially important if you are the kind of writer who does best by writing the part you are in the mood for that day. Those who start at page one and go in a straight line to the final page, always picking up where they left off the day before, will only have to make a notation of the page they are on and the scene they wrote: "April 3, Finished 6th chapter on page 123. Mary Ellen gets blackmail letter. 3½ pages." Aha, you wrote an extra half page. Even that is cause for celebration.

It's a good idea to use a different color folder to hold the pages already written, to distinguish them from the folders that hold your outline.

You've now established a routine. Once you finally sit down at the typewriter, you do not doodle around or wonder what to say. The reason is that you have psyched yourself up before the session. You get the job done a day at a time, telling yourself you don't have to write a whole book, just three pages each day, and you can do it.

In your mind, you play each character's part, saying what you know that person would say. All you have to tell yourself to start the juices flowing is, "I am Evelyn and I am trying to throw myself over the bridge and some man has grabbed my legs. I am screaming at him. So what would I say?" It's the old game of "What If?" "What if he lets go? Then what do I do? Fall toward him or make the plunge?"

When you have gone through your whole list of chapters in this way and have come to the brilliant ending you have been working toward all along, it will be like the great Union Pacific Railroad. Yes, it will be like the moment when the two ends of the long, mighty line of track finally came together and the builders knew they were through. Joy.

FINAL TOUCHES

Now go fill in the gaps, all the places you left blank where you needed to look up a fact or you didn't know which way a certain scene or bit of dialogue went. But that's it. That's all you do. Right then you put the manuscript away to cool. You don't even need to look up those misspelled words yet. Just hide your manuscript in a drawer or closet and relax. You deserve it. You have typed a 270- to 300-page novel. And you did it in ninety days.

And there you have it. You have the *first draft* of what may be a great novel. You are too close to it now, too jaded, too tired of it to know.

Cool It

Do not, repeat, *do not* read any of it yet. So what do you do and where do you go from here? You let it rest for a few weeks, at least. Work on something else for a while. Catch up on your reading. Go on a vacation. Do whatever you need to get a fresh viewpoint, and then suddenly you'll be ready for editing.

TIPS

• Set yourself a daily writing quota of three pages.

• Write during the time of day when you feel most alert. Set aside the same time in the same place every day for writing. Writing should become part of your daily routine.

• Pick a location where you can be productive, whether you require background noise or absolute silence to write.

• Take a few minutes every day before you start writing to visualize what you're going to work on.

• Think positively. Get enthused and excited about writing every day.

• Avoid all interruptions during your writing time.

• Work out dialogue by speaking it aloud.

• Reward yourself after you complete your daily three pages.

• Keep writing—even through writer's block. Switch to another chapter or section of the novel if difficulty persists.

• Count the number of pages you write every day. Just because you wrote extra pages yesterday is no excuse to fall short today.

• Use different color folders to hold your manuscript and your outline.

• When you reach the end of your novel, take time to review what you wrote and fill in any gaps you might find. Check any dubious facts.

• Relax. Let your manuscript "cool" for a while.

7.

Editing Your Manuscript

You have your first draft. You feel safe and secure. Now go to a duplicating place and have a copy made of the whole thing. Make sure the duplicating machine is in good working order and makes a nice, dark copy so you can read it easily. Check that every page is copied. Or, if using a computer, print out a copy, and also put the whole thing on a disk, and carefully label it.

Put this copy in a safe place where you can refer to it later if you make a mistake in editing while you are chopping up your first draft. You can always go back to the first version of some action or dialogue.

Now read your manuscript pretending you are a reader who bought it in a bookstore. Keep notepaper beside you. Jot down any ideas you have for improvement. Mark places in the chapters where you get bored. Mark the places on the manuscript that you especially like. If you think some action comes too soon or too late in the story, make a note about it. Each chapter is still in its folder, so put all the notes about that chapter in the right folder.

One approach to editing your own work is to do nothing except have it typed. Best-selling detective-story writer Lawrence Sanders says he makes few changes once he has his story down. He simply follows his outline and his chapter breakdown, working in longhand, then roughly types it out. The clean, professional-looking draft that goes to the publisher is typed by other hands. "I never rewrite," says Sanders.

On the other hand, Mario Puzo thinks rewriting is everything. He says, "I don't write, I rewrite." James Clavell, whose novel *Whirlwind* sold at auction for $5,000,000, says, "I've always known the art of writing is rewriting."

An extreme of not rewriting was the method John M. Kimbro used to write his forty-book chronicle for Popular Library, *The Saga of the Phenwick Women*. A former Broadway actor, he dictated each book into a tape recorder, acting out in appropriate voices the dialogue. He then sent the tapes to a manuscript typist and delivered the typed manuscript to Popular Library.

Women's fiction author Joan Wolf writes her original draft in longhand—and then edits it as she goes along, typing it herself.

But these are the methods of experienced authors. And of them, the Mario Puzo-James Clavell method is probably closest to what you'll be doing yourself when you edit your first draft.

THE MECHANICS OF EDITING

Here we will insert a few words about using a computer in your writing and editing, and afterward, we'll discuss doing it without a computer. Your goal when preparing a manuscript using a word processing program as opposed to using a typewriter is the same: Make sure the manuscript is as neat, clean and readable as possible.

While nearly any word processing program is capable of producing a good quality manuscript, the two used most commonly on both IBM and Macintosh (and compatible) machines are Microsoft Word or Word for Windows, and WordPerfect. Although the two programs differ in structure, they both have features that are invaluable to the writer. The use of these features entails a new way of thinking about preparing a manuscript. Structuring is done either before or after the manuscript is typed rather than continually as you go along. You set up the format—margins, automatic page numbering, headers and footers if you need them (either automatic or different for different pages), font, type size—either before or after typing. Thus you do not have to think about format at all, unless you wish to deviate from what is standard, for example, 12-point type size. In choosing a font, select one that's clear and easy to read, and avoid fancy and unusual ones. Some particularly readable fonts are Times, New York, New Century Schoolbook and Palatino.

Saving items randomly on ill-marked disks or lumped on a hard disk makes them hard to find later. Better to create a document with a simple title and arrange parts of your novel in separate folders within it. For example, I have this book in a document called "First Novel," and each chapter in a separate folder within it. So it is easy to identify an individual file and possible to apply commands to groups of files according to file type, rather than to each individually, which is time-consuming and risks overlooking an individual file.

There are certain hazards in working on a computer that you should keep in mind. Naturally you should save, save, save and try to protect your computer from electrical surges with suitable equipment. On the literary side, don't rely entirely on the spell checker for proofreading—probably you have wrong verb tenses, unconscious use of cognates, such as "there" for "their" or "it's" for "its," and other errors the spell checker won't catch. George Witte at Picador Books mentioned another hazard: He believes that because it is so easy to revise your work on a computer, writers tend to put down just any version of a thought or idea, intending to go back and revise later—then failing to do so. Even when using a computer, you should still try to get it right and powerful the first time, by forming your sentences in your mind before writing them down.

When using a typewriter rather than a computer, editing need not be a formidable task. If you have used the same word several times in a paragraph or on the same page, think of another, or consult your thesaurus. Write the new word above the old, and draw a line through the old so you can still read it.

If you think you told about something too late in the story, cut that section out with scissors. Keep a lined yellow legal pad beside you and write, "Moving bottom page 6, chapter 12 ax murder scene to chapter 9." When you decide where it goes in chapter nine, add that information: "after stranger goes into barn."

Wait, you are not finished yet. Now put the original page number and chapter in the margin of the piece you are moving. In this case, it would be marked, "ch 12, p 6." This will save endless bother when you are asking yourself, "Now where did I put that murder scene?" Your legal pad will tell you to look in the folder for chapter nine, and the writing in the margin will keep you from having to look at all the cut pieces of paper to find the right one.

Whether using a typewriter or a computer, you may have a lot of scenes moved to different folders and you may not. You may like the way you put the story together the first time.

You may need only a better word here and there. A little more dialogue. The reason for someone's behavior made more clear.

Read your manuscript for plot, for characters, for action. See if it's so compelling you want to keep going. If you don't, stop. Look again. Is it that it needs action at that point? Is this the time for the cops to barge in with guns drawn—at the wrong house? For the kid to be discovered growing pot in the woods behind the house? Don't be afraid to talk out loud when you are editing.

Sometimes what is needed is some dialogue. Maybe the trouble is too much action and not enough talk. Let the characters speak. Or at least break into the descriptions of what the characters are doing to tell what they are thinking. Thoughts can be very juicy. People think about a lot of shocking things they don't dare do. And they analyze people around them with sharp insights that would surprise—if not horrify—the other people. They may act dumb but they know what skullduggery is going on and it's in their thoughts.

If you find parts that are good, compliment yourself in the margin. Write "Great" and run a line along the margin to show how long a passage it is. If it's artificial sounding, write "Sounds fake." If it's boring, write "Who cares?" I think you get the picture. Be pleased that you can spot strengths and weaknesses because then you can fix whatever needs fixing.

A common fault that makes the action flow bog down is pausing to describe someone. You can fit bits of description into dialogue or action. In *How Green Was My Apple*, a detective story that is part of a series published by Crime Club, author Marc Lovell has to get across the fact that his spy-detective, named Apple, is a sympathetic comic figure because he is too tall to be a good spy. Rather than come out and say it, here's some dialogue that establishes this fact, and also characterizes Apple:

Her voice drawling lazily, she said, "If one may ask, how tall are you?"

"Six feet seven inches," Apple said. He gave a smile of apology.

"In your socks?"

"In my bare feet."

"Good heavens," the woman said.

Apple wondered with discomfort if it was proper to use the word "bare" to this type of woman, a thought he then swiftly amended to cover women of all types. Yes, he decided. In this day and age, of course.

Having the courage to make cuts in material that, no matter how interesting or well written, does not advance your story line is an essential part of editing. Steven Linakis, author of *In the Spring the War Ended*, was not afraid to make drastic cuts in his first draft, and discarded almost half of it. But he writes a long first draft.

No matter how you might despair at your first draft, it is essential to have it before proceeding further. Editor and writer Hugh Rawson put it succinctly: "You must have a framework."

EDITING TO PLEASE YOURSELF

Don't get paranoid about how an editor will react to your subject matter. Write it the way you feel you must. It is impossible to guess which way the publisher would prefer something scandalous or shocking treated. If your manuscript is accepted, the editor assigned to your novel will not be shy about suggesting some different way the scenes or action in your plot could be handled or put together to make a more exciting book, or to tone something down.

Each editor has his pet likes and peeves, as you will learn if you deal with enough of them. So don't be afraid to submit your manuscript with your original thinking. First, please yourself. Remember, *you* are the boss.

However, after you have the plot the way you want it—with or without rearrangement—there are other things to do:

Cut out unnecessary adverbs and adjectives. They slow the action and don't really say anything. Take, for example, "She was very beautiful." She's either beautiful or she's not beautiful. Authors used to say "Her beauty rivaled the sun," or other such comments now considered corny and gushing. The same with "Her face could stop a clock." Unless it's being said by a real "country boy" type in your manuscript, what might get stopped is your manuscript from being read a moment longer.

Editor Ellis Amburn says the worst mistake beginning novelists can make is to be boring. And one of the ways they can be is by using trite expressions. The same elements that are used in poetry—figures of speech—can make a description of something a delight to read. Try a comparison of unlike things, never compared to each other before.

Marcel Proust, in *Remembrance of Things Past*, constructs a beautiful metaphor on the effect of time. When one of his characters, Baron Charlus, gets old and begins to totter, he suggests our years are like a set of stilts, and the older we become, the longer the stilts—until first we totter, then fall.

So if something looks boring in your writing, cross it out and look for a fresh approach, or just leave it out.

If scenes aren't needed after all, leave them out.

If characters are not needed, leave them out.

If part of the conversation isn't needed, cut, cut, cut. Or use your pencil or ballpoint pen to draw a line through it. The problem with using a black marker or deleting sections from a word processing file is that you can no longer read what you had, in case you want to rethink it. So save the stuff you take out in a separate file. Marker pens are too final. If there is a long speech or description you think you want to eliminate, just draw a line around it with a pencil or pen and write "Out?" in the margin.

Go slow with self-criticism. One day you may feel so blue that nothing looks good to you. You have to protect yourself from your own moods. On bad mood days, don't cross anything out. Just do something constructive, such as using your thesaurus to see if you can find more colorful words for some you have used and overused. Write the new ones in the margin and circle the words in question. But don't try to find a lot of ways to say "said." Leave "said" alone unless the character is screaming or whispering, in which case, say so.

If you use a lot of participles—"-ing" endings—get rid of them. Use "She laughed." "She cried." Editors don't like "She was laughing" and "She was crying."

It's not the end of the world if you can't edit well. That's why publishing houses hire editors. If they are really impressed with your novel and see there a spark of genius, they will work with you as long as necessary to make suggestions so that you can make the changes. In some cases, the editor will do much of it for you—probably more than you want.

Helen Hooven Santmyer, who was mentioned before, is a case in point. Her novel, . . . *And Ladies of the Club*, originally exceeded the length of Tolstoy's *War and Peace*, and the publisher called for cuts.

Fortunately, Santmyer had a friend qualified to help her with the editing that the publisher, Putnam's, was demanding—a former librarian who lived in the same nursing home. By day, the friend, Mildred Sandoe, would make editing suggestions on how to reduce the manuscript by several hundred pages, as was wanted, and Santmyer would agree. But then, in the night, Santmyer would get up and secretly put back most of the deleted material.

"So what happened?" my coauthor asked Mildred Sandoe in a telephone interview.

Sandoe chuckled. "Eventually, I just bundled it all up the way it was and sent it to the publisher for them to shorten. But I don't believe they did very much." And that is why the Santmyer book still rivals Tolstoy's *War and Peace* in length, each being some 600,000 words long. Santmyer's novel fills 1,344 pages in printed form—three normal books.

An even more extreme case of a writer at sea when it came to editing was Thomas Wolfe. He was absolutely helpless. Everything he wrote seemed important to him, and some of it did read like deathless prose. He turned in thousands of pages on his first novel, *Look Homeward, Angel*.

The manuscript traveled to various publishers in a crate. One editor said that had he unpacked it, it would have been two feet taller than a grand piano. He stopped reading before he finished the first thousand pages because he still had not found the plot. He added that when the book came out, it did not contain any of the sections the editor had read. Somewhere else in the crate was the great best-seller.

The question arises, if his editor at Scribners, Maxwell Perkins, had not done a superb job editing that crate of manuscript, would the world have heard of Thomas Wolfe? The story went that Perkins took the time to plow through the endless pages because he owed a favor to Wolfe's first literary agent, Madeleine Boyd, wife of a noted literary critic.

PUTTING IT ALL TOGETHER

Now it's time to put all of the pieces of your manuscript together to see how it looks with your improvements and, even possibly, your new plot structure. You will need a table to spread out your bits of pages and full pages. When you need to put several partial sheets together, staple or tape them to a sheet of paper. Anchor the rearranged sections firmly to prevent loss and make pages easier to handle.

It doesn't matter how the pages look, just so *you* can read them. When you have cut and fastened the first chapter to have everything in the right place, put it back in the folder and spread out chapter two.

When the whole book is done in this fashion, read it again and see how you like it. If more surgery is necessary, do it. Again, at this point, rely on your own judgment. Editors in publishing houses will have their comments later.

If you like it the way it is, now is the time to type clean copy and look up every word of questionable spelling. (If you're writing on a computer, you may have a spelling-dictionary program that will do this for you.) If you are weak on grammar, now is the time to use the services of a consultant—maybe a schoolteacher, or college English instructor, or professional copyeditor for a newspaper or magazine. If your typing is not good, you might consider hiring a professional typist who is accustomed to book manuscripts. It can be a good investment—every editor prefers an attractive manuscript.

Of course, if you are using a computer and word processor, you will have your novel stored in the computer. You can make changes on the screen—move around parts of your story, add and delete at will—and do this general editing work more easily. I have noticed that my partner, Carol Cartaino, a freelance book editor, saves the material she deletes from manuscripts while editing them, in a separate file. She wants to keep this material available in case she finds another place in the manuscript to use it.

If you're typing your manuscript yourself or running it off on your computer's printer (avoid dot matrix printing), start the first page of every chapter a third to halfway down the page to set it off, and be sure to add the number of the chapter—centered two or three lines above the opening line.

HOW SHOULD EACH PAGE LOOK?

The rules are simple and logical. Type or print on one side of the sheet only, on 8½ × 11-inch paper. You want each page (except chapter openings) to be approximately alike in the number of words so you and a publisher can estimate the total length of the manuscript easily. You don't want too many words on the page so that when the publisher, or the sales manager, is reading it, he will finish each page fast and think of the novel as a "page-turner." I recommend using pica or 12-point type, double-spaced, on plain white noneras- able typing paper. Have a one-inch margin all around, except for the left-hand margin, which should be at least one and one-half inches, or preferably, one and three-quarter inches. The reason you leave more space on the left is so your editor or copyeditor will have room to write comments and suggest corrections if your manuscript is put under contract. Put the page number at the upper right, or upper center—*not* upper left, where it would be covered if pages are paper clipped together. *Never* put page numbers at the bottom of the page, because it's a real nuisance to try to find page numbers at the bottom of a pile of pages in a box.

If you follow these guidelines, you will have approximately 246 words to the page—and can safely round off the total number of words to 250 a page. Here's how this word count is determined.

You will find you have about fifty-three characters to the aver- age line, counting each letter, each mark of punctuation and each space between words as a character. Incomplete lines and dialogue are counted as though they were full lines, because they will use up full lines when your book is printed.

You will probably find you get twenty-six lines to the page, using pica type. Multiply fifty-three characters times twenty-six lines, and you get 1,378 characters to the page. Divide this number by 5.6 (the average number of characters, including spaces between words, occupied by each word), and you get 246, the number of words per page.

To adjust for *elite* type, which is smaller, just allow *two* inches for the margin on the left, and set your typewriter for a fifty-five- character line. Allow *two and a half spaces* between each line, and again, you will have a page of about 250 words. And you will again be producing an easy-to-read manuscript—a page-turner.

One of the things most annoying to a publisher is to receive a manuscript typed with a worn-out ribbon. It is almost an affront to be expected to read something that looks faded and tired. Editors read constantly. Don't strain their eyes! Using a nice clean, dark ribbon that makes a manuscript look crisp and fresh is some of the best advice I can give you.

Your name goes only on the title page, which shows the book's title in the center, with your byline under it. At the lower left or right of the title page, print your real name, if you are using a pseudonym, your address and telephone number.

Don't put anything on the top of each page but the page number. Anything else you might include would have to be crossed off each page by your editor, or the publisher's typesetter might set it into type.

While you are doing your second draft, you can stick to the routine that has seen you through the writing of the first draft. That is, sit down at your typewriter or table at the same time you did for three months. It has now become your habit, and a good one. Type your three pages of clean copy a day, but this time while looking up any words you need to in the dictionary.

Within a reasonable amount of time, you will finish your second draft. Now you may stop, or you may want to do a third or fourth draft. If you are a perfectionist, and find it hard to stop picking away at your work, remember the comment of the great artist Picasso: "I don't finish my paintings, I abandon them." But eventually you *are* finished! Congratulations!

Now, how do you present your product? Don't staple each chapter together. Staples rust. Don't paper clip them together. Paper clips rust. *Don't put it in a binder of any kind*, or your editor will never take it home to read because it's too heavy to take all at once.

Don't do anything but put the whole manuscript in a stationery box. That is the *only* professional way to present a manuscript. If you don't have a box from which a ream of paper was taken, you can buy such boxes at stationery stores or copy shops.

Your novel is born and it's time to let go and send it on its way to a literary agent or publisher.

WHAT IF IT DOESN'T SELL?

What if you do everything you can—give it your best shot and edit and clean copy the manuscript—and nobody wants it? You thought it was good. You couldn't believe how good it was. Your agent liked it, but twenty-two publishers said "no" and the agent doesn't think she ought to submit it any more. The publishers say nobody is reading that particular type of story these days. Or they just don't like it and they don't say why. They may say, "It just isn't quite what we are looking for," or, "It doesn't suit our present needs." A particularly frustrating comment is, "It's okay, but I don't love it."

So what do you do? You have several possibilities. The first is to carry on, curse a little and vow to show them! Then, throw the manuscript in a drawer where you can find it in a few years, and for the present, forget it. Start plotting your next novel. Write the next one with the same three-page-a-day routine that got you through the first.

Now you're proving you're made of the right stuff, and your chances of making it the next time have increased. Comfort yourself that you are in good company. Irving Stone was turned down by no less than seventeen publishers on his first novel. Several said, "Who cares about the life of an artist?" He put the novel away and wrote a second one, which was published. Hardly anyone can remember what the first published one was. But the first one he wrote—*Lust for Life*—the one no one would publish, became a big best-seller in 1934, when Doubleday finally took a chance.

Today, the book—and the late Irving Stone—hold a small niche in publishing history for having improved and popularized the genre called "fictionalized biography." Before Stone wrote his novel based on the life of Vincent van Gogh, that genre had not been used for years.

REWRITING AND ADDITIONAL WORK

Another possibility is that rejection will cause you to dig in and try to improve your novel further. When is such additional work justified by the hope of an eventual sale? I would say only when you have some objective reason to think you are on the right track, but not quite there—such as encouragement from an agent, several near-miss rejections or sincere praise of your work by some obviously qualified person, such as an established professional editor, writer or critic. Or maybe you are simply very stubborn and determined.

You might, in such circumstances, consider trying to find a "book doctor," either an editorial service such as those listed in *Literary Market Place*—The Editorial Dept, founded by former trade book editor Renni Browne, was used by one of my clients—or an individual professional freelance editor who works with authors and agents.

Typical of many such obviously qualified people is Joyce Engelson, whose sage advice is mentioned elsewhere in this book. She has written novels and prize-winning short stories herself, is a former editor in chief of major publishers and now is a freelance editor in New York who works with authors, agents and publishers.

Freelance editors are not ghostwriters; they simply provide you with extensive, detailed objective criticism and try to point you in the direction of rewriting that will make your work acceptable to a publisher. Their services do not come cheap, and there is no point in going to one unless you are prepared to listen to tough, objective and coldly stated criticism—and promptly pay the necessary cash.

One such book doctor was Darrell Husted. He had been an editor with Prentice-Hall, Scribners and other publishers and had several paperback original and hardcover novels of his own published. Though Darrell died not long ago, here are some of the timeless comments he made to me about editing your own work:

> What should shape a book is what appeals to an editor who has the power to get it published. Beautiful writing is useless unless you have hooked the reader, and early on. You have to seduce the reader, and neophytes forget the reader doesn't know where you are aiming.
>
> Get all those loose ends tied up. Readers won't pay $24.95 for a slice of life. They want a story. Don't go off on tangents. Take out unnecessary characters; remove events that have no consequences. Characters should not show up, then disappear. If they are supposed to disappear, they should not show up again without explanation. Authors should offer *specifics*—any office clerk can make general pronouncements.
>
> Good books are cohesive. Their authors express their ideas in a well-formed universe. Form is shape: *form*ula. Fiction explains life better than any medium including history. It makes events comprehensive and interesting and brings form to events for the reader.
>
> Fiction is *entertainment*, and if it isn't, it's nothing. If a novel is entertaining, the sky's the limit for adding other elements—but entertainment is first. Form in the novel is

elastic—works by Dostoevsky, Proust, Jacqueline Susann, Sidney Sheldon all have been successful.

Writers should turn on the reader on page one and put their best writing near the beginning of the manuscript, or they'll never hook book editors, who will simply stop reading. Your characters should be interesting—if they are, you are way ahead of the game—plots can be fixed, but there is not much an editor can do about uninteresting characters.

One device Husted used to help a writer think in more depth about a character was to ask the author the character's birth date. He then looked up the character's horoscope in *It's All in the Stars, A Sun Sign Horoscope for Every Birthday*, by Zolar, the astrologer. He then posed a question to the author: "Here are your character's qualities according to Zolar's horoscope for that birthday. Is Zolar a good astrologer? Are these the qualities of your character?"

This exercise forced the author to consider how much he knew about the character, and reflecting on the question, to enlarge his knowledge of the people in his novel, or at least bring the knowledge to full consciousness.

The following anecdote, which Husted told to authors to further reinforce his point, was, he said, possibly apocryphal, and he didn't remember where he had read it: Ibsen was reportedly asked by an admirer of his plays, "Why does Nora in *A Doll's House* have dark hair, when she is Scandinavian, and most Scandinavians are blond?"

Ibsen replied, "Well, Nora's father went to Provençe when he was a young man, and there met Nora's mother, a beautiful French woman with dark hair. They married, and he took her back to Scandinavia, where Nora was born. Nora inherited her mother's dark hair."

"But Mr. Ibsen," the admirer protested, "none of that is in the play!"

Ibsen said, "What difference does that make? A fact is a fact."

Darrell Husted believed it is not too much out of line even to think of a character's grandparents and get to know them as well as their offspring.

So maybe persistence and rewriting can be the answer for you.

My favorite story of why you should hang on is the real-life saga of Inga Dean, which has the happy ending of Dean seeing her first book published, *Memory and Desire*.

Well, it wasn't exactly her first book, and therein lies the story. Dean, who lived in Washington, DC, finished her first novel in 1970, and it bounced around to possibly twenty publishers before she stopped submitting it. The fact that she was the daughter of famed journalist William Shirer was of no help, as she would not trade on his name.

Determined to get a novel published, Dean started another one and had gotten to page 700 before she realized it was "out of control."

As she told my coauthor, "There was too much of everything—plot, time span, characters." The writing was interrupted by her husband's retirement and their move to Lenox, Massachusetts. Then, Dean said, "I took the manuscript out of the closet and tried to save it but some months later realized what I now had was a thousand pages of unusable drivel."

This time Dean did not bother to submit her new manuscript. She carved it up and saved some of the action and all of her main character, a character she had been living with in her mind for eight years.

Now she started again. A new plot with only bits of the old. She also changed the occupation of her heroine from "a failed artist to a not-too-good restaurant critic of a third-rate magazine, who used to be a not-too-good painter." Persistence paid off, and this time a publisher—Viking—said yes and asked only that the length be cut from 600 manuscript pages to 350. At this point, she had written three drafts of the manuscript over eight years, but she plowed through it again.

"When *Memory and Desire* finally came out in the summer of 1985, I had to laugh at their description of me as 'a talented *new* novelist,'" Inga Dean told Fran. "I had been at it fifteen years, had written not one but three novels and God knows how many manuscript pages." Then she added, "Tell your readers I'd do it again."

SELF-PUBLISHING

If you try to get advice on whether to self-publish a manuscript that no publisher seems to want, most people will say, "Don't do it." But if you are determined to go ahead anyway, based on your own faith in your novel and the opinions of several people you trust, do at least read up on the subject (some books on self-publishing are listed in the "Further Reading and References" section at the end of this book) so you'll have a realistic idea of what you are getting into.

With that caution firmly stated, now let me tell you a story that will gladden the heart of every first-time author who has felt dejected and bruised from those constant rejections.

Aliske Webb had written a novel that was inspired by her passion for quilts. She called it *Twelve Golden Threads: Lessons for Successful Living From Grandma's Quilt.* Over a hundred publishers in Canada and the United States rejected it. Her husband had faith in the book, and encouraged by him, she decided to self-publish 3,000 hardcover copies.

But where could they sell them? At quilt shows, of course. They sold their home in Toronto and toured the States as well as their own Provinces, from county fair to county fair and quilt show to quilt show—setting up a little stand and living in a mobile home.

The book sold remarkably well, and when sales reached 25,000 copies, Aliske Webb went to Sunburst Publishers, a small publishing company in Lancaster, Pennsylvania, hoping to place it as a paperback. Suddenly, everything fell into place and hardback companies expressed interest. In an auction, HarperCollins won out over three other houses, signing Webb to a four-book deal—each book to be built around quilts.

Golden Threads was released in the United States in May 1996, then a Japanese publisher grabbed it as well and produced a 62,000-copy first printing. Webb wasted no time. She set about writing her second novel, *Scrap Quilt Memories,* using a laptop computer as she traveled, in order to meet her 1997 deadline. Her third story was already running around in her mind with its title—*The Phoenix Quilt.*

TURNING UNUSED RESEARCH
INTO A NONFICTION BOOK

What if you have put a lot of research and energy into your first novel and it doesn't sell right away? Maybe you can use the same research as the basis of a nonfiction book—and gain writing experience and make some money in the process. Then you can write an improved version of your novel later.

Does this idea startle you? Consider the experiences of Clyde Burleson, who started writing as a forty-year-old Houston, Texas, ad agency president. In 1975, newspapers began to publish leaks and fragments of the amazing true story of how the CIA and Howard

Hughes secretly built a giant, new kind of ship, sailed it into the Pacific and had recovered, from three miles deep, a whole sunken Soviet submarine.

Since Burleson was fascinated by technology, he followed the stories and did some research. He wrote a twenty-one-page outline and sample chapter of a novel to be based on what he learned, entitled *Project Evangeline*. His agent, James Seligmann, showed it to me in my then-new job as a senior editor at Prentice-Hall. I was intrigued by Clyde Burleson's research, but was not prepared to go out on a limb with a contract for an unfinished first novel.

But most *nonfiction books* are sold to publishers from an outline presentation and a statement of the author's qualifications, and only written after the contract is signed. So I asked Burleson to write a presentation for a nonfiction book based on his research. He agreed, and Prentice-Hall signed the book. After a great deal more research, including three months of travel and interviews, he wrote a lively nonfiction work, *The Jennifer Project*, filled with previously unpublished information about this unique secret undertaking.

With nonfiction, the key to sales is *quality of information* on an interesting subject. Information rules the field. Good writing helps sell the book, but is not essential as long as the writing is passable. So publishers are willing to speculate on a good book presentation, before the book is written, if the author seems qualified. With fiction, the *quality of writing* is paramount, which is why editors and publishers want to see a whole first novel.

The Jennifer Project sold out its first printing of 20,000 copies, and ultimately around 23,000 copies were sold. It was also published in Spanish, Portuguese, Danish and Japanese editions. It earned a favorable full-page review in *The New York Times Book Review* and more praise elsewhere. Burleson went on a three-week, eight-city promotion tour, starting in New York with an appearance on the *Today* show.

Maybe you think we're getting a long way from the subject of writing a novel. But we aren't. Clyde Burleson says that when he finished writing his nonfiction book, he returned to his novel, *Project Evangeline*. "The facts were so much more interesting than my original speculations based on a small amount of information that the story got much better."

His agent continued to offer *Project Evangeline* to publishers, and it was sold to Carlyle Books and published as a mass-market paperback. Seligmann also placed it with Mondadori in Italy and

Lademann in Denmark, where it became a major book club selection circulated throughout Scandinavia. The Carlyle edition earned royalties above the advance, and the foreign editions earned additional money. And Burleson got to see his book "everywhere—in airports, bookstores, drugstores"—one of the greatest pleasures of the author of a mass-market paperback.

TIPS

• Make a high-quality copy of your manuscript—immediately.

• Read through your manuscript, noting both ideas for improvement and parts you especially like. Put the notes for each section in the corresponding chapter folder.

• Type your manuscript on a computer or typewriter if you have not already done so. Make sure your manuscript is neat, clean and readable.

• Avoid dot matrix printouts.

• Save each chapter in a separate document when using a word processing program.

• Save your work often, to minimize your loss if the computer should malfunction.

• Proofread your manuscript carefully. The built-in spell checker on your computer can make mistakes.

• When editing a typewritten manuscript, write neat corrections on the manuscript itself.

• The amount of editing depends on the author. Some make drastic changes; others hardly revise a word.

• Spice up a dull scene with dialogue.

• Incorporate description into dialogue.

• Cut unnecessary words, scenes and characters.

• Avoid trite, overused expressions in your writing. Find new ways to convey ideas.

• Replace participles ("ing" endings) with strong verbs.

• Don't try to guess what an editor wants to see. Write to please yourself.

• Type a revised copy of your manuscript. Use 12-point type, double-spaced, on good quality 8½ × 11-inch paper.

• Leave a one-inch margin on all sides, except for the left-hand margin, which should be at least one and one-half inches.

• Number pages on the upper right or upper middle of the page.

• Calculate the number of words in your manuscript.

• Include your name and the book title on the title page, along with your address and phone number.

• Send your manuscript to the publisher in a stationery box.

• Listen to the advice and criticism of editors and agents. Consider hiring a professional editor to help with rewriting.

• Self-publishing is a risky, yet sometimes rewarding, way to see your book in print.

• Consider using your research to write a nonfiction book.

8.

Selling and Contracts and Money, Oh My!

In *The Wizard of Oz*, Dorothy chants her special refrain based on her fear of coping with unknown dangers, "Lions and tigers and bears, oh my! Lions and tigers and bears. . . ."

The publishing world is indeed a kind of Land of Oz, where anything can happen—like getting a six-figure advance on your first novel. Or $3,000. Or $15,000. Or $30,000. Or being turned away at the door and coming away empty-handed. So much depends on locating the right wizard. And who are the wizards? The agents, of course.

Don't feel too hurt if an agent says she is not interested in handling your first novel. Agents have quirks and preferences. They love this kind of book, hate that kind of book. Some agents are sympathetic and will treat budding authors with kindness, even giving a little advice when they refuse to handle someone's work. Others are blunt and almost seem cruel to the sensitive newcomer.

Often the source of their crossness or abruptness is that they are already overloaded with unsold fiction. So if an agent says she is overloaded, you can make a note to try again in six months or a year, when the situation may be different.

Keep in mind that different agents have different sales styles. One is to play hard to get—to act as though dealing with anyone so lowly as a potential client is to extend a rare privilege. Such a role requires the agent to act skeptical of your claims. If the agent is playing this role, she acts as though she has such pricey merchandise from other novelists that she doesn't have to deal with anyone but the most select writers—and hints that even they have to crawl a little to enter her sanctum.

Naturally, if you—a new author—brush against someone of this type, you will get a little scared. Just remember that even in the most tough-guy organizations, there have to be a few nice guys to balance the act, so things can go better *if* you reach the right person.

Publishers respect agents because agents *do* have power—the power to enrich them by giving them major new books. Some super best-sellers are worth more than whole publishing companies. And agents can also impoverish a shaky publisher by selling to it, for a lot of money, a clinker that seems like a good bet, but which in fact will absorb the publisher's limited capital in a futile effort to make the book go.

The thing for you, an author, to remember, whether you are dealing with agents, editors, publishers or anyone else whose business is supported by books, is that without authors, they would be nowhere. Even if *they* don't keep this central fact in mind, *you* should. Your importance as a budding member of the class that supports the book publishing industry, and entertains and educates countless millions of readers, should be a source of pride to you.

My coauthor, Frances Spatz Leighton, author of more than thirty books, says, "Your best defense to protect yourself in dealing with agents and editors is to be like a toasted marshmallow, crisp and tough on the outside, while maintaining your warmth and softness on the inside—the softness that gave you the sensitivity to understand your material."

A brutally realistic note on the subject of why a writer needs an agent was struck by the late John Cushman. He himself had been on both sides of the negotiating table—first as an editor at several publishing houses and then as a literary agent. As quoted by *Literary Agents of North America*, Cushman frankly admitted, "As an editor, I was hired to help authors make their books better, and at the same time to take financial advantage of them."

While Cushman's views may have seemed a little harsh, they didn't prevent editors and publishers from liking him even while he was protecting his clients from them. For one, James O'Shea Wade, an editor and former publisher, used to meet Cushman every Friday afternoon, without fail, at the Harvard Club for drinks and exchanges of information on the latest wizardry in the publishing world.

When I called Jim Wade to reminisce about John Cushman, he told me a story about another editor-turned-agent with whom he had dealt, Knox Burger. Burger loyally represented New York Police Lieutenant William J. Caunitz for years through many rejections, hanging on and offering him editorial guidance as Caunitz continued working on his novel of inside stories about police life. Burger sold it to Wade, originally for a small down payment, with more to come when it was finished. When the publishing company with which Wade was associated dissolved, Wade remained interested and brought it with him when he joined Crown Publishers. Wade's judgment was vindicated. After he did additional editorial work with Caunitz, Crown published the novel and it sold over 40,000 copies in hard cover. It also got a $300,000 reprint deal from Bantam for paperback rights. It has sold over 1,000,000 copies. The title: *One Police Plaza*. And another writing star was born.

So you see, often when you look into the history of a successful first novel, a literary agent is very much in evidence.

WHAT AN AGENT CAN DO FOR YOU

I agree with John Katzenbach, author of the very successful thriller, *In the Heat of Summer*, who said that if you try to bypass agents and sell the book yourself, you are "increasing the difficulty."

That is true. An agent runs interference for the author. An agent knows the likes and dislikes of various publishers and does not waste time, as new novelists frequently do, sending a manuscript to a publisher who has a blind spot for that kind of book. An agent knows editors at the publishing houses, runs into them socially, has lunch with them and can make a more casual approach sometimes to see if interest can be aroused. And the editor or publisher knows that even the most lowly, beginning agent is performing a valuable service— screening out manuscripts and projects not worth considering, a service the publisher would have to pay dearly for if he did it himself.

And then comes the money game. A new writer may say, "I don't want to look like a money grubber. I just want to get this book published." Well, be happy that agents *are* money oriented. It is their desire, their duty and to their best interest to get the best deal, the biggest advance that can be worked out with that publisher. Agents know when to hold "auctions," which means send the manuscript to a half-dozen or more publishers and see who makes the best offer by a given date the agent sets.

Also, *before* the book is published, the agent has been busy trying to sell excerpts of the book to magazines who might be interested in that type of story. If the sale is made, the agent must arrange to synchronize the story's publication date in the magazine with the publication date of the book.

After the book is published, the work of the agent continues in that he tries to monitor and encourage paperback deals and to make foreign sales. And New York agents usually have connections with Hollywood agents for making a movie or TV sale—or in many instances handle these offers themselves.

It's not easy to get a novel before the TV or movie cameras. In an article in *The New York Times*, "Hollywood and the Novelist—It's a Fickle Romance at Best," Edwin McDowell quoted Judy Hotchkiss, story editor for East Coast production at MGM/United Artists: "The figure we use is that one in fifty fiction books gets optioned for the movies, but only one in two hundred actually gets made into a movie."

This seems a reasonable figure for theatrical movies, because if you divide the five thousand books of fiction published each year by two hundred, the result is twenty-five. But if you add in TV movies and ones produced solely as videos, it would be considerably higher.

At a meeting of a literary agent's association I attended, a panel of producers, scouts for movie companies, story editors and agents discussed at length the mounting delays and woes connected with getting a novel made into a theatrical motion picture. They agreed that fewer and fewer books are made into general-release movies. The wisdom expressed by the panel at the end of the meeting was, "If you want to see it in your lifetime, go TV."

AN ADVANCE SUCCESS STORY

Jacquelyn Mitchard had less than a hundred pages of her first novel written when Viking offered a half-million dollars for it as part of a two-book deal. She took it. She also accepted $3,000,000 for a movie to star Michelle Pfeiffer, and Peter Gruber had outbid producer Ron Howard in his option offer. And what was Mitchard before lightning struck? A freelance reporter who, as she put it, "wrote everything for anybody to pay the bills, even warning labels for spray paint."

Mitchard had written the first chapters of her book from notes she kept in a Tupperware container, but now she was too badly in need of money to spend any more time on it. She had five children to support after her husband had died of cancer.

She took a chance and sent it to her agent, Jane Gelfman, explaining she would need $10,000 to live on if she was going to finish the book. Eventually a phone call came, and it was Gelfman: "I'm going to tell you something that will change your life."

So what was the manuscript about? The story line was that a three-year-old boy is kidnapped from a hotel lobby and the family is panicked. As Mitchard described it to Jeff Giles of *Newsweek*, her story is not lurid. "*The Deep End* isn't a novel about violence done to children," she said, ". . . but about violence done to the human heart."

Viking's judgment in taking a chance with Mitchard was certainly confirmed when her book, *The Deep End of the Ocean*, became the number one best-seller on *Publishers Weekly*'s and other lists in the fall of 1996.

AN ADVANCE IS ONLY THE BEGINNING

Don't worry if your first book does not command a big advance. If the book is a success, you'll make it up on your next book. Anyway, the advance is only the beginning of possible earnings. If the book is published in hardcover first, there may be a paperback rights sale, a movie sale, book club sales, condensation, sales of magazine excerpts and income from foreign rights. And the number of copies sold makes a difference. As soon as the book has earned back the advance through a royalty on each copy sold, you start to get checks for your royalties on additional sales.

John Katzenbach, mentioned earlier, received a modest advance for his first effort. But he was grateful to Atheneum for publishing it at all, after the turndowns he received. Then the paperback rights were sold for $250,000—a bonanza to be split between author and publisher. On top of that, he received a movie offer.

I will not give you a false picture and say more than a few novels receive an advance big enough to change the author's lifestyle. Many advances for a first novel on a subject of general interest are in the $5,000 to $10,000 range. Historical first novels, which are much longer books, usually receive more, while first romances and other genre novels often get less—$3,000, but sometimes $7,500 if you are lucky.

However, successful romance writers, in the long run, can make a lot of money, as witness author Danielle Steel, whose works appear like clockwork on the best-seller lists week after week, year after year.

HANDLING YOUR OWN WORK

Writers of romances don't have to have agents because editors of these books are willing to read unagented works, and the contracts offered to first romance novelists are apt to be pretty standard, agented or not.

Publishers often help budding romance writers learn the formula for a romance book, as was the case with Mary Kilchenstein of Rockville, Maryland, who sent her first effort—*Bed of Roses*, under the byline Jean Faure—to Berkley. It was returned with the comment that the characters were too true to real life and many suggestions on how this could be remedied.

Kilchenstein found it too painful to rewrite her book, so she threw the manuscript in a drawer and started a new one, paying close attention to the rules of the road in romance writing. She sent that in. Now came the news that her hero was just not quite "heartwarming" enough. As Kilchenstein told reporter Sheila Moldover of *The Journal*, a Virginia newspaper, "I added a chapter where they went to the zoo and he bought her cotton candy. Then they went home, and he did the dishes. That made him heartwarming."

Even if your book is not a romance, you may elect to act as your own agent. I know several authors who have had whole careers without an agent, or who only used an agent occasionally. Others get started without an agent and turn to an agent later. And in part two of this book, you'll see that several of the authors profiled started without agents, including one whose first novel was a major best-seller.

Sometimes there is a more dramatic reason behind the lack of an agent. You may *have to* do without an agent because of your temperament. Agent Richard Curtis told me the story of an author he represented who constantly called and complained that her editor was asking her to make too many changes. So in selling her next novel, he warned the editor, "She doesn't like to make a lot of changes, so go easy on the editing." The result was that the author then called and complained, "My old editor helped me a lot, but this one is so lazy she makes me do all the work."

Though one of the advantages of using an agent is her knowledge of publishers' preferences, you can find some of this information yourself with a little detective work. Look at the "Acknowledgments" page of novels in the general category of yours. Usually these pages are at the beginning, sometimes at the end, of the novel. Often the author will offer a special "thank you" to his editor. Articles in writer's magazines such as *The Writer* or *Writer's Digest* also identify editors' interests. Since editors move around, a good way to learn where they are now is to look in the "Names and Numbers" section of the current edition of *Literary Market Place*, which lists names of people in publishing and tells where to reach them.

Handling your own work, you'll probably spend a lot of time poring over *LMP* and directories such as *Novel and Short Story Writer's Market*, listed in the back of this book. Their listings tell what publishers say they are looking for.

A simple kind of market research you can also do is to go to a public library and look up the names of publishers of novels in some way similar to yours. Check the year of the copyright. If you find that particular publishers have done *several* of your kind of book in the last three years, then these publishers are obvious targets for you.

For example, though many publishers publish some mysteries, or an occasional one, St. Martin's Press, Walker, Mysterious Press, New American Library, Scribners and Henry Holt consistently turn out mysteries, a few by new writers.

And by looking on the title pages of the books, you may note an editor's name, such as "A Thomas Dunne Book." He has his own imprint at St. Martin's Press.

Librarians who do buying and bookstore buyers often know what kinds of books a publisher has been succeeding with lately, so enlist their aid.

Don't forget the book reviews in your local paper and in *The*

New York Times Book Review, Los Angeles Times, Chicago Tribune, and *Washington Post,* among others. And study the ads, because the ads show which books the publishers particularly value, and how they think of them. From the reviews and ads, you can get a reading on which publishers like which kinds of novels. You might even want to subscribe to *Publishers Weekly,* the trade journal of the book publishing industry, or read it in your library to learn inside information about what new publishing companies are being formed. It will also tell you which editors have just moved to new jobs.

If you get discouraged marketing your own work, consider what Robert Oliphant did. Reading in *Publishers Weekly* that Clyde Taylor had just formed a new agency (later merged with Curtis Brown), he wrote a letter suggesting that since Taylor was a new agent and he was a new author, maybe they should work together. Taylor not only placed Oliphant's novel with a publisher, but interested Reader's Digest Condensed Books in using it as one of their selections. He then arranged for film agent Warren Bayless to place the movie rights. The novel and film were *A Piano for Mrs. Cimino,* with Bette Davis starring in the TV film. Oliphant later wrote a *Publishers Weekly* article about his first-novel experiences, in which he called Clyde Taylor "Mr. Laconic" and Warren Bayless "Mr. Warm," a good description of two agents' selling styles.

SHOULD YOU TRY TO FIND AN AGENT?

In considering this question, ask yourself whether or not you like to have other people handle important financial and sales matters for you. Or do you prefer to handle such matters yourself? Do you take the advice of an investment adviser or make your own financial decisions? Do you consult a lawyer from time to time? Would you use a real estate agent to sell a piece of property or try to make the sale yourself? Do you prefer to balance your own checkbook, keeping it up to date? Do you get someone else to do it, or do you postpone doing it at all? In sports, can you take the advice of a coach?

In other words, can you *delegate* important responsibilities to others, or are you so nervous and concerned that things be done exactly as you wish that you prefer to handle important matters yourself?

If you decide you need and want an agent to help you with

your writing career, you have to face the fact that finding an agent is sometimes just as hard as finding a publisher. Even though *Literary Agents of North America* lists over eight hundred U.S. and Canadian literary agencies, some of these are small operations, some specialized and some only accept clients by referral. Some just don't accept new clients.

Literary Market Place lists over two hundred agents. Another list can be found in *Guide to Literary Agents*, published by Writer's Digest Books, Cincinnati. The Manhattan Yellow Pages, under the heading "Literary Agents," lists about one hundred names, addresses and phone numbers of agents. About half of these are the principal literary agents of the United States. Besides these fifty based in New York, a few more major agents are based in Los Angeles, Boston and Washington. The reason most major book agents are in New York is that that city is the headquarters of most trade and mass-market book publishers, although increasingly, literary agents are moving out of New York. So you might investigate whether one has an office nearby, by looking in the yellow pages of cities near you.

Many literary agents belong to the Association of Authors' Representatives Inc. (AAR), 10 Astor Place, Third Floor, New York, NY 10003. For a small charge, AAR will supply you with a list of its members, with names, addresses and phone numbers, together with its canon of ethics and a very brief description of what an agent can and cannot do for you. If you call AAR at (212) 353-3709, a recording will tell you how to get its packet of information; or you can write to the address above, enclosing a self-addressed, stamped envelope, for the same information as is on the recording. The agents I met there when I was a member seemed competent, professional and well informed. The organization is less useful to agents who live outside the New York area, so while there are members from other cities, most of the members are New Yorkers.

Any agent you contact will have her own sales methods, sometimes idiosyncratic to the point of eccentricity. Can you face the fact that you will have to rely on an agent to tell you whether or not your work is being submitted, and to which publishers? Can you put up with your agent's personal approach, which may involve her seeming to withhold your work from what you regard as major publishers? Can you let your agent decide whether your work is more suitable for paperback or hardcover? Can you take it when your agent holds out for a higher advance royalty guarantee, possibly killing an already good deal? Can you bear to wait while your agent haggles with the publisher over small details of the contract? And can you trust an agent to collect your money, deduct a 10, 15 or 20 percent commission—agents vary in the commissions they charge—and promptly send you the rest? A famous agent of the past described an agent as a sort of benovelent leech—he said that while the agent took part of the author's income, he had noticed that authors with them generally did better than those without them.

Whether you are looking for an agent or publisher, you have two appropriate ways to approach them—through referrals or through queries.

Referrals

With either agents or publishers, good sources of referrals are published authors, lawyers, contacts you make at writers conferences or writers groups, professors of English or creative writing, businesspeople who deal with agents and book publishers, bookstore owners, reviewers, magazine and newspaper editors. Take advantage of whatever opportunity your alertness presents to you.

But don't be surprised if some people are reluctant to refer you to their agents or publisher friends! Having, or knowing, an important agent or publisher is regarded by many as being part of an "inner circle," and traditionally, outsiders are hazed a good deal when they try to break into any established group. It's up to you to think of a way to get around this problem.

Queries

Lacking a referral, the next best route, whether you are approaching an agent or a publisher, is to write a query letter. An ideal query is a one-page, single-spaced, typed business letter with short paragraphs that describe your novel, your qualifications and perhaps, briefly, why you think it will succeed. With this you may, if you wish, include a brief, two- or three-page outline or synopsis of your novel, plus two or three chapters.

The outline can be single- or double-spaced, but as described earlier, the sample chapters *must* be double-spaced. Do date your query letter. *Don't date your outline and sample chapters*—such dates quickly grow stale. Send out the whole thing, *packed flat*. No binder is necessary, but do paper clip the pages of the outline together so that it won't get mixed up with your manuscript. Enclose a self-addressed stamped envelope (called an SASE) big enough for return of your materials. Mail in a *sturdy* padded envelope, First Class, to one or more agents. Or to one or more publishers. Send the original of your letter and clear photocopies of your outline and chapters. It is underwhelming to an agent to receive a photocopied letter—I just throw them away.

Multiple submissions of unsolicited queries are perfectly okay, when they are introduced by individually typed letters. If an agent becomes interested, he may ask you to withdraw other submissions. One way to do this is to call all the others and ask them to reply within two or three days, as someone is very interested.

If a publisher asks you to withdraw other copies of a multiple submission, just laugh unless he makes a firm offer.

But if you actually sign up with an agent or publisher, it would be courteous to write immediately to the others to whom you have submitted and request return of your materials—no reason is necessary.

In writing a query letter, remember you are engaged in business correspondence, so be brief. The person receiving it is pressed for time. When you remember that the person you write may get thousands of queries each year—most of them unprofessional or illiterate and *very* few even truly worth a reply—you can see why *your* letter must be outstanding.

Make sure your query is typed perfectly, contains no errors of grammar or spelling and is filled with facts. The reason a written query is better than a telephone call is that it can be passed around to several people. Remember, you are dealing with *book* people— that is, people who prefer the *written* word as the best means of communication. Also, you are a writer, not a professional speaker, so probably you will be able to put your best efforts more easily into a good letter than an oral pitch.

Carol Cartaino, an experienced book editor, told me an anecdote that powerfully illustrates the point that publishing people prefer reading rather than listening. At an editorial meeting, an editor read aloud a detailed report on a book project, and some excerpts from the book itself. Cartaino found herself, and a couple of others around the table, leaning forward and saying, "Let me see it," even though they had just heard it.

If you decide to try telephone queries, be ready to talk. Have notes in front of you. State your name, your reason for calling and the nature of your novel quickly and succinctly. Is your novel a historical romance? Of what period? Does it have a man or woman protagonist? Or is it a family saga? Thriller, mystery, juvenile, literary or what? Tell these facts right away. Have the title in your notes and on the tip of your tongue—don't be worried about someone stealing your title.

Don't apologize or say, "I know you get a lot of queries, but . . ." Yours is a business call—one businessperson calling another with a business proposition that can be worth a lot of money. If the person you reach suggests you send a written query, agree, hang up and send it immediately, referring to your telephone call and its date to begin the letter. If the agent or publisher says she isn't accepting submissions, hang up and try someone else.

Above all, don't be long-winded even if you detect some interest. You are using the valuable business time of the person who takes your call, and people who receive sales calls don't suffer fools gladly. It might help to practice the call first with a friend experienced in sales, or even alone.

Here is an effective query letter from an author in search of an agent:

(On author's letterhead with date, address and phone number)
Collier Associates
(address)

Sir or Madam:

> I am an ex-Marine, a Vietnam veteran, and an attorney. During the early 1970s I defended Marine drill instructors accused of boot camp brutality. Today, ten years later, the papers still carry stories of DIs charged with training abuses. The questions are always with us:

>> What kinds of hardship may be justifiably inflicted when molding men to fight and survive in modern guerrilla warfare?

>> Is there a point at which observance of individual rights in training shortchanges our troops in later combat?

>> Are drill instructors really such monsters?

> I have written a novel about one such incident, a court martial of a drill instructor for murder. Against the background of a society that to an ever-increasing extent preferred to "make love, not war," I have told the story about people charged with making war and

the uncertainty and self-doubt that was the legacy of the Vietnam experience.

Entitled PAYBACKS, my story provides insights into the rigors of Marine boot camp, the tension of night combat, and the natural drama of a trial for a man's life. I have enclosed an outline-synopsis, a summary of the novel, a brief biography, and copies of the first three chapters, which introduce the reader to the main characters: Sargeant Markey, the drill instructor charged with murder; Michael Taggart, the defense counsel disillusioned by his own experience in Vietnam; and Veronica Rasmussen, the cynical reporter so opposed to the American role in Vietnam. I hope these chapters will make you want to read my entire manuscript.

Sincerely,

Christopher Q. Britton

CQB:njk

Enclosures

When I got this letter from Christopher Britton, together with "outline-synopsis, a summary of the novel, a brief biography and copies of the first three chapters, which introduce the reader to the main characters," I read it immediately. It was clearly and professionally typed. Its first paragraph engaged my interest, establishing the author's qualifications, then flowed into three intriguing questions. Britton immediately followed up, telling in one paragraph a great deal about his novel. He wound up with the title and a request for a reply.

After finishing the letter, I immediately began to read the enclosures with high hopes. I was not disappointed and quickly called the author, requesting that he send the whole manuscript, together with more detail about his background. I became his agent. After he did some additional work on the novel, it only took a small number of submissions before I placed it with Donald I. Fine, Inc. *Paybacks* was published in hardcover about two years after Britton's letter to me, and about a year later, Warner reprinted it in a mass-market paperback edition after paying a substantial guarantee.

Novelist Christopher Britton's letter also answers a question I frequently hear: "How much sample material should I show?" The answer is, "Enough to introduce the main characters and to get the main story line of the novel underway."

YOUR AGREEMENT WITH AN AGENT

If an agent offers to represent you, he will want to be your exclusive agent, usually for some minimum period of time. It is to your advantage to keep this minimum period as short as possible, such as six months, or at most a year, in case you and the agent prove incompatible or the agent fails to sell and loses interest. Your agent will also want to handle the dramatic and foreign rights to your novel and its first serial rights. This is reasonable, as the agent invests time and his own expenses (to an agreed extent) in marketing your work.

Some agents use a written agreement; others rely on oral agreements with you. All will want to insert an "Agency Clause" into your contract with a publisher. Here is a typical agency clause:

> *All sums of money due under this agreement shall be paid to the Author's agent, _____ , 000 Madison Avenue, New York 00000, and receipt of the said _____ shall be a good and valid discharge of such indebtedness, and the said _____ is hereby irrevocably empowered by the Author to act in all matters arising from this agreement. The Author does hereby irrevocably assign and transfer to _____ , and _____ shall retain, the sum equal to _____ percent (_____%) as an agency coupled with an interest, out of all monies due and payable to and for the account of the Author under this agreement.*

My own policy is to have oral agreements with authors I know well and have dealt with over a period of years. With new clients who are strangers before they approach me or I approach them, I prefer a written agreement. Here are some of the elements I try to include in every agreement, and some notes on them:

1. I become your exclusive agent for not only your books, but the dramatic rights to your work.

2. The only works of yours I can collect commissions from are those put under contract while I represent you (whether I made the sale or you made it alone makes no difference—it's

just *when* the deal was made that matters)—not things you sold before you engaged me or after we have parted company.

3. If I sell a book of yours to a publisher, I get to be the agent of it, forever, for dramatic rights and foreign sales. To make dramatic rights sales and foreign sales, I can use coagents.

4. Money earned by your work is paid to me, not you. I then deduct my commission and pay you your share, promptly (which means *after* the check has cleared in my authors' account). Alternatively, if the publisher will agree (and some won't), I arrange for the publisher to split your earnings and pay your share directly to you and my share directly to me. However, this arrangement doesn't work with foreign publishers and foreign agents, so with foreign contracts, I have to receive the money and disburse it as described above.

5. If you ask me to make copies of your work, or I order up to twenty books of yours from your publisher to use for rights submissions, or I send you something by Express Mail, or I otherwise engage in some unusual expense at your request, you must pay the cost. (Some agents will want to charge you for additional expenses, such as reading fees or postage.)

6. I become your exclusive agent for some agreed-upon period of time, and after the end of this period, the agreement runs on indefinitely until you fire me or I resign. But even if our agreement ends, I still get commissions from earnings of agreements made while I was your agent, and I still get to handle dramatic and foreign rights to books published under those agreements.

7. I'm not responsible if your work is lost, stolen or damaged.

Most agents charge either 10 or 15 percent as their commission for U.S. contracts, and 20 percent for foreign contracts. When your agent uses a dramatic rights coagent, your agent and the dramatic rights coagent usually split the 10 or 15 percent commission, so this costs you nothing extra. But if the deal is a small one, the dramatic rights agent may grumble at only 5 or 7½ percent, and you may have to agree to pay him 10 percent, or allow him to deduct some minimum flat fee.

There have been many changes in the agent scene in recent years. Not only are there many more agents than there used to be, but more agents than ever specialize in particular genres. For example, Dominick Abel represents many mystery writers. Where there used to be two agents' associations, the staid and conservative Society of Authors' Representatives and the youthful and freewheeling Independent Literary Agents Association, now they have merged into the middle-of-the-road Association of Authors' Representatives Inc. Even some old line agencies, like Harold Ober Associates, now charge 15 percent, but others, like William Morris Agency, still charge the one-time standard 10 percent commission.

How can you tell if your agent is a good one, and honest? I don't think you can tell absolutely—after all, even the most famous and respected people and corporations are sometimes convicted of crimes. But you can ask such questions as how long the agency has been in business, what some of its recent sales have been, who some of the writers it represents are, how money is handled, what publishers it deals with, what organizations it belongs to and, of course, what the commission is. Don't be put off if you learn the agent is recently established—just ask what the agent did before. He may have been an important editor or executive from a good publisher, highly experienced in handling book deals.

If the agent uses a written agreement, you might want to find a lawyer to look at it. Ask the lawyer in advance how much he will charge for this service. Or you might want to show it to an author who uses an agent. Above all, don't hesitate to ask the agent to explain any part of the agreement you don't understand before signing it.

BOOK CONTRACTS

If you don't use an agent, you should get an attorney's advice on a contract offered to you by a book publisher. While, in my opinion, it would be best for you to make the effort to seek out an attorney already experienced in book publishing contracts, finding such an attorney might be hard if you live in a remote place. You might ask your local attorney to find the name of such a specialist attorney for you.

Your contract with your publisher is such an important document in your life as a writer that I must say if you really want to understand it, without an agent or attorney, or at least an experienced author to guide you, you should get and read book-length treatments of the subject, such as the legal guides in the list of recommended books in the back of this one. Even if you do this, you'll find you only learn some lessons by experience. After many years in the book business, I'm still learning myself.

So what follows is a brief description of book contracts and a few main points you should watch out for, not a definitive guide.

Typical trade books or mass-market book publishing contracts specify such things as the name of the author (and any pseudonym), the title of the work, its length in number of words, when and in what condition it is to be delivered, how copyright is to be registered (in your name, preferably), the publisher's exclusive and nonexclusive territories, the advance against royalties, the royalties paid (and whether they are paid on the retail price of the book or "actual cash received" by the publisher—an inferior arrangement), a definition of different kinds of sales for which there will be less royalties, the subsidiary rights granted to the publisher (such as book club and quotation rights) and the division of earnings between author and publisher from these rights, your warranty that the book is original or your property and contains no libel or invasion of privacy of another person or other unlawful matter, when and how often statements and payments are to be rendered to you by the publisher, the time period the publisher has within which it must publish or lose the right to do so, how many free copies you will receive and at what discount you may buy additional copies, an option on your next book, what happens if you fail to deliver a final manuscript or it is unacceptable to the publisher, and provisions for termination (and thus getting back your rights) if the book goes out of print, plus other elements. Publishing agreements vary from two or three pages to the twenty or more pages in Simon & Schuster's contract.

As an agent, my philosophy is that you must plan for success. If you have an agent, the agent will probably want to give the publisher only what the publisher actually does well itself. If it is a hardcover publisher, the agent would try to sell hardcover rights only—and retain for you, and sell separately, such other rights as paperback, audio, magazine, foreign, dramatic, electronic storage and transmission, etc.

Of course, with a first novel, the agent probably would not often be able to actually achieve such a deal. So the agent settles by at least holding back for you first serial, foreign, and movie-TV-dramatic and allied rights, but leaving paperback rights under control of the publisher. The hardcover publisher ordinarily gives you half the paperback earnings. If the book is a success, all or part of the retained rights can be sold separately, often for good sums of money (except that first serial must be sold beforehand).

On the other hand, if you have no agent, *someone* must market these rights—you could try to do it yourself, or you could leave the rights in the hands of the publisher and let it market them for you—with the provision that it gets a share.

The problems with the latter arrangement are (1) the publisher will hold your earnings from subsidiary rights until your advance is covered by your earnings, which may be never, so you don't get anything from, say, a subsidiary rights deal for a modest British edition contract; (2) the publisher only pays you twice a year, and even then usually waits several months after the end of a six-month accounting period to do it. This means you can be rich on paper (say the publisher made a giant paperback deal) and not have a cent in your pocket for many months.

You can find ways around these problems, but it may be difficult if you represent yourself. If you do represent yourself, you should probably focus on the obvious—the amount of the advance royalty and the amount of the royalty paid on each copy sold.

How much you get for an advance royalty is strictly a matter for negotiation. The more the publisher wants your manuscript, the more money you can get—if you hold out. Usually, for paperback genre first novels, the amounts mentioned previously, $3,000 to $7,500, will not be subject to much negotiation, but it never hurts to try. Longer works, like a historical romance or historical novel, certainly should get more—possibly up to $10,000 to $15,000 in a routine case, depending on whether the publisher regards it as a potential lead or second-lead title.

Hardcover first novels usually get $5,000 to $10,000 or more—sometimes much more, particularly when an agent is involved and is very excited by the novel and editors agree that it is exceptional (witness Jacquelyn Mitchard's advance of $500,000 cited earlier). You'll just have to try to feel out the situation if you are representing yourself.

The reason the amount of the advance royalties is so important to you is that this is the only money you can be sure of earning from your book contract. The advance should be a "nonreturnable guarantee," and it is the inducement the publisher offers you to sign the contract. Even if the book sells only a few copies, you get to keep this money.

After the book is published, each copy sold should earn, under the contract, a royalty. Ideally, this royalty will be computed as a percentage of the *catalog retail price* of the book. This way of figuring royalties is vastly superior for you to figuring royalties based on a percentage of "actual cash received by the publisher" for each copy. Naturally you would rather get your royalties as a percentage of the retail, rather than the wholesale, price. The publisher will keep an account of the sales of your book, and the royalties earned, in your "royalty account." When the royalties earned equal the advance royalties paid you, the book has "earned out," and all additional royalties earned are yours, after the end of the next accounting period.

For example, suppose your advance was $10,000, and your book is published in hardcover at $20 retail price. If your royalties are 10 percent of the retail price, that is $2 a book. When 5,000 copies are sold, your book will have earned out its advance. When one more copy is sold, the publisher will owe you $2 additional. If 4,000 more are sold, the publisher will owe you $8,000, and your total earnings on the 9,000 copies will be $18,000—$10,000 as advance royalties and $8,000 as later royalty earnings.

This example is rather simplified. In an actual contract, some of the royalties might be less than 10 percent because, among other reasons, the books were sold in Canada at a reduced royalty rate; and some of the royalties might be more, because your contract may provide that you get 12½ percent royalties for all copies sold over the first 5,000. Be sure and study the fine print of royalty provisions!

If the novel seems likely to be published in hardcover first, try to get your publisher to pay royalties of 10 percent of the retail price of each of the first 5,000 copies sold, 12½ percent on the second 5,000 and 15 percent for all copies thereafter.

If it is to be a "trade paperback," probably the royalties will be less: either 6 or 7½ or sometimes 10 percent of the catalog retail price for the first 10,000 or maybe 20,000 copies sold, and possibly some higher royalty for more sold.

If yours is a mass-market paperback original, depending on the company and your bargaining position, you may get anywhere from 4 to 10 percent of the cover price for the first 100,000 or 150,000 copies sold, and an escalation to a higher royalty, or series of escalating royalties, for increasing quantities sold. A typical contract of this sort would pay 6 percent for the first 150,000 copies, 8 percent for the next 150,000 and 10 percent for all over 300,000 copies. Getting that final stage, 10 percent, might come hard.

If you do not have an agent, and have no experience with magazine sales, it would probably be better to let the publisher handle the first serial rights. Though some publishers are not ashamed to ask for 50 percent of the money for these rights, you may be able to get them down to 25 percent, or the 10 percent I consider fair.

Unless you have some reason to think you can handle the foreign rights effectively yourself, without an agent you should probably let the publisher handle them, in exchange for a 20 or 25 percent share to the publisher.

I would advise you to retain the movie-TV-dramatic rights in every instance—you can always try to get an agent or lawyer to handle these later if there is any demand for them. If you let the publisher handle them for a 10 or 15 percent share, the publisher would usually just turn them over to an agent in any event. If you can manage to retain audio and electronic rights, splendid, but publishers seem increasingly determined to hang onto them, even in agented contracts.

For your protection, the agreement should include a "bankruptcy" clause that makes you a secured creditor if the publisher becomes bankrupt. And there should be a provision that you may end the contract if the book goes out of print and the publisher refuses to reprint it. If possible, you should restrict the rights of the publisher to edit and change the book without your permission, beyond simple copyediting, and you should try to get the right to approve the title of the novel if it is changed.

Any option on your next book should not be much more elaborate than "on terms to be agreed," and the period in which you have the right to submit your next book should begin, at the very least, on the publisher's acceptance of your final manuscript. If possible, strike out any option clause altogether if you think you will be a prolific writer.

Whether you have an agent or an attorney or both, read the contract carefully yourself and try to understand it. If you don't, discuss it with your editor. But remember that the deal itself is the most important part of it, not the details. As one publisher with a not-so-perfect contract, but a reputation for running a large advertising campaign for each of his books, remarked, "Authors are paid in dollars, not percentage points." He was pointing out that with his big promotions, the author could make more through big sales, even if the royalty percentages didn't escalate and the publisher kept a sizable share of rights earnings, than if the author had an agented-type contract with another publisher who did little promotion.

SHOULD YOU GO TO A LARGE AGENCY OR A SMALL ONE?

This is a familiar question. As a person who has sometimes operated alone and sometimes with a partner or a couple of associates, I only know the small agency scene from the inside. But as an editor, I dealt with the largest agencies as well as small ones. The question is deceptive. What you should ask is, "Do I believe my individual agent can do the best possible job for me?"

In reality, the agent can only maximize the profits from the work she handles—there is nothing magical about the agent or the size of the agency. What sells is the property—the biggest agent can't sell a piece of junk any better than the beginner can who has just switched from being a rights assistant for a publisher. If you create a great property—your first novel—your agent, large or small, can sell it, and probably, with enough effort, you could, too.

SHOULD YOU PAY A FEE TO GET AN AGENT TO READ YOUR FIRST NOVEL?

Some agencies charge a "reading fee," and these fees can vary from a small payment the agent has imposed to keep too many beginners from making submissions to quite substantial amounts. As I have sometimes charged a fee and sometimes not, I can say that in fact the charging of fees doesn't seem to deter authors from submitting works.

The attraction fee-charging agents have is that they usually, in exchange for the fee, provide some kind of an appraisal or criticism even if they reject the work, and those agents who don't charge a fee might write across a query letter, as I do when I'm in a hurry, "Sorry, not for me," or, "Sounds okay, but not my kind of thing," and stuff it immediately in the return envelope to go back to the author. I consider this better than the alternative, a form rejection slip.

The question that arises is, Is criticism bought for a fee worth anything? I have to say that I think it is, and if you can't get a reading any other way, and can afford the fee, it might be worth your while.

To an experienced person in publishing, such as an editor or agent, it is not surprising that most reader's reports sound alike, with criticisms such as poor characterization, much irrelevant material, lack of consistency, poor focus, shifting point of view, weak plot line, wordy, filled with clichés, etc. No matter how tactfully and positively the criticisms are made, or at what length, these are such common flaws that a good report is bound to mention them. It would even be possible to prewrite paragraphs in a word processing program and print a report lightly customized from such canned paragraphs.

SHOULD YOU PAY AN AGENCY
A FEE FOR EDITORIAL WORK?

If an agency also offers editorial services for a fee, I really don't have firm advice for you. As discussed in the previous chapter, certainly editorial work can sometimes turn an unsalable work into a salable one. What you have to ask yourself is, "Can *this* agent make the difference?"

The question in my mind is whether, in some instances, *anybody*, no matter how well intentioned or well qualified, can truly help—for love or money. Often it is better to start over on a new novel rather than dwell endlessly on trying to improve an old, much-rejected one.

I am not against a writer paying for help of various kinds or for the privilege of rubbing shoulders with other writers and people of the publishing world—even if it is only the fee for joining a local writers club. Knowing the isolation many writers face, I believe it is important that they meet creative people as well as editors, publishers and agents who deal with creative people behind the scenes of publishing.

What are the options open to the lone writer? Dozens of writers conferences are conducted on campuses and other sites around the country—for a reasonable fee, you even live in a college dormitory. Besides the writers clubs and agencies, writers schools and extension courses offer editorial assistance. Surely they could not all remain in existence year after year if they did not fill a need.

Naturally, in such a large clutch, there will be a few bad eggs.

It is a caveat emptor situation—buyer, beware. So before you send any money, try to check out the organization—maybe with the Better Business Bureau—or at least find out how long it has been in existence. Some writers conferences have been going on successfully for many years, and I and other agents are sometimes paid an honorarium and expenses to speak at them. Though I always resolve to harden my heart and not pick up any beginners to represent at them, in fact, I usually end up with at least one new client, because talent and originality are hard to ignore.

A final word is to be sure you understand what service is being offered. Real help in getting you published? Or just friendly contacts with writers and editors? Or psychological support? If you want the answer to be "all of the above," you'll probably have to join several groups.

The work of a literary agent—selling and licensing literary rights to literary property—is an esoteric occupation. This was brought home to me convincingly when I was visiting a fashionable summer resort and at a cocktail party met a socially prominent dowager. She asked me what I did, and I said I was a literary agent.

"And what, might I ask, is a literary agent?"

"Well, a literary agent sells or licenses rights to literary property, just as a real estate agent sells or licenses rights to real property."

"Hah!" she said. "I don't believe there could *be* such an occupation," and stalked off.

TIPS

• Consider hiring an agent to help you sell your manuscript. Some types of novels have more need of an agent than others.

• Agents can help negotiate your advance, or up-front payment, when a book is sold to a publisher. Most advances for a first novel range from $3,000 to $10,000.

• If you choose to work without an agent, you must identify potential markets for your work yourself. Examine other publications in the same general category as yours for ideas. Writing and publishing industry magazines offer clues about editors and publishers who specialize in your genre.

• Use resources like *Literary Market Place* and *Novel and Short Story Writer's Market* to identify possible publishers for your work.

• Librarians and bookstore buyers can tell you what types of books have succeeded recently for certain publishers.

• Book reviews show what kind of books a publisher is promoting.

• If you do decide to enlist the help of a literary agent, there are several reference sources and literary organizations to help you find one.

• Referrals from published authors and others in the publishing industry are useful when seeking an agent or publisher.

• A query letter, a short business letter describing your novel, is another way to contact agents or publishers. Sometimes writers also include a two- to three-page outline of the novel, or the first few chapters, in their queries.

• Multiple submissions of unsolicited queries are perfectly acceptable.

• Don't withdraw other copies of a multiple submission unless a publisher makes you a firm offer.

• A telephone query should also be brief, professional and fact-filled.

• If you do enlist an agent, keep the initial contract period brief, in case you and the agent prove incompatible or the agent fails to sell your work.

• Understand the terms of your contract with your agent or publisher.

• Study the details of your royalty provisions. It is to your advantage to retain as many rights as you can.

• Investigate an agency or writers school that offers editorial assistance. There are many helpful organizations out there, but all fulfill distinctly different needs.

9.

The Publishers and Editors

Authors and agents talk of publishers and publishing houses, but what they are really talking about are the editors—the backstage stars of your show, the persons who hold the fate of your novel in their hands. Yes, they—the editors—check it out with their superiors, and maybe the president of the company himself has a hand in deciding whether or not you get published. But the president usually would not even have seen your manuscript if it weren't for the editor. Even if you submit your work directly to the president, he will almost certainly turn it over to an editor.

"Each editor is a mini-publishing house," one author told me in astonishment, after I had introduced him to a number of editors who were considering his book at the same time. He added, "These people aren't ordinary business representatives of their companies. They are only interested in how my book will look on their lifetime list." And one editor did add his title to *her* list of credits.

Editors are judged by their "track records" of picking good-selling books and attracting and putting under contract books that sell. Editors may solicit you, if they hear of you, and often are in contact with agents, asking what is new and good.

After the contract is signed, it is the editor who studies your manuscript page by page, asks for clarifications, new twists and various changes. And it is the editor who decides when the manuscript is ready for publication and for the printer.

It's interesting to know that editors are a comparatively recent development in the publishing business. In the 1920s edition of *The Truth About Publishing*, British publisher Stanley Unwin advised an author, after he had finished his handwritten "fair copy" to take it to a good typist, who would correct it for punctuation, spelling, sentence structure and grammar—and it would be ready to publish. The "good typist" of the past is the editor of today.

You might encounter two theories of editing: the British and the American. John Beaudouin, formerly editor in chief of Reader's Digest Condensed Books and now a publishing consultant, says, "English publishers, by and large, assume that the book is the author's sole creation and it is the publisher's duty to execute and publish it, whereas American publishers are inclined to offer numerous criticisms and suggestions for improvements—to help the author, by their way of thinking, make the book better."

The editors you will meet on these pages, and/or have to work with in real life if your novel is put under contract for publication, are not the "hands-off" British, but American book editors—a nosey, opinionated, book-reading breed who think, often with some justice, that only they know what the public wants. Fortunately, they don't *agree* on what the public wants, and since there are a lot of them, you have a fair chance of finding one who thinks she knows that *your* novel is what the public wants.

It's a widely held view that editors and publishers are part of some sort of liberal conspiracy, and in fact, many editors are liberal. But there are also some conservative editors and some completely nonpolitical ones.

Many editors are women. So if you are a woman hater and write a misogynist novel, they won't like it—unless, as happened with Ileene Smith, an editor at Summit Books, one of them regards it as a brilliant book. She was happy to acquire and help Summit publish *Stanley and the Women*, by Kingsley Amis, even though some angry women thought it shouldn't be published because of its depiction of women characters.

It's only practical for an editor or publisher to look for works that appeal to a wide variety of readers—and to avoid turning off whole classes of readers (not to mention reviewers and librarians) as potential buyers of your book.

So for business reasons as well as considerations of common decency, comb your manuscript free of ethnic, religious, gender and racial slurs and stereotypes. Stereotypes have no place in good writing in any event.

Editors are proud of their place in the literary world and of the budding novelists they have launched. Ellis Amburn is proudest of his 1970s discovery of Belva Plain, whose first novel, *Evergreen*, gave rise to a new subgenre, the Jewish family saga.

Every book Belva Plain has written has become a big or bestseller but when Amburn met her, she was an unpublished grandmother in New Jersey, married to an ophthalmologist supportive of her struggle with her manuscript.

As Amburn told my coauthor, "In the evenings I was teaching a class in writing and publishing at the New School for Social Research. I asked Plain if she would like to come to class regularly and let me and the class edit her novel in public, so to speak. She was taking an awful chance, but she was a good sport and agreed—and that's how her first book was edited.

"It did not always go smoothly. Once she and I had a furious argument in front of the class about some bit of proposed editing, and the class was distressed. But then one of the students called out, 'Hey, that's part of the process. There's no need for us to get excited.' They laughed and settled down and presumably learned something as Belva and I finally worked it out."

Amburn did not edit Belva Plain's later books because she stayed with Delacorte Press but he moved to another publisher. She has proved herself to be an enduring writer—in the summer of 1996 Delacorte published her novel *Promises*.

The publishing world is never at rest. The chairman and chief executive officer of The Putnam Berkley Group is Phyllis Grann. She started as a secretary at Doubleday, was an editor at Morrow, then David McKay, and became a senior editor and vice-president at Simon & Schuster, where among the notable authors she launched was Mary Higgins Clark with her first novel, *Where Are the Children?* When the merger of Putnam and Penguin was announced in the fall of 1996, it was also announced that Phyllis Grann would be the head of the new company.

The climb up the editorial ladder is not always easy. Genevieve Young told me she had to work a number of years as a secretary at Harper & Row before becoming an editor and editing the bestseller *Love Story*. But once started, she continued successfully at Lippincott, then was a senior editor and executive at Little, Brown, and after a stint as editor in chief of Literary Guild, retired as editorial director of Bantam.

Well-known literary agent Georges Borchardt, addressing a group of publishers, commented on the changeable publishing scene by saying, "Each morning before I can conduct business, I must find out where the players are today."

In contrast to Phyllis Grann and Gene Young, Robert Loomis, a vice-president and executive editor of Random House Adult Books, has reached the top by staying put—he has been at Random House for forty years. While he says only about a third of the books he buys are fiction, some of the authors he has edited have succeeded by staying put with him. Pete Dexter, whose first novel was *God's Pocket*, stayed and a dozen or so years later won the National Book Award with *Paris Trout*. Others among the authors whose work he shepherds are Laura Hobson and William Styron. At Random House, he told me, until very recently, there were no editorial meetings— all he had to do to get a manuscript or project accepted was to get only one other top person to agree to make an offer. Also, he says, at Random House, the editors don't ask the sales department for input in advance of a buying decision.

When you, after you are an established author, try to call your agent or editor between noon and 2:30 or even 3:00 P.M., you may find they are "out to lunch." These luncheons are an important part of doing business in the publishing world. A few editors and agents, however, resist this routine and have sandwiches at their desks during quick business meetings. If your editor asks you to this unglamorous kind of desk luncheon meeting, don't be insulted—it's just one of the perfectly acceptable publishing styles of behavior.

Your next invitation may be different. You may, as an author, find yourself invited to lunch by a publisher. It's a good sign he is interested in your book. But don't become bedazzled. I remember the first time I made a multiple submission to publishers back in the 1960s. My client was taken, in turn, by two major editors to very elegant lunches at famous and expensive French restaurants, and later both made an offer. We also had a third offer from an editor who never went to lunch. I suggested we make a deal with one of the three editors, and the author replied, "No, no, make more submissions, so we can have more fancy lunches!" We ended up with the editor who *didn't* wine and dine him.

HOW MUCH OF A NOVEL DO YOU HAVE TO WRITE BEFORE SELLING IT?

I firmly advise that you write your whole first novel before a publisher sees it, even if an agent has seen part of it and encouraged you to go on. As editor Ellis Amburn explains it, "The first-time novelist has no track record. That writer had better create the whole story so that I can see how it was handled and how the plot was resolved. Remember that a publisher spends a great deal of money launching a first book, and with that risk, he really must know what he is getting."

But there is always an exception. One agent, Harriet Wasserman, was so impressed with the first hundred pages she had seen of a beginning novelist that she gave it to a particular editor she thought would appreciate it, Jonathan Galassi, then at Houghton Mifflin.

Galassi liked what he saw and Houghton drew up a contract that gave author Alice McDermott a $12,500 advance to be paid in three parts—an immediate payment, an installment at the midpoint and the final part when the job was completed. Then Galassi switched to Random House and the budding author had to decide where her loyalty lay, with the editor or the publishing house.

She decided to go with her editor, and Houghton's advance was reimbursed. Of course, had Random not gone along with Galassi's desire to guide McDermott through her first book, she would have had no choice but to stick with Houghton and take whatever editor was next assigned her. She later followed Galassi to Farrar Straus & Giroux, where he became editor in chief.

HOW DOES A PUBLISHER DECIDE WHAT TO DO ABOUT YOUR MANUSCRIPT?

More than half the manuscripts that are offered to trade book publishers come from literary agents or lawyers acting as agents. Others come in because editors show interest in an author's query. And many are simply sent in unheralded, or are hand-delivered by the author. Such manuscripts are called "over-the-transom" or "unsolicited" submissions.

"Solicited" manuscripts come from every direction. Sometimes from within the publishing house itself, brought in by someone who has taken an interest in a new writer—an editor, executive or other employee, perhaps a salesperson, publicist, clerk, secretary or even the janitor.

If anyone, such as your attorney, agent, friend, teacher or mother-in-law—or you yourself through a query—has asked someone at the publishing house whether he wants to see your novel, and the person at the publishing house says yes, then your novel becomes a solicited submission.

Solicited submissions receive better treatment than unsolicited ones, in most cases. Unsolicited submissions are often routinely returned unread if the publisher has a policy (to save money) of not considering them. Or they may be turned over for reading and appraisal to a very junior person, such as a recent college graduate taken on for a trial period as an employee.

Fortunately, sometimes even if a junior person gives your manuscript a bad report, others such as the editors or editor in chief will have second thoughts and might actually glance through the unsolicited submissions to make sure something of real interest is not being overlooked. But you have no assurance of this, because the volume of unsolicited submissions is large, and experience has shown that many are hopeless—obscene, illiterate, unprofessional, racist, incoherent or colored by such odd religious or philosophical bias as to be of little interest to a large audience. Because of editors' built-in readiness to say no, many possibly okay works are returned after only brief inspection.

To show how accidental and casual the treatment of unsolicited manuscripts can be, I'll tell you a story from my own experience, without revealing the author's identity. When I was a busy editor of hardcover books at Prentice-Hall, a manuscript of a novel came in addressed to me, but by a person I did not know. I presume the would-be author took my name from a directory, such as *Literary Market Place*. I looked at it casually, decided it was unsuitable for hardcover publication and told my secretary to return it with an individually typed, polite form letter.

But instead of returning it, she began to read it during her lunch hours, and when she finished it, passed it on to another secretary to read. When both had finished it, they approached me and said, "This is good. You shouldn't just send it back with a form letter. If we can't publish it, Oscar, why not at least tell him where to take it?"

More because I appreciated the fine secretarial help I had received than because I respected their literary judgment, I took the manuscript home and read it over a weekend. I realized they were right. It was a perfect paperback original. So I sent it back with a letter suggesting the author take it to a certain paperback publisher, whose headquarters happened to be near where he lived. He did. They published it as a lead book successfully and sold the British rights also for a goodly sum, of which the author got a share.

Solicited manuscripts are handled by more experienced editors, and the editor who gets your manuscript is now the key person in determining your novel's welcome or expulsion from that publishing house.

Even so, the busy editor might first have someone else read the novel for him and write a brief report. This person might be an assistant editor or an "outside reader," that is, some freelancer who will read the novel and write a report, or even the editor's spouse. Regardless of whether the report is positive or negative, usually the editor will make at least a brief inspection of the work.

This brief inspection might be to read the first few pages, read at random in the manuscript and possibly skip to the end. *Therefore, each page of your work must be excellent,* so that no matter where the editor's eye falls, the work will attract his attention—"hook" him so he wants to read more.

If the manuscript survives this initial cursory inspection, usually the editor himself will read it carefully—or read as long as it holds his interest.

Again, if your novel survives these tests, the editor will then begin to prepare a case for and against the success of your book. If the case for it is stronger, he will begin to try to interest others in the publishing house in it—the editor in chief, the sales manager, the publicity director, the rights director and so on.

This can be a formal process, in which the editor writes up an elaborate proposal that compares your novel to best-sellers or other successful works, makes an estimate of sales (or an informed guess based on experience) and points out its promotional virtues. He may have to circulate this proposal, get comments from others and then defend the manuscript in an "editorial conference," that is, a formal meeting of those who have decision power.

Or, in a system used by some other publishers, he may have to get the approval of only one other person, such as the publisher or president of his company. Then the editor is free to go ahead and make an agreed-upon offer to publish—an offer that would include an advance against royalties and contract terms.

Keep in mind that publishers are inundated with manuscripts and have little patience with slipshod work. That is why it is really important to eliminate trivial drawbacks, such as poor spelling, a poor typing job, dog-eared pages, too-narrow margins, lack of double-spacing, or typing on both sides of the paper.

Poor spelling means more expensive copyediting and delay while this work is done. Poor typing means the manuscript will not photocopy well to submit to book clubs and may have to be retyped—expensive and time-consuming. A dog-eared manuscript looks as though other publishers rejected it. Narrow margins or single-spaced format makes it hard to edit. A manuscript typed on both sides of the paper would have to be tediously photocopied, as composition of type is only done from manuscripts on one side of the sheet.

These drawbacks, plus other doubts, in combination with strong competition from professional-looking manuscripts, may add up to the judgment: "It's too much trouble to publish this work."

But say you make it. You sign with the publisher, the long process of editing and copyediting is behind you and the book is scheduled for publication.

Is it all clear sailing now on a trip to fame, success and megabucks? A lot depends on the next step.

WHAT ABOUT PUBLICITY FOR YOUR FIRST NOVEL?

Your publisher may or may not be prepared to spend much time and publicity money on a beginner's work. In the old advertising jargon, he may "run it up the flagpole and see if anyone salutes." If your novel gets a good advance notice in *Kirkus Reports* (a publishing newsletter with advance reviews) and in *Publishers Weekly*, or if a good paperback or book club sale happens, or if book buyers happen to like the jacket and blurb and a good number of copies are ordered in advance by bookstores, then the publisher may promote vigorously. What she is doing is following the theory of pouring gasoline on an already burning fire. But suppose these good things don't happen right away. What then?

Many writers don't know that there are specialized public relations consultants who can be hired by *writers* to get publicity for a new novel. So, rather than take a chance that you will be disheartened after you are published and get only a few reviews, no advertising and scattered distribution, you can try to do something about it in advance and hire someone.

According to Lisl Cade, a New York public relations consultant for authors and publishers, who was formerly publicity manager for Harper & Row and director of publicity for W.W. Norton, good reviews are the most important publicity a first novelist can receive, because they can affect your whole career. Other kinds of publicity, such as press stories, radio and TV interviews and autographing parties, can reinforce the good impression of reviews but are of less importance in the long run.

No one in the publishing business can promise or accurately predict that you will get *good* reviews. But a skilled public relations person can greatly increase the chance of your getting *many* reviews simply by advocating your novel with letters, press releases and phone calls. And if you get many reviews, people, including editors, will say for years, "Oh, yes, I heard of that."

For someone like Lisl Cade to help you most effectively, the time to start promoting your book, she says, is several months *before* publication—at least four months before for the actual publicity work, and a couple of months before that for planning and making arrangements. She and most others in this field will only accept author clients if they like the author's work and can envision how they can succeed in publicizing it.

So you may have to shop around. The arrangement is to negotiate a monthly retainer with a publicist for some agreed-upon number of months. In addition to the retainer, expenses must be paid— travel, press kits, photographs of you and your book, many long-distance phone calls by the publicist, postage and messenger fees. Unless your publisher is cooperative, you may have to buy sets of advance bound proofs from her, and even buy copies of your book beyond what your publisher planned to send out for review.

If your publisher shares your publicist's enthusiasm, she may pick up all these expenses and do even more than you thought of doing yourself. Naturally, if your publisher *tells you* of the very extensive plans for review mailings, and has helped you secure important advance quotes from famous authors and personalities, and asked you to set aside time for a promotional tour, then you may not have to do anything on your own.

But say the publisher makes no promises, seems to have no promotion plans. Then *your* publicist can do it instead. After getting advance quotes, advance reviews and initial reactions to your novel, your publicist may be able to secure additional publicity for you, such as radio, TV and press interviews, and a book tour. To do this, he will have to work with you to figure out an angle interesting to the media—an angle connected with your book, but not just based on what's in it. New faces are news. Having a lively personality helps.

Your publicist will look for a real story, not concoct one, to make you newsworthy, a story you might not realize you are carrying with you all the time—such as how you wrote your Doomsday novel in a fallout shelter. Or you may be able to publicize your mystery story by talking about your adventures on your neighborhood Crime Watch.

Sometimes the publicity story can be very obvious, yet still exciting. When Lisl Cade publicized *Six Days of the Condor* for W.W. Norton, the story was that this first novel by the young James Grady had been retrieved from the "slush pile" by editor Starling Lawrence. It was "from unknown to author of a best-seller bought by Robert Redford to be made into a movie." That campaign was so powerfully effective that I bought and read the book myself and went to the movie.

To publicize *Fields of Fire*, the first novel of the much-decorated Marine Corps hero, James Webb, Patty Neger, then publicity director of Prentice-Hall, arranged a long publicity tour in which Webb discussed the public's neglect of Vietnam veterans. But first she laid the groundwork by circulating good advance quotes from well-known writers, sending out many advance bound proofs, and by telling reviewers she met with that the publisher considered it an important book. Good reviews, the powerful publicity and good subsidiary rights sales gave the publisher obvious reason to do sizable printings and advertise the book, and the first-time author was launched successfully. In 1997 Webb's fifth novel, *The Emperor's General*, was acquired by Broadway Books for what *Publishers Weekly* "Rights" columnist Paul Nathan reported as "a happy point between $500,000 and $1 million."

Fate helped publicize the first novel *Don't Embarrass the*

Bureau, by former FBI agent Bernard F. Conners. The novel was critical of the FBI, and when J. Edgar Hoover died practically on its publication date, the *Today* show invited Conners to appear. In a long interview, he predicted and advocated reforms for the FBI a new director might introduce—women agents, black agents and agents from other minorities, plus relaxed dress codes, among other things.

Often a publisher will devote little or no apparent effort to publicizing a mass-market paperback book. A good cover and big printing is the name of the game instead. When the first novel of Niel Hancock's fantasy quartet, *Circle of Light,* was scheduled to be published, he visited the editor in chief of Popular Library, Patrick O'Connor, and said, "I have some ideas. What are your plans to publicize my book?"

O'Connor replied, "I'm glad somebody has plans to publicize it, because we intend simply to publish and distribute it." And that's all they did. But editor Karen Solem (later editorial director of Silhouette Books and now an agent at Writer's House) had recommended that O'Connor authorize the expense of a famous cover artist. He agreed, and with nothing more than a beautiful cover and wide distribution to introduce the series, *Circle of Light* became an enduring seller.

If this review of the world of writing, agents, editors and publishers has seemed unduly depressing, don't despair. Read on and learn how some other novelists, both famous and still striving, got their start. Remember, *they* were first novelists once, too.

TIPS

• Editors and publishers look for books that appeal to a wide, or established, audience. They tend to steer clear of manuscripts containing misogynist themes and religious, racial or ethnic stereotypes.

• Write your entire first novel before showing it to the publisher.

• Solicited manuscripts generally receive more attention than unsolicited manuscripts do.

• Even a solicited manuscript may receive only a cursory inspection, so every page of your manuscript should be excellent.

• In addition to promotion by the publisher, authors themselves can hire someone to do publicity work for their books and bolster sales.

Part Two

HOW TWENTY-THREE NOVELISTS BROKE INTO PRINT

10.

They Weren't Always Superstars: How Six Famous Novelists Got Started

Novelists are made, not born. And if you look at the lives of even the most famous of them, you will see that they are *self*-made. When you read the elegantly packaged books of authors who are international celebrities, they may seem seamless and perfect, like those of Mary Higgins Clark. Not so, not so.

Surely his freshman English teacher at Mississippi State University could not have predicted that this student who barely squeaked by with a D would become "The $25 Million Man" of literature in the 1992-93 *Forbes* list of high-earning Americans, John Grisham. And it's hard to imagine Stephen King, writer of multiple bestsellers, facing rejection slip after rejection slip. Or to remember that sophisticated sex-and-celebrity-book-queen Jackie Collins started to write because of her anger at male writers.

Why were they different? Why did *they* become superstars? The answer is superior strategy. They found what they could do and did it again and again. After a quick look at a half-dozen authors whose names to publishers spell money in the bank, we'll examine twelve others. These twelve have been carefully selected from among the authors I or my coauthor know personally because their lives and work illustrate the most vital points you need to know in building your own success. And finally, we'll let you listen in on "Conversations with Five New Novelists."

JOHN GRISHAM

He was an obscure Mississippi lawyer who practiced law in the small town of Southhaven. He and his wife lived in a two-bedroom house so cramped that his computer was set up in the laundry room. But John Grisham would teasingly assure his wife, Renée, that one day he would be buying her bottles of wine that sported corks.

Determined to get ahead, he ran for state legislature and was elected in 1983. Now he was busier than ever, often working ten or twelve hours daily with his two careers and a third—fatherhood— with the arrival of a son, Ty, in 1984.

The same year, 1984, while at the Desoto County courthouse, he happened to hear the testimony of a pathetic twelve-year-old child who had been raped. It gripped him in a vise, and he could not get it out of his mind. What if that child were his? That rapist would surely not be alive to see another daybreak.

What if the little girl were only ten? What if this? What if that? That very day Grisham sat down with a yellow legal pad and started outlining a novel. There were two rapists—not one. They were rednecks and drunk and the child was black. And the overwrought father cannot wait for justice but kills the men in a back stairwell of the courthouse, shooting them down with an M-16 after their bail hearing.

Bit by bit the twenty-nine-year-old lawyer worked on his story, writing it all in longhand on legal pads, telling no one but his wife. And now he kidded Renée that it didn't matter if it sold, he just wanted to point to a pile of typed manuscript pages in his office and casually tell friends and clients, "Oh, that's a novel I wrote."

It took three years to finish. He frequently got up at 5 A.M. to get a little writing done before going to the office. And in recesses and lunchtime at the courthouse or state house, he would find a vacant room and turn out a page or two.

He didn't need to research a small town trial. He knew how it went. And he knew the types of men he needed for his lawyers—especially the white lawyer who defends the black father partly from conviction and partly for what the publicity about the big trial can do for his career. Grisham put it all in—the intimidation of witnesses, the media blitz, the harassment, the client stealing.

And then it was done, and there was a neat stack of manuscript pages in his office. He knew he needed an agent—that was the routine, he learned at the local library. So he made a list of all the literary agents he could find—some fifteen or twenty—and sent his first three chapters of *A Time to Kill* to all of them.

Those who bothered to make a comment said that novels about lawyers and courtrooms were hard to place. Publishers didn't want them. They were dead. Only one agent saw the potential of the courtroom drama. The late Jay Garon, an independent agent who then had an office in an upper-story apartment on Central Park West in New York, picked up the phone. Legal novels had not been selling lately, but it was time, he said, for the pendulum to swing in the other direction. "Send me the whole manuscript," he directed. Grisham was elated.

But as time moved along, it was beginning to look like all those nay-saying agents had been right. One after another, the major publishing houses told Garon, "That's a dead subject." And what was most annoying, Grisham kept calling Garon to ask, "Have you sold it yet? Have you found a publisher?"

To get Grisham off his back, he said, "Now is the time to start writing another book. Quit calling. I'll call you."

And eventually he did. Even after some fifteen or so turndowns, Garon kept beating the bushes and managed to get a small publishing house, Wynwood Press, to bring out the book, which it did—very quietly—in 1988. Wynwood printed only 5,000 copies, but the books weren't moving. Grisham, himself, bought 2,500 copies of *A Time to Kill* and used them as Christmas presents as well as passing them out to the courthouse crowd and his legislative colleagues.

But he still had piles of books in storage. A friend who served in the Mississippi legislature with Grisham, Bobby Moak, suggested that they load up Grisham's old Volvo and sell the book themselves at ladies' garden club meetings and libraries. They put the price down to $10, but they still could not find many people seeking courtroom drama or John Grisham autographs.

Looking back, Bobby Moak told Kelli Pryor of *Entertainment*

Weekly, "It was hell getting rid of those dadgum things. . . . A trunkload got wet and mildewed, so we just took 'em to the dump." The irony is that first-edition collectors are now paying from $3,900 to $5,000 for those Wynwood copies of the book, and a further irony is that Wynwood Press went out of business, while Jay Garon made so much money from just handling Grisham's book and movie deals he could afford to buy several vacation homes. He deserved it.

In fact, the world still might not have known the name Grisham if agent Garon had not decided on a bold move to try to get Grisham's second novel, *The Firm,* launched. He did an end run around the whole publishing world and took the book straight to Hollywood where Paramount bought movie rights, to star Tom Cruise. So far, the movie has grossed over $260 million worldwide.

As for the book rights, Garon still had a little trouble landing a major publisher for Grisham's second book, but eventually Doubleday said yes, offering $600,000, and found itself with a run-away best-seller. *The Firm* sold more than seven million copies, spent 46 weeks on *The New York Times* best-seller list and became the top-selling novel of 1991. It was translated into twenty-nine languages.

Meanwhile, Dell picked up *A Time to Kill* for paperback. It became a best-seller, and as of 1996, Dell has sold over five million copies. Then Doubleday brought out a new hardback edition of *A Time to Kill,* which of course also became a great best-seller. But the greatest triumph for Grisham and Garon came when the book that nobody had wanted and that had ended up on the city dump sold to Hollywood for $6 million. Everything Grisham writes earns many millions.

Counting all his list of legal thrillers that have been published in just eight brief years—1988 to 1996—John Grisham has over 670 million books in print worldwide.

It has been speculated that he just might be the most commercially successful author in history. You could also say that success has not changed him. Except for that huge Victorian house on a hill outside Oxford, Mississippi, with its sixty-seven-acre spread he moved to. And those bathrooms with silver vases of lilies and roses. And except for the tennis court, the croquet court, the swimming pool. And except for the ballpark he built in a pasture. And except for some quarter horses. And except for a full-time housekeeper and a maintenance man.

Those are the externals. But as a man, he definitely has not changed. He still shaves only once a week—Sunday before church. He still teaches Sunday school when he has the time, and he still coaches Little League for his son, who turned twelve in 1996, and encourages his little daughter, Shea, who is two years younger and into soccer, to keep up her practice.

What is the secret of Grisham's vast success? His books succeeded because you, the reader, feel it could have happened to you. As Grisham himself explained his technique, "You take a sympathetic hero or heroine, an ordinary person, and tie them into a horrible situation or conspiracy where their lives are at stake . . . they could be killed." Grisham also keeps in mind that the pace must be kept fast: ". . . no flashbacks, no long descriptions about relationships." And it doesn't hurt that we are in a litigious time, when everyone reads and hears about dramas in courtrooms.

JOHN LE CARRÉ

Britisher David Cornwell has single-handedly turned the view of the modern superspy 180 degrees, from handsome, young, wenching, cold-blooded killers, à la Ian Fleming's James Bond, to lonely, middle-aged men, unsure of the value of their spy work and hating violence, à la George Smiley.

But when his first book was published in England by Gollancz in 1961, he didn't really expect much of anything to happen. He was just grateful that it was in print and that he'd been able to get something off his chest—namely, his view of the spy world. After all, his life was littered with failed enterprises. And if his book failed too, it wouldn't matter. He wasn't using his own name anyway. He had spotted the name John le Carré on a London shop window.

David John Moore Cornwell was his real name, and he had failed as a teacher, a painter-illustrator, a drifter and, finally, a secret agent of sorts for Her Majesty's Foreign Service.

Actually, he had also failed as a writer if you were to believe his teachers at one of the many preparatory schools he had attended. He had been a lonely lad whose father owned racehorses and forced his family to live "an itinerate life." As David Cornwell remembers it, he wrote a short story on a subject that he knew something about—a poor, exhausted racehorse that was whipped brutally by a heartless jockey who cared only about winning. To little David's anguish, the headmaster called it "trash." And other teachers concurred.

Yearning to be a part of the academic world, le Carré went to Eton College after graduating from Oxford. There he worked as a tutor in German and French. He did not fit in and felt pressured to leave in two years. He tried his hand at another skill—art—but again found himself floundering. Unable to figure out where he belonged, he drifted around for several years taking whatever job he could find.

In 1960, on impulse and in desperation, he answered an ad seeking men for the British Foreign Service. Disillusionment set in almost immediately as he learned what spying and spies were all about. But this time, he did not run. Instead, he used the time it took to commute by train from his home in Great Missenden, Buckinghamshire, to the London headquarters to write a novel showing what the life and work of a spy was *really* like—seedy and sad.

Call for the Dead was his first novel, and its main character—hardly a heroic type—was scruffy, overweight, middle-aged, weary, disillusioned with his secretive, dangerous profession and saddled with a wife who cheated on him. George Smiley was his name. Six years after the book was published, Hollywood decided it liked Smiley's name, but not the name of the book. James Mason played Smiley in the film, called *The Deadly Affair*.

By this time, the John le Carré name had appeared on two more books. But not sure whether his first book's success was just a fluke, Cornwell had hung on to his position and had even been advanced to second secretary of the British embassy in Bonn, Germany.

The second book was *A Murder of Quality*. It had enabled Cornwell, through George Smiley, to get out all his pent-up feelings about the "intolerant, chauvinistic, bigoted" public schools he had attended. But it was the third book, *The Spy Who Came In From the Cold*, that made his pseudonym a household word and gave him the accolade of "The Spymaster." In this book Smiley is only a secondary character, but the so-called hero is again a jaded, bitter spy who is called back to the home office after the murder of his last East German contact.

Only then did David Cornwell feel secure enough to quit the foreign service and take up writing as a full-time profession. Books seemed to pour out of him—*The Looking Glass War; Tinker, Tailor, Soldier, Spy; Smiley's People*, to name a few. Honors were heaped on him—the Somerset Maugham Award, the British Crime Novel of the Year Award, the Edgar Allan Poe Award, among many others.

The only time he stubbed his toe was when he tried to write a straight novel—the story of a businessman's extramarital love affair. One reviewer's comment on the 1971 book summed it up for almost all reviewers: "a disastrous failure." Cornwell hastened back to George Smiley. Even at this writing, Smiley is alive and well in books that continue to go into new printings every year. And so is "John le Carré," whose name appears on the 1989 book that topped the best-seller list, *The Russia House.*

In 1996, Cornwell took a leap into the future with the spy story *The Tailor of Panama*, published by Knopf. The reader glimpses tomorrow's history, as le Carré develops a cloak-and-dagger plot featuring what happens December 31, 1999, when the Panama Canal is taken over by Panama.

The question remains, How much are Cornwell's *heroes* patterned after himself? Cornwell won't say, but facts speak for themselves. Like Smiley, Cornwell is rather shy and lives in seclusion on a cliff in Cornwall. Like Smiley, he had an unhappy marriage. In Cornwell's real life, he divorced the mother of his three sons and married a woman who bore him another son. And he does admit that *The Perfect Spy* is patterned after his own parent and that writing it finally enabled him "to jump over the shadow of my father."

There are two messages you can get from looking at Cornwell's career. One is to write what you feel strongly about, even if it goes against the accepted norm of the day, which is what Cornwell did when he invented Smiley. The second is to look around you and draw on the people you know—even if that person is yourself.

STEPHEN KING

Stephen King was not crowned the king of horror stories with his first manuscript. He survived the pain of having four novels and about sixty short stories shot down before he was finally anointed and given the keys to the kingdom of his chosen genre. *Then* riches were heaped at his feet.

His is a story of persistence, energy and narrow specialization. He built towering success on a very small foundation: A collection of paperback fantasy-horror novels was almost the only thing of value left behind by his father, a sailor, who left home when Stephen was three. These influenced the boy at a tender age, so it became natural to try to write in this genre.

There was no hint of a writing career in King's early jobs as janitor, mill hand and laundry worker. But he did get a scholarship, and graduated in 1970 with a B.S. from the University of Maine. When he settled into a serious job, it was as a teacher on the high school level for a private school in Maine.

King became more closely allied with the world of creative writing when he married a poet, Tabitha Spruce, the following year. King started writing at a furious pace, not stopping even though short story after short story—and his novels—were turned down.

Finally, in 1974, Doubleday accepted one of his novels, *Carrie*. It only took one book to make King famous. *Carrie*, a horror story about a girl with frightening telekinetic power, was made into a movie. And since 1974, top-selling books have been pouring out at a prodigious rate just as though King were still trying to get started— *Cujo*, *The Stand*, *Dance Macabre*, *The Talisman* (with Peter Straub), *Christine*, *Salem's Lot*, *The Shining*, *The Dead Zone*, *Firestarter*, *Night Shift*, *Skeleton Crew*, *Pet Sematary*, and others such as *Thinner*, written under the pen name of "Richard Bachman."

King has had more than one book on *The New York Times* bestseller list simultaneously—in early 1986, he had three. After more successes, the 1990s found King still whirling merrily along on his writing spree. And his dual writing personality of Stephen King and Richard Bachman showed no signs of ending. In 1996, he insisted that two of his manuscripts be published the same day—*Desperation*, by Viking, under the Stephen King byline, and *The Regulators*, by Dutton, under the byline of his other personality, Richard Bachman.

King, speaking for both personalities, insisted that the books were twins and so should have equal treatment with birth on the same day. And he would not permit Dutton to go ahead with its plan to say on the cover, "Stephen King writing as Richard Bachman." That's how protective he is of his alter ego. The result was that the two publishers launched a $2 million joint marketing campaign, and eager fans bought the package containing both books.

The sales gimmick was that the two covers fitted together, having been made from a Mark Ryden canvas cut in half. To the left is the cheerful Bachman view of a village, but the cover to the right shows the ghoulish dark side of the other half of the village, with a slinking coyote and frightening symbols.

King confessed to Judy Quin of *Publishers Weekly* that there is a little voice inside him that suddenly speaks up and directs his career, as in the case of the decision to write the twin books. "I did it because the Voice told me to do it," he told her. ". . . The Voice doesn't talk very much, so when it does, you have to listen."

Whatever turns him on, the results are spectacular. With the publication of his novel *The Green Mile*, as a serial in six separate volumes, he had all six on the mass-market best-seller list at once in September 1996, prompting mutterings from authors and publishers that he was monopolizing the best-seller lists. Daisy Maryles opined in her column, "Behind the Bestsellers," that "King fans are most probably checking out Evelyn Wood's speed-reading courses to keep up."

No matter what name he uses, no matter what publishing tricks he resorts to, as long as Stephen King makes the reader shiver with fear and apprehension, he'll have all the readership he could want. Someone has said that reading one of his books is like going to a Halloween party.

What's his secret? I think it is that he works hard and fast. To King, this work record doesn't seem prodigious. To him, it's just the natural speed at which he works, and it only seems unusual, he says, "to someone who doesn't write as much as I do." So far he has stuck to his chosen narrow field of specialization, still building on the foundation of his modest inheritance—that paperback collection of fantasy-horror books left by his father.

The success of Stephen King shows that you can succeed by contributing to a body of existing literature that you admire.

ROBIN COOK

He's on leave from Massachusetts Eye and Ear Infirmary in Boston. But the infirmary needn't hold its breath. It's safe to say the good doctor won't be back because he is now the leading practitioner of a writing category called "Medical Mystery Thriller."

Dr. Robin Cook was well on his way to a lucrative medical career when something befell him, so to speak, that would cause his dramatic career change. He had studied medicine at Columbia and Harvard universities and had even spent the year of 1972 teaching at Harvard Medical School as a clinical instructor.

After graduating from Columbia in 1966, he had spent two years in Honolulu as resident in general surgery in Queen's Hospital before returning to the continental United States and eventually becoming a resident in ophthalmology at Massachusetts Eye and Ear, and finally a staff member in 1975.

So what happened to make him change the course of his career? Boredom made him do it. Uncle Sam had suddenly tapped him on the shoulder and he found himself in military service, stationed on a submarine. Or rather *in* a submarine. Far from shore he had endless time and nothing to do but examine what was in his own head.

Cook decided to write a novel that would show the general public the ugly truth about medical schools and hospitals and the men and women struggling to become doctors—the horrendous hours they must stay awake and the horrendous sights they see of gore and pain and the horrendous competition they face and the horrendous decisions they must make while in a sleep-deprived state. And much more.

At the end of the naval tour of duty, he returned to the medical world with two new things: a rank of Lieutenant Commander and a manuscript that was almost ready to show a publisher. He didn't bother with an agent and went directly to publishers—after all, he was used to making judgments and he was pleased with the end result, which he called *The Year of the Intern*.

When, after just a couple of rejections from publishers, Harcourt accepted the manuscript, he was almost sure he must have written a best-seller. The rude awakening came when the book debuted in 1972 and did not make the list. Cook was determined to find out why. What did best-sellers have that his opus didn't?

He approached the problem as he had learned to do in medical school, dissecting several dozen best-sellers—especially suspense novels—and studying everything about them. And gradually he knew what he must do. He would tap into the desire of people to be a little frightened, a little better educated or made privy to some bizarre situation in the field of medicine. Or to be made a little nervous and anxious about whether the good doctor or helpless patient will be saved from the evil forces unleashed in the medical world. Could he do it?

He had the background in medicine. He enjoyed suspense novels. He liked to teach and alert people to dangers in the future. It all added up. He would carve his own niche, the aforementioned Medical Mystery Thrillers.

It took Cook five years to write and place his first book written with all the things he had learned about best-sellers foremost in his mind. It was a scary tale named *Coma* about a black market in the sale of human organs. A young female intern is confronted with mysterious deaths on her first day at a Boston hospital.

She knows what is going on, but the police will not believe that certain medical people are involved in this conspiracy. No one will believe her. And now the criminals are after her, and she is in mortal danger. And bodies are being warehoused in a vegetable state.

This time his publisher was Little, Brown, which brought out the book in 1977.

And what was the verdict of reviewers, you ask? Did his formula succeed? The answer is beyond his wildest dream. Charles J. Keffer in *Best Sellers* was impressed with how Cook's descriptions of medical procedures kept the reader deeply involved. "I do not think anyone can beat the suspense and the story line development throughout this novel," he said.

Mel Watkins of *The New York Times* praised the plot for its "escalating cycle of terrifying events that keep the action moving."

The paperback rights alone sold for $800,000, and the movie that followed grossed $50 million.

Now Robin Cook had his best-seller. He had arrived at the age of thirty-seven. With his third book, *Sphinx*, he went to Putnam, and now he had found his publishing home. He stuck to Putnam through a whole string of books that popped out at the rate of one every year or two, and in one year, two—*Harmful Intent* and *Vital Signs*, both published in 1990.

Turning his back on Wall Street, Cook invested in his own good life, acquiring one luxury home after another—a six-story Beacon Hill townhouse in Boston worth about $4 million, a condo in Trump Tower worth another $4 million, a retreat in Martha's Vineyard valued at $1.8 million and another condo in Naples, Florida, which he himself estimates is worth $5 million.

His string of best-sellers and movie sales attested to the fact that Robin Cook's formula of *medicine, mayhem and murder* was a mega-million-dollar one, and he has had some ten additional hits, through *Chromosome 6*, in 1997. It was estimated that by 1996, he had earned some $15 million from books and TV miniseries.

Cook has been faulted by various reviewers for his characters who "lack depth" or are "cardboard thin" or even "wooden." But with compelling plots like his, he can, as the saying goes, cry all the way to the bank.

Robin Cook has acknowledged that he would like to learn how

to develop deeper character delineations but, as he told Jean W. Ross of *Contemporary Authors*, "My books are written as mystery thrillers and not written to be compared with Henry James or any other more literary writer."

MARY HIGGINS CLARK

Mary Higgins Clark is famous for her suspense novels with their recurring theme of evil menace abroad—sometimes to children, sometimes to women. Even her titles are full of foreboding: *A Stranger Is Watching*, *Where Are the Children?*, *The Cradle Will Fall*, *A Cry in the Night*, *While My Pretty One Sleeps*. But it didn't start that way.

In fact, Clark's story should give heart to every middle-aged homemaker and mother who dreams of becoming a famous author. Her dream became urgent when suddenly, after fifteen years of marriage, her husband died and she was left with no insurance and with five children to feed and raise.

She had been a flight attendant for Pan Am before marrying, but returning to her old career with its constant travel was impossible. And the careers of her parents did not interest her—her father ran a restaurant in Manhattan and her mother was a buyer.

Clark had always known she could write, and she had good secretarial skills. She graduated from secretarial school and college summa cum laude, and so she turned to writing. She had written some short stories before (she sold her first one after several dozen rejections) and she turned to short stories again, but it was not profitable enough. She began scriptwriting for a radio program to help pay the bills.

As it turned out, radio writing was the best training she could have had for developing her writing skill. "It taught me to write tightly," she says. Each script was only four minutes long, and in that time, she had to tell a whole story.

It took several years for Mary Higgins Clark to feel ready to tackle a book. She chose an upbeat theme—a biography of George Washington. It was published by Meredith Press in 1969, just five years after she had been widowed. The title was misleading—*Aspire to the Heavens*. She can laugh today as she recalls that bookstores placed it in the section labeled "Religion." The size of the printing was only 1,700 copies. But she had learned the importance of titles and of following your own interests.

It took six years for Clark to be ready to publish again, but this time she chose fiction. And this time she had a provocative title and a provocative theme—children being menaced. To add to the intensity of the suspense the reader feels, all the action takes place in one day. The book was *Where Are the Children?*

Mary Higgins Clark wrote this first suspense novel at the kitchen table every morning from 5 to 7 A.M. before getting her younger kids off to school. She was now forty-seven. Her advance from Simon & Schuster, where Phyllis Grann was her editor, was a mere $3,000, and three months later, she and her children were sitting around trying to figure out how to come up with the college tuition one of them needed, when the phone rang. It was her agent, Pat Myrer, to say that Dell paperback was offering $100,000 for the paperback rights. Bill Grose of Dell had been sitting on his bed with one shoe off when he began looking at the manuscript. "He says he didn't take off the other shoe until he had finished the whole story," said Myrer, laughing. "Congratulations."

The second thriller, *A Stranger Is Watching*, did even better. It earned over a million dollars for paperback rights plus a movie sale to Metro-Goldwyn-Mayer. Its action takes place in three days.

Clark's third thriller, *The Cradle Will Fall*, became a CBS-TV Movie of the Week, and she has been a top-money writer ever since. In fact, she set the literary world on its ear in 1988 when she signed the first eight-figure contract in publishing history. As her current agent, Gene Winick, explained, "The deal is for five books—four novels and a collection of short stories. The minimum she can collect is $10.1 million. But the payment can go up to $11.4 million."

The message here for the first-time writer is not to be distressed if the first book doesn't make it. Clark's first book, she is the first to admit, was a financial flop. But it helped her get her bearings. Then she moved in another direction into a field that was uniquely her own, and she has not strayed from it ever since.

Just what does she do that holds us rooted to her books until we turn the final page? According to Jean White of *The Washington Post*, everyone can identify with Clark's characters. "She writes about terror lurking beneath the surface of everyday life—ordinary people suddenly caught up in frightening situations as they ride a bus or vacuum the living room."

And where does she get her plots? Out of newspapers. Out of the blue. You've seen those full pages of personal ads in newspapers and magazines by persons seeking dates for shared fun, romance, friendship or a "long-term serious relationship." Well, Mary Higgins Clark saw them too and they inspired her to write *Loves Music, Loves to Dance*.

New trends in today's world served as springboards for several Clark suspense novels. The growing number of people finding it necessary to lead hidden lives protected by the government's security program triggered her mind to write *Pretend You Don't See Her*. In vitro fertilization became the basis for *I'll Be Seeing You*. But it's not just a simple process. "For each of my novels, I do extensive research," she says. She enjoys every phase of writing and has no intention of retiring. "Someone once said if you want to be happy for a year, win a lottery, but if you want to be happy for a lifetime, love what you do. That's the way it is for me."

Clark also enjoys the process of moviemaking and goes to the set to watch and even sometimes experiences a walk-on part with one line or no lines. Two of her books were made into movies for the big screen, and three became TV movies.

"When you sell a book for televison or a feature film, you are in effect giving up your child for adoption," she says philosophically. "You wish it well, but lose control."

And whatever became of her five children, you might ask? They turned out remarkably well. One son, Warren, is a municipal court judge; one daughter, Marilyn, a superior court judge. Son David is president of Celebrity Radio, working with syndicated programs. Daughter Patty is an executive assistant at the Mercantile Exchange.

And to Mary Higgins Clark's great joy, one child followed in her footsteps—her daughter Carol. The byline Carol Higgins Clark, as of this writing, appears on three suspense novels, *Decked, Snagged* and *Iced*. They feature a female sleuth named Regan Reilly.

It has already come to pass that mother and daughter had bestsellers simultaneously. *Publishers Weekly* reported in May 1996 that mother Mary Higgins Clark had one book on the hardcover fiction best-seller list—*Moonlight Becomes You*—and one on the mass-market list—*Let Me Call You Sweetheart*—which was joined by daughter Carol Higgins Clark's paperback, *Iced*.

JACKIE COLLINS

Jackie Collins is one of the newer galaxy of literary stars to deal in the erotic. But her field and fame lie in writing about Hollywood— its sex and sin, its flash and trash and glitz.

My coauthor, Fran Leighton, met her in Washington, DC, when Collins was on a promotional tour for her book *Lucky*.

Collins told reporters frankly that she had originally chosen her theme because of her anger at Harold Robbins. She was sick and tired, she said, of what Harold Robbins did to women. He made them weak. His men were strong and had only to look at a woman to get her "to fall backwards into bed with him." She said, "I decided to do for women what Robbins had done for men." In Collins's books, women are the strong characters and *women* decide who will jump into bed with them. "My women are the aggressors," she said.

Her theme of aggressive women demanding a lot from life and getting it has made her a multimillionaire. Book after book has found a spot on the best-seller list as well as in movies and TV miniseries— *Hollywood Wives*, *The Bitch* and *The Stud*.

The sister of movie and TV star Joan Collins, Jackie, too, tried her hand at acting but regarded herself as "an out-of-work writer" rather than an actress. But even as she started writing her first book, back in the 1960s, she did not aspire to be a literary writer. "I'm a street writer," she says. "I write the way people talk, the way they think." As she tells it, she was politely invited to leave school when she was fifteen, and she never went back. She left her home in London and came to Hollywood to stay with her sister.

Her first novel, *The World is Full of Married Men*, raised enough eyebrows to assure that her second book, whatever it was, would also be published. That book was *The Stud*, and sister Joan, needing a starring vehicle to help her lagging career, chose it. (Joan also starred in *The Bitch*.) But Jackie did not become a writing star overnight. Her apprenticeship was a long one spent jotting down conversations overheard in restaurants, such as Ma Maison, and at parties where would-be starlets sat around in Jacuzzis to wait for the best offer and where guests were served cocaine on silver platters.

No, Collins was not a prodigy, writing her first novel as soon as she was kicked out of school. She didn't write it until she was twenty-five, and she still gets her material the same way—listening in on conversations or making the most of the latest gossip her friends keep her posted on by phone. If she ever wrote a nonfiction book about Hollywood, she says, no one would believe it. That's because it would have to include such stories as the one told her by the son of a famous movie star who learned about sex looking out his bedroom window, watching his parents and their guests play "change partners" at a poolside party.

Jackie Collins, it is said, has turned the milking of Hollywood into a fine art and is feared and courted by the Hollywood crowd. Viewing up close what happens to families and family life in the milieu of the movie colony, she wrote not only *Hollywood Wives*, but also *Hollywood Husbands* and, finally, *Hollywood Kids* as part of her list of more than a dozen titles.

Collins writes only what she cares about and frankly admits that with each book, she has a ripping good time. So, commercial as her novels may seem, the truth is that commerce is secondary. She has discovered a way to write tellingly about what she knows best and is most interested in and tell it the only way it can be told fully—in fiction.

Jackie Collins is a true successor to Jacqueline Susann, author of guess-who celebrity fiction such as *The Valley of the Dolls*. About Susann, one of her publishers, Bernard Geis, told me he thought her books succeeded because, "My wife says reading them is like listening in on a party line." Jackie Collins has added sight to sound.

11.

Writing About
What You Know

1. FROM BOOKKEEPER TO NOVELIST

Steven Linakis
author of *In the Spring the War Ended*

> "*Readers of* Catch-22 *may find this a superior novel.*"
> Eliot Fremont-Smith, The New York Times

> "*And it's a powerful enough book to cause much more of an agonizing reappraisal of our war effort than that earlier conversation piece,* The Caine Mutiny, *which by comparison reads like, and has the effect of, a polite literary exercise.*"
> Samuel I. Bellman, Los Angeles Times

> "*As important as any novel I've read about the way it was in World War II.*"
>
> Lester Goran, Chicago Tribune

"Makes Norman Mailer sound like Louisa May Alcott."
Albuquerque Tribune

"Best first novel of the season."

Richard Kluger

With the proceeds earned by his first novel, Steven Linakis, graduate of Hell's Kitchen, school dropout and self-taught bookkeeper for a hardware firm, bought, among other things, a $6,000 Yamaha nine-foot concert grand piano with genuine ivory keys; a $15,000 stereo system, which included Bozac concert grand speakers and Marantz-9 amplifiers; a four-bedroom ranch house on an acre of Long Island, complete with lawn sprinkler system; two new cars; and a mink coat and other furs and clothes for his wife.

How did Steven Linakis (pronounced "Lynn KNOCK iss") come to write such a moneymaking work the first time out? By living it first during and after World War II, then brooding on it for fifteen years and, finally, being goaded and pushed by his enterprising and talent-nurturing aunt into actually getting started.

I remember my first meeting with Linakis well. I was a beginning literary agent, working out of my apartment on East 72nd Street in New York. The telephone rang. An imperious voice trumpeted, "Os-kar! This is Madame Callas. My nephew is writing a novel. I have arranged for him to bring his work to you on Monday afternoon at 2. Good-bye!" Bang went the telephone. I didn't know how to reach her to call her back. And I had to think that perhaps I should look over her nephew's novel. After all, Evangelia Callas had already shepherded the operatic talent of two daughters, one of them Maria Callas.

Steven Linakis was delivered into the world in 1923 by a midwife at Bellevue Hospital in New York City. When he was five, his father and mother separated, and he didn't see his father again for more than fifteen years. His mother supported them by beading dresses—artistic but laborious work. Much of his childhood was spent at 434 West "Fifty-Toid" Street, as his Irish streetmates used to say.

The streets of this part of New York, called Hell's Kitchen, were a hard school. Most of his male contemporaries who made it to adult life went to prison, except for a few who went into the Army. Young Steven managed to stay clear of the law. Some of the time he lived with his aunt, Evangelia Callas, and played games with her daughters, Maria and Jackie. In his fourth book, *Diva, The Life and*

Death of Maria Callas, he wrote that living with the young Maria Callas had its hazards:

> I seriously doubt that Maria knew or sensed that her mother had preferred to have a boy when she was born. She did believe herself to be a fat, ugly duckling and thought that Jackie was preferred over her, which may have been why she was so assertive, precocious, competitive and even a bit of a tomboy.
>
> Once when we were both about twelve years old, Maria said it was her turn on roller skates. I made the mistake of telling her it was my turn. She knocked me over, yanking the skates right off my feet. The corner of my mouth was split open and later I had to have three stitches. She wasn't in the least sorry. It had been my own fault. It had been her turn.
>
> Another time, I had fallen off a backyard fence. She let me lay there and wouldn't do anything, although I knew my arm was broken. I had to promise not to say it was her fault. I would have promised her anything, and I had to swear it before she went to get her mother.

After grade school, Linakis attended Chelsea Vocational High School until he was seventeen. In retrospect, he regards only one day of his high school career as valuable—that was a day when a school teacher "rapped about life." He then went to, and dropped out of, the High School for Aviation Training, on Manhattan's east side, where he received training in the workings of "obsolete 600 horsepower Consolidated engines."

After leaving school, trying to do some writing ("Toilet seat writing: as long as no one knocked on the door") and holding down manual labor jobs outside New York City, he was drafted into the Army during World War II when he was nineteen.

It was during his sojourn in the U.S. Army and its aftermath that he gained the book-worthy experiences that many years later led to this conversation with his aunt:

> "Is it a nice love story?"
>
> "Don't know if you can call World War II a love story," I said.
>
> She was very interested and whenever she called after that she would ask how the book was progressing.

"Oh, it's coming fine," I would say. "Keeps me awfully busy." From the sound of it, I had roughed out a 500-page manuscript. I got quite good at talking about the book, when I hadn't committed even a single word to paper.

After basic training in the Army, Steven Linakis was sent to the Firth of Clyde in Scotland, then to the south of England, near Bournemouth.

On D day, he was part of the invasion of France, landing at 6:15 A.M. on Omaha Beach, "Dog Red," as part of the First Division, 16th Infantry. Describing his experience, he said, "Parts of people were all over you from explosions. I thought I was wounded—was in a state of shock. I think some of our own stuff was hitting us. Our planes bombed three miles inland. The German defenders were just a home guard unit—their first line outfit was on maneuvers. We were stuck on the beach a long time anyway."

Then, from June until September, he and his outfit "walked, crawled and drove across France—I never got laid once." They reached Belgium September 7, and he believes his unit was the first to invade Germany.

At the battle of Hurtgen Forest ("Statswald was the actual name of the woods," he remembers), his unit had 70 percent casualties. The protagonist of *In the Spring the War Ended*, Nicholas Leonidas, remembers Hurtgen in a flashback:

. . . when I heard that patient screaming, then those hard cracks of lightning, and Johnny talking about the Hurtgen, in my mind I'd been back to the last assault on the Hurtgen after the kraut had finished us. Then it hadn't been that patient screaming, but Lt. Miller and that was after we'd been lost and running, and the tall fir trees were all down, shattered and splintered white. The kraut mail had kept coming in and all the forest exploded behind us, yellow and red, and everything stank of high explosives and the dead.

We'd made it to the clearing all right when they hit us again. Only it wasn't the kraut this time. Our own heavy mortar was falling in a tight pattern, spreading phosphorus, white and hissing. It hit me like a hot iron, scalding. Then Miller screamed and we both were screaming.

Miller tried to stand on his knees after he'd been hit. I rolled in the mud, while Miller still screamed, and then the mortaring just stopped. Then you really heard him. All of him smoking, his face blistering, and him screaming, and his eyes trying to see. I tried to push him down into the mud. He jerked away from me. Going on one knee and then the other, he kept trying to get up, screaming all the time. I'd never heard a man scream like that.

I had to sit on him to work the morphine. I tried his, but it was too shaky. The pain shriveled me and I broke the needle. Then I tried mine. I got it into him all right, but it didn't do any good. I yelled for the medics. There weren't any medics. A squad of infantry came through. They got us to battalion aid. All the time Lieutenant Miller was screaming that they should shoot him. He had the stink of a burned tire. He was blind all right and his face was black with red blisters. It took several medics to hold him down and cut his clothes off.

A medic said to me, "Are you hit?" I said I didn't know.

"Wrap him up," said another. "He's going into shock."

"He is like hell," said the first.

"Are you all right?" asked another. I said I didn't know.

On the floor, somebody pulled the heavy cartridge belt and webbing away and yanked off my coat. Somebody else was cutting away the field jacket and pants.

"Look at that," said the first medic. "Like a million cigarette holes, right down to his longjohns. The mud cut off the oxygen."

Steven Linakis was sent from a field hospital to a base hospital, and after he had recovered partially from his wounds, on Armistice Day—the day commemorating the end of World War I—1944, he went AWOL, personally ending his own participation in combat in World War II.

Initially, wandering around in rear areas, he was horrified and furious at seeing five-gallon jerricans of gasoline being sold to the black market, while battlefield vehicles were stalled for lack of fuel.

But as he gained experience in hiding out and adopting disguises, he began to participate in the black market himself to finance his fugitive life. He stole and sold trucks, jeeps, coffee, shoes, parts. He took part in a scam involving confiscation of food stamps worth millions and ended up with $5,000. He stole parachutes from airports—from B-56s, B-50s—and found that stealing from American planes at British-protected bases was easiest, as the British guards didn't seem, he thought, to care what happened so long as their own planes were left alone. A parachute could be sold, for its silk, for five thousand to fourteen thousand Belgian francs, then worth forty-four to the dollar.

He was apprehended at least a dozen times by the MPs, and escaped—once from Mannheim prison, a medieval fortress complete with moat. Of the fifteen who made the breakout attempt with him, seven were killed. He was in Paris Detention Barracks, in prison garb—maroon ODs and yellow helmet liner. He was severely beaten by MPs several times, and the atrocities he later described in his novel were either experienced or witnessed. He says the conditions in the prisons were worse than those of "the real war."

In retrospect he says that "criminality is very strange—you can justify anything."

For a year, he lived this life on the run, behind the lines in France and Belgium, from November 1944 to November 1945. When he was caught at Liege, after becoming one of the most wanted men in Europe, a whole MP platoon was sent to escort him, manacled hand and foot, to prison. For thirty days, he was kept in solitary confinement, handcuffed, at a site near Waterloo. The MPs who caught him were given, he heard, ninety-day furloughs as rewards—rewards, he believes, sanctioned by orders from General Eisenhower.

At his trial on a general courts-martial procedure, on Valentine's Day 1946, Linakis was "charged with every military offense in the book, except rape and treason—including murder, which I never committed."

He felt lucky with his sentence of twelve years in prison. He knew some sentenced to twenty years for being AWOL for two months. While at Paris Detention Barracks, he had seen Private Eddie Slovik escorted out on the way to being shot for desertion under fire. Linakis attended his own trial shackled hand and foot and guarded by two MPs armed with Thompson submachine guns.

In the Spring the War Ended is a fictionalized, picaresque, but often true account of his adventures (and things he saw and learned) while AWOL, coupled with flashbacks of actual battle experiences. This fact was unknown to me when I was the book's original agent and to his publishers—he only revealed it in an interview with a UPI reporter well after the book was published.

What were the changes that transformed Steven Linakis from a twenty-one-year-old AWOL soldier, sentenced to twelve years in prison, to a novelist praised by major media, published in eight countries?

The first of these changes came about in Lewisburg Federal Penitentiary, in Lewisburg, Pennsylvania. Instead of being a wanted felon on the run, he entered the more orderly life of a Federal prison. On Friday, September 13, 1946, Linakis and two hundred other general military prisoners arrived in New York on a "Liberty" ship after a sixteen-day trip from Hamburg. It was the first time he had seen the United States in more than three years. The prisoners were taken to Ft. Hamilton, and Linakis was given a dishonorable discharge from the Army. All his decorations were removed from his record: the Silver Star, three Purple Hearts, four Battle Stars and the Arrowhead for D day.

Guarded by a line of MPs with machine guns, they were escorted to Lewisburg and turned over to the prison authorities.

Lewisburg seemed a paradise after what they had been through. When the prisoners arrived, its great hall of a dining room had the melody "Claire de Lune" playing over loudspeakers. They were given plates, and the plates were piled high with spaghetti. "Take all you want," they were told.

"We ate like animals," Steven Linakis recalls.

In Lewisburg, he met some notable inmates: the Lustig brothers, of Longchamps, serving time for tax evasion; Steve Menna and other members of organized crime (it was at Lewisburg that he first heard the then-code word, "Family," to refer to those in organized crime); and Serge Rubinstein, a Wall Street financier in for draft dodging, whom he protected from prison fights.

After six months of depression and inaction came the second change. He decided to try to use his time in prison to make something of himself, and began to read. Before going to prison, his reading tastes ran to adventure stories, such as those published in *Airways* magazine. Now he tackled *Studs Lonigan*, the three volumes by James T. Farrell; the works of Steinbeck and Hemingway; and, most impressive to him, the work of John Dos Passos—*Three Soldiers*, *The U.S.A.* He did not like Hemingway's work at first, but came to appreciate it after he began to write himself.

The third change he owed to public-spirited university people. He studied with a group of tutors from Bucknell who came to the prison. Linakis took classes in writing from an English major. His early efforts, which he submitted to magazines, were rejected. But he got detailed responses, mostly encouraging. Actually, he was not himself convinced he was a writer, because what he was reading was so much better than what he wrote. He initially chose subjects far afield from prison or what he had experienced; for example, he wrote a story about India, based on a *Time* magazine article. When you are in prison, he says, you want to escape by writing about faraway things.

But occasionally he wrote about the war, and some of his work was published in the prison magazine, *Periscope*. He had a run-in with an associate warden about his war stories. The warden said, "Don't write about the horrible things in war."

"I wrote reams," he says, "and still have a 300-page handwritten manuscript I wrote then." His own characterization of his writing at that time is that "the description was good, but the dialogue was wooden." He also began to play the piano—two rooms at Lewisburg had uprights, with another piano in the auditorium—though he had "two bum fingers from shrapnel."

By the time Linakis left prison, his life had new meaning through a "marvelous concentration of learning."

He was paroled from Lewisburg and returned to New York. When he visited West 53rd Street, he was "amused at how small and dirty it all was—the five-room railroad flat." He got a job in a zipper factory and rose to foreman. He didn't like factory work and sold vacuum cleaners for six months, was a foreman at a plastics factory and was a deliveryman for the David Schumacher company. He met and courted his first wife and was humiliated when he had to take her to meet his parole officer to get permission to get married. They were married in 1951, and nine years later, with no children, were divorced.

During this time, he stopped writing and began to study the piano, taking five years of formal instruction at the Greenwich School of Music. I believe his study of music is another change that helped him develop as a novelist. In many instances talents don't seem to come singly, but are many and varied in creative people. In Linakis's case, he is a professional writer, is quite a good piano player and has still another talent I discovered in an embarrassing way when I visited him at his Long Island ranch house after the success of his first novel.

Soon after I arrived, I became increasingly aware of a beautiful painting on the wall of his living room. As I had been a professional painter for fifteen years before going into the book business, and had particularly admired the work of Vincent van Gogh, I became very nervous as I realized that what I saw before me was a *painting*, not a reproduction. The brush and palette knife strokes were those of van Gogh. The size of the painting was exactly right. It *was* a van Gogh! I knew by then of Linakis's criminal record and his prison sentence. I became very nervous. He had always been scrupulously honest with me, and I also knew that at his job as a bookkeeper for Mutual Electricity and Machine Co., he had been trusted to make the company's bank deposits and withdrawals. But this was a *real* van Gogh!

Trying to keep calm, I said, "That is a very fine van Gogh you have there."

He replied, "Yes, I got it from the Metropolitan."

That was where I had seen it!

"How did you get it out?" I ventured.

"Oh, I stole it," he replied.

"How?" I asked, my worst fears confirmed.

"A little bit at a time," he replied. "They wouldn't let me copy it in the museum same size, so I went and examined a little part of it each time and came home and duplicated it on a same size canvas."

I believe that Linakis developed his extraordinary total recall— a skill that helps him write excellent dialogue (and that helped him copy the van Gogh exactly)—partly through his musical training.

While he was still a bookkeeper, he noticed a newspaper story about his aunt Evangelia Callas, being employed to help in a store that had been newly opened by the Gabors, and he got back in touch with her. She was then writing her own memoirs, published as *My Daughter Maria Callas*, with the help of a ghostwriter.

I was destined to meet Linakis through Madame Callas. As a salesman for her publisher, I was assisting with her book's publicity. We liked each other immediately, though I have to admit I was a little intimidated by her. She was a natural matchmaker, and when she learned that I was married, she was somewhat thwarted as to how she could return the hard effort I was putting into making her book a success. But as I wrote earlier, she finally did match me, when I became an agent, with her writer-nephew Steven.

As Linakis records it with light and satirical pizazz in *Diva:*

One afternoon, she called and said she had marvelous news. A marvelous man, a marvelous friend of hers, was extremely interested in my book. I caught the name of Oscar Collier, but I wasn't sure whether he was a publisher or a literary agent. She told me to join her on the East Seventies that Monday afternoon to meet him and, of course, to bring the manuscript.

Here it was a Friday. I was hung. I'm sure Litza told him I had a 500-page manuscript that was sheer genius. I couldn't very well go empty-handed. So over the weekend I typed out twenty-six pages, which weren't half bad, but I didn't think they were all that good either. Still, it came easily enough. Maria had her traumas. I had mine: World War II.

I suppose I was curious about this Collier. He turned out to be a literary agent who, very impressively, was handling people such as James T. Farrell. Collier was tall and . . . soft-spoken. He gushed a bit when he greeted my aunt, but he didn't seem all that interested when I was introduced to him. I could just imagine what was going through his mind. Every aunt considers her nephew talented, and Collier was going to have to go through that bore. I was amused by it all.

Collier was a little cold when he asked me how much MS I had.

"What?" I asked.

"Manuscript," he said curtly.

"Oh," I said. "I've roughed out about five hundred. But I only brought a sample, mainly not to waste your time and to see whether or not I had it."

He took my address and phone number, saying he would get back to me as soon as he read it. Then he was happily talking to Litza again.

Before I ever got home, Collier had called. When I returned his call, the first thing he said to me was, "How much more of this do you have?"

"Why?"

"It's not bad. Quite good, in fact. If the rest is like this, I can sell it tomorrow."

"You kidding me?"

He wasn't in the business of kidding anyone, and he wanted to know when he could see the rest of the MS, amending that by saying, "Manuscript."

The hell of it was that out of a downright lie that grew,

I became an author, a rather perverse way of contributing oneself to literature.

So the fourth change that occurred in Linakis's life is that he was pushed by a nurturing family member into realizing one of his dreams. I was sorry to learn, from Steven Linakis, that his flamboyant, fascinating "Litza" died in Greece in August 1982 at age eighty. We should all be lucky enough to have such a relative!

At the end of the phone call Linakis described above, he told me that he needed time to polish his manuscript, and that he would be back in touch with me in a few months.

He began to get up at 2:30 or 3:30 in the morning and write until 6:30 A.M. He commuted to work for an hour and a half, worked eight hours and commuted home for another hour and a half. He participated in family life with his second wife and children somehow while writing more on weekends. Altogether, it took him fourteen months to write a 700-page manuscript, using a space and a half between lines. The 315,000-word novel started with VE Day and ended as the protagonist, Nick Leonidas, was being taken from Brussels to be shipped back to prison in the United States.

When it was partly finished, he showed me a sizable portion, together with a terribly written outline of the rest, and I began to show it to publishers: Pocket Books, Scribners, Viking, Knopf. At Knopf, Ashbel Green replied that it really was a Putnam's book.

I recommended that Linakis have it read and criticized by a freelance editor, Darrell Husted, who gave him a report and analysis. The comments made by the editors who saw the novel, and by Darrell Husted, were probably the fifth change that helped Linakis become a published novelist—he proved willing and able to take professional advice.

I submitted the manuscript to Peter Israel, then editor in chief of G.P. Putnam's Sons, after having described Linakis to him at lunch. Israel rejected it, sending a long, well-thought-out letter of criticism explaining why he was rejecting it.

Linakis enrolled himself in a class Israel was holding at Putnam's, for a $75 fee, in order to get to know more about the editor's ideas. He gained confidence in Peter Israel from the sessions and began to feel that Israel was the one person he needed. So he started a correspondence, replying point by point to the criticisms Israel had made in his rejection letter. He didn't just take no for an answer.

After some back and forth, his new agent, James Seligmann, to whom I had sent him after closing my agency to take a job as head of a small general trade book publisher, negotiated a contract with G.P. Putnam's Sons. The contract was for a $2,500 advance against royalties, payable $500 on signing, $1,000 on completion of a first draft and $1,000 on acceptance of a final draft.

He submitted small sections of the novel to Israel through his agent as they were completed. He describes Israel's editing as "do-it-yourself editing," though Israel did correct his grammar. There would be indications of "awk" (awkward, section to be rewritten), "cut?" (suggestion to delete), and "Let's talk" (leading to discussions of what Linakis had meant to say, and was it necessary and desirable?). He had worked now more than fourteen months on the novel, the last six with Peter Israel. With the advance money, he bought furniture and a color TV.

The manuscript was slimmed down from 700 pages, 450 words each, to 376 manuscript pages—which came out as 346 book pages. "When it comes to shortening," Linakis says, "Hemingway is a good teacher." Linakis's hardest work was on the dialogue. He began to listen closely to what people were saying and how they said it—their cadences. The dialogue, he says, must reflect your feeling, plus what the character is saying. It is necessary to interpret, rather than quote. "You have to make your characters smarter or dumber than life; you have to feel it and know when it is good by the sense and flavor. Musical training helps." At times his drafts got too Hemingwayesque, and then he drew on his observations of how Steinbeck and Dos Passos wrote.

Linakis believes that much of the power of his novel came from his anger. But he couldn't write it while angry. He had to *recall* his anger coolly, analytically, and think of what really happened, from both sides. Above all, he says, the novelist must read and study how other writers achieved effects like the ones he wants.

Peter Israel recommended the novel to movie producers and foreign publishers, even though Putnam's, as is usual in agented contracts, didn't control those rights. James Seligmann took on a coagent to help him handle movie rights, and used his coagents abroad to negotiate foreign rights contracts. Peter Israel generated interest in others by calling the book "one of the best of the three thousand first novels that have crossed my desk."

Putnam's auctioned paperback reprint rights, and Dell won at $49,500. Book clubs turned down the novel because of the strong language. *Man Magazine* ran a piece of it as a first-serial-rights sale. Foreign editions were published in France, Holland, Germany, England (hard- and softcover), Sweden, Denmark, Spain and Japan. It was a best-seller in Holland and earned royalties well beyond its advance.

Larry Turman, producer of *The Graduate*, optioned movie rights, with $35,000 paid on the option vs. $200,000 purchase price. Though the film was never made, Linakis realized over $75,000 in option money and a settlement and earned $500 a week plus expenses for quite a period when Turman brought him out to Hollywood to try to write a new screenplay after the one by William Goldman didn't fly. Linakis didn't care for Goldman's version of his novel. He said, "I felt like a bird came into my house, took everything I owned, then shit on my grand piano." Turman warned Linakis that, "Doing a screenplay of your own novel is more painful than doing an appendectomy on yourself."

Peter Israel left Putnam's shortly after *In the Spring the War Ended* was published. Putnam's took out a full-page ad in *The New York Times Book Review* and a small ad in the daily *Times* for the book. It received many glorious reviews, except for severe pannings in *Time* and *Library Journal*. Hardcover sales were in the six- to seven-thousand range. The Dell paperback reprint was moderately successful, and several years later, Popular Library reprinted it in still another edition. Altogether, he estimates he made over $200,000 from his first novel.

Steven Linakis offered some reflections on writing: "Write about what you know—cheat from it, but use it as a base. You must hit a nerve for the best of writing.

"What is a novel? A piece of yourself—but just a piece—not the whole picture. A novel is the tip of the iceberg. Never give it all away.

"A story must have structure. If you find repetition in your writing, cut it away, but leave some if it works. Put it all in at first, then trim it away. You can't see the whole story until the whole thing is written—then you can see the structure. Put it away to cool, then see what you have got.

"Start with what's interesting to you—others will believe your story better if you are interested in your material.

"Fiction is more truthful than nonfiction. Nonfiction has trouble with lawyers. Fiction is nonfiction, nonfiction is fiction today.

"Today's publishers have a fashion industry mentality. The old

Scribner's-Maxwell Perkins world doesn't exist any longer. Books are pieces of goods that will sell. Nobody cares about art anymore— but it sneaks in once in a while anyway.

"Procrastination and delay are castrating.

"Agents did help me, but most are cold bastards and not very smart.

"The effect of my success was to turn my life topsy-turvy, and I have some regrets. It caused family problems. Writing is a lonely, unsure existence. Writing is the easy part, though—the problems you have to deal with are the reviewers and the industry. I have been dissuaded from a number of books. But if you stick to it, it can work."

Beginning novelists can learn many lessons from the experiences of Steven Linakis. To me, the actions that contributed most to his success were these: He acquired a marvelous concentration of learning through reading good novelists. He developed his ear and memory by studying music. He allowed himself to be pushed into action by a nurturing, interested person. He proved willing and able to take professional advice. And he didn't take no for an answer— probably the most important lesson any budding creative person can learn.

2. FROM SPOOK TO SPY NOVELIST

George O'Toole
author of An Agent on the Other Side

> "George O'Toole writes about the CIA with authority: He served as an intelligence officer in that organization for three years before leaving to devote full time to writing. He is an expert on the use of computers in intelligence work. His other interests include parapsychology, which has long absorbed him; cryptography (he has invented a cryptographic device); and flying light aircraft. 'But,' he says, 'some of my most interesting accomplishments are, unfortunately, classified.'"
>
> Flap copy from the hardcover edition

George O'Toole, who later changed his writer's name to "G.J.A. O'Toole," had the opposite task as a novelist from that of Steven Linakis. Linakis wrote a picaresque autobiographical novel that was a rearrangement and development of his direct experiences. He had to select from those experiences, enhance them in a true-to-life but powerful way and arrange them into a plot.

O'Toole, who had been an intelligence officer for the Central Intelligence Agency for a few years of his career, had signed, casually, when he joined, a form agreeing for all time to show the Agency anything he wrote that might even remotely be about the CIA or things he had learned while working there, and not to include materials the CIA forbade.

Up to the time his first novel was published, there had been no court case testing this agreement, and he had actually forgotten he had signed it. Nevertheless, since his novel was about a fictitious CIA operation, he decided he had better show it to the Agency, to make sure he had not inadvertently revealed material the CIA wanted to keep secret. This decision turned out to be a good idea, because later, in a court case on *The CIA and the Cult of Intelligence*, by Victor Marchetti, the courts affirmed that the pledge he, Marchetti, and others had signed was enforceable by law.

O'Toole sent his manuscript to the Agency through a friend who was still working there, and it came back without any requests for changes or deletions, though, he said, "I was intrigued by the paper clips that had been left attached to certain pages."

So George O'Toole's task was to write a novel that wasn't true in any way, shape or form—a work that was truly fiction, and contained only such facts about the CIA and the "spook" world as were known from previously published material—yet still would seem to an outsider true to life and very revealing of inside information.

In an "Author's Note" inserted at the end of the novel, he says, "*An Agent on the Other Side* is a lie. Lying, however, like most human endeavors, can be done either poorly or well. Inspector Spinka gives us his two criteria for a good lie: It must contain many elements that are true, and it must include something so improbable that it seems it could not have been invented. In that sense, I have tried to make the story a good lie." However, he concludes this three-page author's note by adding, "Things, after all, are often not what they seem to be," and thereby leaves the reader freshly tantalized. Is there truth, after all, in the novel? This is a proper final note.

O'Toole got the idea for his novel when he read a Soviet paper on parapsychology that said the Reds encouraged psychic research. He began to wonder how the psychic could be used in an espionage operation—to hoodwink the other side.

He had also become interested in the situation in Czechoslovakia when, after ending his CIA service, he published a paper in *Computers and Automation* that had mentioned, in his biographical sketch at the end, that he had been with the CIA. He received a letter and a request for a reprint from a Czech correspondent, and later an invitation to visit Czechoslovakia. From friends he learned that the person who wrote to him was working for Czech or Soviet intelligence agencies, so he decided to decline the invitation.

Because of these events, he began to follow the news about Czechoslovakia and studied the Soviet invasion of that country with close attention. The invasion happened during the period he would have been there had he accepted the invitation.

He wove these two themes into his novel, looking around for possible characters. At the time, he was working for a company that made educational films, so he chose a person from that industry for his protagonist. He then devised characters based loosely on people he had met in the CIA, being careful that the resemblances to real people were not close enough to be "actionable." He based his main female character, a medium who received messages from "the other side," on his reading about a famous woman medium, altering her in personality and appearance to fit into his developing novel.

He selected the idea of the CIA becoming involved with mediums as something highly unlikely to have actually happened—but since it was known that the Soviets were experimenting with parapsychology, the idea was credible enough to use in a thriller. Here, from the book jacket, is his publisher's description of the novel:

> A superthriller, involving the CIA, international intrigue, the use of psychic power for conveying messages from a dead man.
>
> In the summer of 1968, on the eve of the Soviet invasion of Czechoslovakia, a lovely young woman with psychic powers approaches the CIA and claims to be in touch with the spirit of a dead Russian spy. As evidence she offers the detailed secret Soviet invasion plans.
>
> But there's a hitch. The CIA learns that another medium in Prague, a celebrated one, has been selling identical information to West Germany. And it could only have come from the same dead spy! To unravel this strange web, the CIA taps John Sorel, a young filmmaker, who starts his investigation under cover of his work in films. Overnight he finds

himself involved in a plot complicated by internal, double-dealing double agents, murder, and strange occurrences in the world of the occult on both sides of the Atlantic, including a spine-chilling séance in a Bohemian castle.

The inside view of the CIA at work in this exciting tale is fascinating and perhaps only partially fictional.

To write this first novel, George O'Toole took a six-month leave of absence from his work and lived on accumulated savings. After finishing it, he queried six publishers, writing a long—"too long," he says now—letter addressed to the "Editor in Chief." The novel was rejected by Burroughs Mitchell at Scribner's, Hal Scharlett at Doubleday, John Willey at William Morrow, William Targ at Putnam's and editors at Walker & Co. and Dutton.

After reading an article in a writer's magazine on how unsolicited manuscripts are only published "once in a while," he decided he must find an agent. He secured the list of agents who are members of the Society of Authors' Representatives (SAR) and began to read *Publishers Weekly*. In Paul Nathan's *PW* column on rights and permissions, he read that Seligmann & Collier had handled the first novel—*Don't Embarrass the Bureau*—of former FBI agent Bernard F. Conners. O'Toole wrote an inquiry letter to James F. Seligmann. Seligmann passed this letter on to me, as a person more interested in such novels. I wrote away and sent for it, liked it and arranged to secure five copies for a multiple submission.

Within two weeks, while George O'Toole was attending the Bread Loaf Writer's Conference, Eleanor Rawson of David McKay called and made an offer, which I recommended O'Toole accept. The contract provided that $1,000 would be paid on signing, and since McKay wanted him to work more on the novel, $1,000 on acceptance of one-half the manuscript, and $1,000 on acceptance of the whole work—$3,000 total as an "advance against all earnings." He became something of a hero at Bread Loaf!

One of the pleasures of "writing about what you know" is putting into your novel satirical passages about the world you are describing. O'Toole included in the novel a couple of pages of very funny material about a CIA agent who was a failure, but because of the situation, was pushed on through various stages of his training anyway. He kept failing "Breaking and Entering."

He had to do that part of the course several times, and became a familiar figure in the Baltimore lockup. Finally, because he was an embarrassment to all concerned, he was permitted to graduate on the strength of a forced entry into a grain warehouse in a tiny Virginia hamlet, and the successful evasion of the town's eighty-year-old constable.

His training record was not scrutinized too closely because a big to-do then being planned had created a great demand for case officers. After a brief vacation he was flown to a secret base in Guatemala to assist in the training of a group of Cuban refugees to land on the southern coast of Cuba. When the invasion was finally launched, Hagarty had the task of coordinating the air support over the Bay of Pigs.

O'Toole's editor called me to complain about the material involving this comic character, Hagarty, and O'Toole's stubborn support of it. I have to admit I defended it vigorously, saying, "After all, where else can you learn about the air support officer at the Bay of Pigs?" McKay left the material in.

The book had only modest sales, and O'Toole says it was not very widely distributed. It received very few reviews. But Dell reprinted it in a paperback edition, and Arthur Barker Ltd. published it in England. It was translated into Italian and published in Italy by Mondadori. Through Seligmann & Collier's dramatic rights coagent, Warren Bayless, a modest movie option was negotiated with screenwriter Joseph Boyd, who paid $1,875 for nine months' option time. Boyd extended the option nine months more for $1,875 additional, after which it lapsed with no movie made and the $25,000 purchase price unpaid.

Altogether, George O'Toole made about $10,000 for six months' work, which was acceptable—he had been making about $22,000 a year at other work. And the book later made a few thousand more when it was reprinted in paperback a second time by another publisher.

Though he received somewhat higher advances and earnings from his subsequent books—*The Assassination Tapes* (nonfiction), *The Private Sector* (nonfiction), *The Cosgrove Report*, a highly acclaimed novel, *Poor Richard's Game*, a historical novel about spying during the Revolutionary War period, *The Spanish War*, a history, and two books on the history of American intelligence and spying—those later books took much more time to write, and O'Toole believes that on a per-hour basis, and allowing for inflation, his compensation rate for writing has remained pretty constant.

Still, one has to wonder, how did G.J.A. O'Toole, computer expert, former naval air cadet, MENSA member, cryptographer and one-time CIA intelligence officer, turn to writing for a career?

What has probably made him a professional writer, though he sometimes threatens to give up the occupation, is the same force that made him leave the CIA: "There were no policy differences— I had exhausted the possibilities of my job. I came in to do certain things, and got them done. I didn't want to stay and just mind the store." Small wonder. He is an exceptionally bright person. When he took an intelligence test so he could join MENSA, he was rated as having an I.Q. in the top .001 percent. He has sought work that is interesting enough to stick with, and to date has found it in being a writer.

About writing, he says, "Writing about what you know is knowing about what you write." He likes to write in the morning and says he works well for a short period of time after sleeping. When he lacks inspiration, he takes a nap. During periods when he wants to work constantly day and night, he alternately writes and naps.

About the necessity of research, even when writing fiction, he says, "I can't expect the reader to suspend disbelief when I can't suspend my own disbelief." Sometimes when he writes he hears "a voice inside speaking it."

12.

Collaborating With an Expert

Nan F. Salerno
author of *Shaman's Daughter*, in collaboration with Professor
Rosamond M. Vanderburgh

Summary Report

Title:	Shaman's Daughter
Submissions:	*Twenty-eight by an agent, all rejected* *One by Nan F. Salerno, as arranged by a friend, to Prentice-Hall*
Advance royalty:	*$10,000*
Hardcover sales:	*20,000+ copies*
Reprint rights:	*Dell Books, $137,500 guarantee equally divided between authors and publisher. Used as a Dell lead title, 800,000 first printing.*

Book clubs:	*Book-of-the-Month Club alternate selection; selection of Reader's Digest Condensed Books of Canada*
Foreign rights:	*French hard- and softcover editions, Danish edition, serialized in Norwegian magazine*
Author's earnings:	*About $74,000, split 50-50 between the authors*

It all seemed to happen so naturally. A friend called me, said a friend of his had written a good novel; I read it and loved it, recommended it for publication, and everybody else in the publishing house I worked for loved it, too. We did publish it, and it succeeded. Even the title, *Shaman's Daughter*, came from the authors, and nobody even thought of suggesting another.

And listening to Nan Salerno's account of how *Shaman's Daughter* came to be written as a collaboration between her, a writer, and Professor Rosamond M. Vanderburgh, an anthropologist, the collaboration seemed to happen very naturally, too. Salerno's daughter, Michele, was attending the University of Toronto and was fascinated by the accounts of Ojibwa Indian life told in Professor Vanderburgh's anthropology lectures. Michele related the stories to her mother and said they ought to be in a book for the general public.

Nan Salerno wanted to write a children's book and went to see Professor Vanderburgh to arrange to use her material.

But Vanderburgh said, "No, no, that's already been done. What is needed is a novel about the everyday life of Indian women."

So before the visit was over, Nan Salerno and Rosamond Vanderburgh agreed to collaborate on such a novel. They got together occasionally and wrote and telephoned each other with new ideas and progress reports. Over a two-year period of intermittent work, they produced the novel. Together they constructed the basic plot. Salerno did the writing. Vanderburgh supplied information to be woven into the story, sometimes vetoing ideas, incidents or plot twists Salerno added that were not appropriate or authentically representative of the real lives of women of the Ojibwa groups Vanderburgh had lived with and studied.

It's a heartwarming story of two nice people getting together and putting together a good book that naturally succeeded because of its quality. Seems easy as rolling off a log, doesn't it? Quality will tell.

But when you look at the story behind the story, it takes on a greater complexity—an incredible chain of coincidences, extraordinary preparations, the most powerful qualifications, good luck and

determination in face of apparent failure. Of course, without the
lyrical beauty of the novel, the coincidences would probably never
have happened, so both the story and the story behind the story
are worth study, especially by a beginning novelist who is looking
for good material and finds that such material might best be acquired
through collaborating with an expert in the field.

But first, I'll deal with one of the questions I'm often asked as
an editor, literary agent and publisher: "How do you split monies
earned by a collaboration? What's fair?"

Nan Salerno and Rosamond Vanderburgh never troubled themselves over that question. They just assumed from the beginning
that it was an equal effort, with earnings, if any, to be split 50-50.
As it turned out, their only written agreement was the publisher's
contract they both signed, which provided that each would get 50
percent of the author's earnings. I say "author's earnings" because
in most book contracts, the "author" is defined as all those who write
a book, whether one, two or more. The 50-50 split is the most usual
and ordinary one, easiest to understand and justify when people
start out together.

Problems with that arrangement arise when one partner of a
collaboration comes into it with a lot of work already done, or when
one partner has much more weight or commercial clout than the
other. Or when, sometimes, one partner has already spent a lot of
money on research or related travel. Or when the project will involve
a good deal of expense (copying, typing or retyping, for example)
for one partner and not the other.

The only procedure I can suggest to those deciding on the percentage each partner will get is that each should frankly say at the
outset what she thinks is deserved and openly argue for her case.

That argument, and the stubbornness of each partner, will determine the final formula. Sometimes it will be 50-50, other times 60-
40, 75-25 or an even more disproportionate division.

Another solution, appropriate for a collaboration between a
proven professional writer and a person with an obviously valuable
story or powerful name, is an adequate and motivating fixed fee—
probably split into installments (i.e., so much down, and so much on
completion of the job) for the writer, and all remaining earnings for
the nonwriter. In this case the nonwriter may strike it rich, or be
money out of pocket.

Sometimes it seems appropriate to have two different splits—
one of advance royalties and a second for earnings beyond the

advance. I would always recommend that the terms of the collaboration be put in writing, in a plain-English contract understood by each partner, reviewed and approved by an agent or lawyer of each, and signed, even witnessed or notarized.

How did Nan Salerno come to be so well prepared to collaborate with Professor Vanderburgh, when it was the first novel she ever tried to write? Though she suspects she may have had a Native American among her ancestors, she knew little of Native American life before she started *Shaman's Daughter*. The answer may be that her life prepared her to become a novelist.

She began reading at age three. When asked what she read while growing up, she gives the same answer George Bernard Shaw gave when asked what a young girl should read: "Anything I could get my hands on." Her father was an Army ordnance expert, first as a civilian, then, during World War II, as a colonel in the U.S. Army. An only child, she was constantly with her parents, who took her with them wherever they went. If they went to dinner with friends, she was taken along, ate with the adults and was put to bed on a couch, then awakened for refreshments at midnight before the trip home. She says, "I listened to everything and absorbed much of what was said."

As her parents moved from post to post, she traveled with them to Texas, Virginia, Florida, North Carolina, New Jersey, Indiana, Missouri and Colorado. She attended eight different schools before she'd finished high school. Asked what she had learned from so many changes, she replied, "How many ways children can be cruel. It wasn't easy but I never regretted it." She had a sense of separateness and independence: "I never came to regard any particular place as home—I have the whole U.S.A. as my home. And I gained a strong sense of the difference of each region."

But I do not doubt that there was strain in all this change and saw a certain tightening of her lips when she talked of it. I am reminded of the report of a psychologist who studied the effects of stress on children. Under the blows of stress, he found, "Some bend and stretch, some shatter, and some resound like a bell." The strong music of *Shaman's Daughter* is, I believe, Nan Salerno's bell note, still resounding.

Salerno said she sometimes attended public and sometimes Catholic schools—in the country and in big cities. When I asked if she were a Catholic, she replied that her mother believed "attending *any* church is better than attending no church. But I came to admire

Indian religion while writing *Shaman's Daughter*."

Her father finally settled down to work for a stretch of seven years in Washington, DC, and she graduated from high school and attended art school there. She had written her first short story by the age of ten, and continued writing, while also becoming fascinated by art.

As she had gone about the country on her family's travels, she had "educated myself by looking." She was a sharp-eyed child who watched the scenery and the people wherever she went, and describes this child's study of adult interaction with environment as "the beginning of my training as a novelist." Her power of observation was further sharpened by her art training. In *Shaman's Daughter* the reader never feels lost. In fact, the sense of place and atmosphere is so powerful and all-pervasive that her way of including it is almost unnoticed (which I would call good technique). The reader can concentrate on the action because he always knows where he is, what it looks like, how it sounds and feels. Only a few times in the novel does Salerno withdraw this penumbra or fringe of integrated sensation—and when she does, she is able to achieve an out-of-time, out-of-place effect that is very impressive, as when she describes the disorientation of a long water journey.

The way Nan Salerno combines setting, sensation and action is shown in the following passage. Supaya, the heroine of the novel, is twelve, and has been seeking a life-guiding vision for two years. This time, her grandmother tells her, she might succeed, and she has left her house early in the morning.

> Above her a bird called; another answered faintly, and she knew she must hurry to reach the hilltop before dawn. As the trees thinned out, she moved faster and was soon climbing the slope, slipping on the damp, loose stones that rattled under her steps. She felt for footholds and climbed over and around the boulders, pulling herself steadily upward. Gasping for breath, she paused and, tilting back her head, saw the rocky summit silhouetted against the paling night sky and knew she had come too far. Skidding and sliding, she scrambled to her left and down and found the small pocket hidden between the boulders. She sat down on the patch of earth, dizziness momentarily overcoming her. Her pulse throbbed, her forehead was clammy. She had eaten

nothing since midday the day before, and felt an empty, nauseating fear. Perhaps she should go back. Perhaps. . . .

Notice the active verb forms of this passage: *called, answered, hurry, reach, thinned, moved, climbing, slipping, rattled, felt, climbed, pulling, gasping, paused, tilting, saw, paling, come, skidding, slid, scrambled, found, hidden, sat, overcoming, throbbed, eaten, go.* And note at the same time how few adjectives she uses!

Nan Salerno's father asked her, while she was studying art, how she could make a living with it. She investigated the employment opportunities for an artist in Washington, DC, and decided they were very limited, so she became an English major in college. She attended Wilson Teachers College, American University and Catholic University in Washington, and then at the University of Wisconsin was awarded a Ph.M. degree (similar to an M.A.). She has taught at American University, the University of Colorado, University of Illinois and Purdue—English literature, composition, the novel, Shakespeare, poetry. She did not like teaching, saying she regarded the students not as a teacher but as a mother—fascinated and curious about their development or lack of it.

While teaching at Purdue, she met fellow staffer Henry Salerno, who has been a professor of English at the State University of New York at Fredonia for fourteen years.

After their marriage, Nan took jobs as divergent as working in a university steno pool to part-time teaching. The Salernos had two children.

Henry Salerno, while teaching at Purdue, started a magazine to publish original plays called *First Stage.* Nan Salerno was the editor who screened the large number of submissions from all over the world. She managed its actual publication, read proof and maintained its subscription list. This labor of love was a heavy burden of work, and it continued until the year before she began *Shaman's Daughter.*

During those years, she tried writing children's stories, none of which have been published. After *First Stage* ceased publication and her children were grown, she was ready for more writing action.

That was when fate—and daughter Michele—stepped in with an introduction to Professor Vanderburgh.

Rosamond Moate (her maiden name) was born of a British father, who had come to live in Canada, and an American mother, who came from Massachusetts. Though her parents lived in the north woods of Quebec, they traveled to Massachusetts for her birth, then returned to their home in Canada. Rosamond Moate chose Canadian citizenship. Later her family moved to Toronto, and when she completed high school there, she had already decided she wanted to study other peoples' cultures.

But in the 1940s such studies were not available in Toronto, so Rosamond came to the States and entered Radcliffe College in 1944 on a scholarship, taking a concentrated course of anthropology and graduating cum laude.

After a year as a research assistant at Harvard, working with Dr. Ernest Hooten, Rosamond went to Northwestern University, where she earned her M.A., writing her thesis on the influence of southern Africans on the cultures north of the Sahara.

Then, after two years at the University of Pennsylvania, she and another graduate student planned to work toward a Ph.D. by doing fieldwork with tribes in Morocco.

But there was trouble between Morocco and the United States at that time, and the State Department would not approve of two young, single women going there to live.

Rosamond returned to Toronto, where she met Albert Vanderburgh, a young electronics engineer, and married him. He was not enthusiastic about her undertaking foreign travel for her fieldwork, so she looked for anthropological work nearer home.

As it happened, the Southern Ojibwa, who lived around Lake Huron in Canada, had not been studied since the 1930s. While working as a teaching assistant at the University of Toronto in 1965, she began to study them. She had previously worked two years as a curatorial assistant at the Royal Ontario Museum in the Department of Ethnology. In 1967, when the University of Toronto opened its Erindale campus, she joined its faculty, where she has been teaching since and is an associate professor. She and her husband have two grown children.

Every year since 1965, Professor Vanderburgh has done fieldwork among the Southern Ojibwa, and also library research on them. In addition to some fifteen scholarly publications on anthropological subjects, she has written what was originally conceived as a trade book—the biography of an Ojibwa woman, Verna Johnston, entitled *I Am Nokomis, Too*. It was published in 1977 by a Canadian firm. The book has been widely used as a text for native studies and women's studies.

She wrote it to begin to set the record straight about the lives of Native American women, a subject she believes has been neglected by other anthropologists and writers.

I asked Professor Vanderburgh how she had come so readily to accept the idea of collaborating on a novel about the life of a Native American woman.

She replied that the tradition of anthropologists expressing their knowledge in novels goes back to the turn of the century—1890, to be exact—with the publishing of Bandelier's *The Delight Makers*, a story about the Pueblo of the Southwestern United States. The novels of Dr. Carleton S. Coon are part of that tradition. What *was* new, she said, was a collaboration by an anthropologist with a layperson. Despite her scholarly credentials, Professor Vanderburgh felt she lacked fiction-writing talent, and it *is* rare for an expert in a scholarly field also to have novel-writing skill. She recommends collaboration to others.

When I further asked how she could trust Nan Salerno, who had no previous credits as a writer, with such an enterprise, she replied that she felt Salerno's long work as an editor of plays, her teaching experience and her overall air of competence and sincerity were what convinced her. Once Vanderburgh made the decision to go ahead, she did not question it or have second thoughts.

An important principle in such a collaboration, she believes, is that the expert must not stint in offering information for the writer to study, and the writer must study and absorb everything offered.

So Nan Salerno was able to carry on her research in a deluxe manner, as a student under the tutorship of a highly qualified expert. In effect, Professor Vanderburgh gave her a personalized crash course in the anthropology of the Ojibwa. She offered books, tapes, lectures, photographs, a chance to view Ojibwa objects and artifacts and a field trip to an Ojibwa reserve.

In about two years, Nan Salerno and Rosamond Vanderburgh had written their novel and adopted the title suggested by Salerno's husband, *Shaman's Daughter*.

They gave it to a literary agent known to Henry Salerno. The agent made twenty-eight submissions with no offer resulting. When Nan Salerno learned that the book had stalled with a major publisher for a number of months while that publisher had a competing novel with similar subject matter scheduled, she withdrew it from the agent, and they mutually agreed to end their association.

Meanwhile, in Ridgewood, New Jersey, where I was then living, my wife one day took our young son, Christopher, to a storytelling session at the local library. There she met Sandra Scarry, who had brought her daughter, Sioban, to the same event. Children and mothers became acquainted and friendly, and eventually I became friends with Sandra's husband John, an assistant professor of English at Hostos College.

The role of John and Sandra Scarry in bringing *Shaman's Daughter* into print is an important one, and the world is better because of people like the Scarrys: the bustling, busy, creative people whose energy is great enough to do their own important work—both John and Sandra teach full time, and John has authored several English textbooks—and still find the time to recognize and encourage the talent of others.

When I think of the Scarrys, I am reminded of the story of a person watching ants. He observed that a few ants in each anthill were much more active than others. These active ants, which he marked with a little daub of colored powder, strayed off the regular ant highways and nosed into everything around. They took shortcuts and long cuts; they climbed blades of grass and twigs, and simply seemed to go everywhere. They discovered new sources of food, started new trails while the other, more orderly ants ploddingly stuck to established paths and food sources. In a cruel experiment, the ant-watcher removed these few active ants from several anthills. In each case, the colony slowed down and eventually died from lack of food.

If you meet people of this sort, treasure them! Be alert for them, because they will enhance your life, and may even further your career.

Nan Salerno, though discouraged by the many rejections encountered by the agent, sent the manuscript of *Shaman's Daughter* to her longtime friends the Scarrys to read. Sandra Scarry read it first and recommended it to her husband. John Scarry was impressed by it, and by Sandra's strong positive reaction. With Nan Salerno's permission, he asked me to read it, with the request that I recommend a new agent.

When I read the novel, I had to admit that several of the scenes made me cry, and others made me laugh with joy. I found that I really cared about what happened to its main character, Supaya, and her family and friends.

When the Salernos came from Fredonia to visit the Scarrys, I met them.

Nan turned out to be an attractive brunette who laughed easily, yet had a deep undercurrent of seriousness about her, so that her expression changed frequently. I asked her if, instead of sending her book to an agent, I could take it as a submission to Prentice-Hall, where I was then working as a senior editor of trade books.

She agreed. I also asked her to contact her collaborator and to secure her agreement that Salerno would be the member of the team I would work with almost exclusively. I had learned by hard experience that it's better for one member of a collaborating team to act as its spokesperson in dealing with a publisher (or agent, for that matter). Professor Vanderburgh agreed to this procedure.

What happens inside a large- or middle-sized publishing house when a solicited work is submitted to a senior editor? While each house varies, the procedures in the Trade Book Division of Prentice-Hall by which *Shaman's Daughter* was considered are fairly typical of those of larger trade publishers.

As the editor who had brought in the submission, I first told the editor in chief, John Kirk, that I had in hand what promised to be a pretty good first novel.

After completing a second reading, I gave the manuscript to Kirk together with a memorandum recommending it, but saying it needed work. I asked Kirk to be its second reader, as he was an experienced fiction editor with a strong interest in finding new works of merit. Had he been very busy at the time, or primarily interested in other forms of literature than novels, I would have sought other opinions instead, either in-house, or from outside readers.

He read it quickly and reacted very positively, though he agreed that it needed editorial sharpening. He promised to help with the editing and offered some good insights on points needing attention. He gave me permission to write and circulate a proposal that the company make an offer to publish the manuscript.

Using the form the company used for that purpose, I wrote up the proposal that Prentice-Hall publish the work. I described the authors' qualifications, briefly described the content of the manuscript, projected the market for the book and what readers it might appeal to, found out sales of similar books recently issued by other publishers, estimated minimum and maximum sales and guessed at possible subsidiary rights sales.

The proposal and the manuscript were then circulated to the marketing director, the sales department, the publicity director, the head of production and the subsidiary rights director. Each wrote comments on the proposal form—estimates of sales by the marketing director and sales department; estimates of review potential and other publicity by the publicity director; estimates by the production department of the cost of manufacturing it as a hardcover book at different levels of initial and reprint printing quantities; and estimates of likely book club, reprint rights, serial and foreign sales by the subsidiary rights department. As I was, by then, intensely interested in the novel, I handed the proposal and manuscript personally to each person who would comment on it and made a little speech to each praising the manuscript and urging that it be read promptly.

They all loved it! They found it good enough to read to the end, which assured me the book had broad appeal.

Armed with these positive indicators, I returned the manuscript and completed proposal form to the editor in chief. After conferring with the president of the division, he gave me written authorization to offer a $10,000 advance royalty to the authors and negotiate a contract along terms we agreed on. We decided to offer a favorable contract, similar to what would be negotiated by an agent, as we hoped the authors, particularly Nan Salerno, would become significant writers and would want to stay with our publishing house if their book succeeded.

The authors accepted the offer and signed the contract. Part of the advance royalty was paid on signing, and the rest was to be paid when the authors completed revisions to the publisher's satisfaction.

The editor in chief and I made a number of editorial suggestions—none major—to tighten the narration of the story and maintain suspense in key sections. As I edited each portion of the manuscript, I sent it with a longish letter to Nan Salerno explaining the reasons for the proposed changes.

Before I began, however, I had a phone conversation with Nan that may shed some light on the editor-author relationship. I told her that an editor, in making suggestions, was not a hostile critic putting down an author, but was rather more like a friend conspiring with the author for the book's greatest possible success; also, that the author should feel free to reject any of the suggestions made, and argue freely in favor of, and thus explain to the editor, the original version, as expressions of the author's insights and intentions.

Without this understanding, it would be impossible for the editor to express his possible ignorance, insensitivity and even ineptitude to the author, just as the author had exposed her views and insights, and possible failings, in submitting the draft manuscript. In addition to being a very experienced reader and student of the structure and appeal of books in general, the editor is a stand-in for those who will later buy and read the book. As such, he treasures his ignorance as well as experience, because no reader has a perfect preparation for a particular book, and what confuses or fails with the editor may well confuse and fail with the ultimate consumers, the readers of the book who determine its success or failure.

The editor, usually a person who has chosen the profession out of a love of reading, is first and foremost a *reader*, a consumer of books. For a novelist to have a successful dialogue, the necessary give-and-take, with his editor, the novelist must first regard the editor as a reader or fan and ignore the notion of the editor's power over the writer's business success. The relationship, to be successful, must be one between equals. Editors *must* find, and get along with, many types of authors. And unless you, the author, are interested in self-publishing—a rough road for a first novelist—you must work with an editor at a publishing house. Just remember the equation has two sides, separated by an equals sign, and you'll find it easier.

In the case of *Shaman's Daughter*, the editor-author relationship went smoothly, and Nan Salerno promptly revised the manuscript, keeping in mind the ideas expressed by me and by John Kirk, but using them in her own way—in fact, improving on our suggestions many times.

Her relationship with the book's copyeditor (the editor whose job it is to correct English usage and spelling, smoke out inconsistencies and omissions, find clichés, etc.) was a little tense at times, as Salerno herself was a former editor and English instructor, but quibbles about commas were resolved, as were other small points of style. Most publishers are willing to allow a novelist more latitude of style than would be granted a nonfiction author.

When the book reached the next stage, being set in type, Prentice-Hall ordered one hundred "BOM's"—page proofs of the book bound with a paper cover. These were sent to other authors, anthropologists, bookstore buyers, book clubs, paperback reprinters and major reviewers who need plenty of advance notice of what a publisher regards as a "big book."

The mailing produced some favorable comments from other authors. Two of these comments—one from Anna Lee Waldo, author of the best-seller *Sacajawea*, and one from anthropologist and author

Dr. Carleton S. Coon were selected to be printed on the back of the book's jacket.

Dwight Myers, one of Prentice-Hall's most active and influential salespeople and an expert on writings about Native Americans, helped assemble the list of those to receive the bound proofs. The editorial department was delighted with his active help, as he had great influence with the other salespeople who had to distribute the book to bookstores and book jobbers. Authors are often distressed to discover that publishers have to sell their books to their own salespeople!

As the question of how to deal with a publisher's sales force is eventually faced by every published author, I will interject here some pointers on this important subject. The key principle: Cultivate the publisher's salespeople in a friendly, positive, but not overly demanding, way.

The best thing you can do for them is to provide them with information: the names of bookstore people you know, local authors or critics who admire your work, businesspeople who might make bulk purchases of your work for special purposes, interviewers who might want to invite you to appear on radio or TV and librarians who are your friends and supporters.

But don't push the salespeople too hard, or they will begin to duck you and stop returning your calls. Remember they have a long list of other books to sell, too. And keep in mind that they must obey the orders of their superiors about what to push. If your book is not in a key store, remember that there could be a very good reason why the store isn't handling your book.

For example, the store might not have paid its bills to the publisher, and hence not be able to get credit from the publisher. Or, if the store is part of a chain of stores, buying is probably done centrally, and the local salesperson might not be able to influence whether or not the branch handles your book. If a bookstore clerk, buyer or owner says, "Oh, that salesman never calls on me," or, "She visited but never mentioned your book," stay cool, and say, "Then why don't you order it from your wholesaler? They probably have it."

In my experience—and I've been a publisher's salesman and sales manager—publishers *never* refuse to sell to a creditworthy bookstore, so *if* the salespeople in fact didn't call, it was probably for a sound reason. And a bookstore owner can always get a book in stock if she really wants to do so. There is no advantage to you in getting involved in problems between a publisher and a bookstore.

If your friends say, "I went to three stores and nobody had your book," investigate. But be skeptical—they might not want to put out the money to buy a copy.

All of that said, I will admit now that publishers often do an abysmal job of distributing a first novel, or any book. A famous author of nonfiction best-sellers told me that one of America's largest and best known publishers only sold slightly more than a thousand copies each of his first three books, all novels. That's the kind of business publishing is, and the possibility of such results is one of the hazards of authorship.

If a friend or relative really wants to help, he should go into a bookstore and ask for a copy of the book. If the store has it, fine. If the store doesn't have it, he can ask the store to order a copy for him, thus calling it to the store's attention in the most positive way possible. It is particularly good for the friend or relative to bring in a good review and say, pointing to the review, "Do you have this book? I'd like to buy one."

In the case of *Shaman's Daughter*, the sales department had some positive news to help their people place the book in bookstores: the jacket quotes, the fact that Book-of-the-Month Club selected the book as an alternate (and in Canada, that Reader's Digest Condensed Books of Canada would use it as a selection), and that a major sale of reprint rights had been arranged.

Prentice-Hall's subsidiary rights director, John Nelson, had touted the book to paperback publishers, and before publication, had staged an auction of paperback reprint rights. Dell Books made a "floor bid with topping privileges" for a substantial sum, which was accepted by Prentice-Hall. This meant that Dell would have the right to make the last bid in the auction, and if its last bid exceeded anybody else's by 10 percent, Dell would get the reprint rights to the book. The highest bid made by another publisher was $125,000, and Dell chose to top it, so Dell acquired the book for an advance royalty guarantee of $137,500, an excellent reprint deal for a first novel.

The sales department was able to impress bookstore buyers with this display of confidence in the book's commercial potential.

Prentice-Hall of Canada was delighted to have a good book coauthored by a Canadian to add to its list, and pushed the book in that country.

On the negative side, the price of the book proved a little too high for major rental libraries. And review coverage, while largely positive, was not as widespread as all had hoped. *The New York Times Book Review* and the daily *Times* did not review the book.

But over 20,000 hardcover copies were placed in bookstores, and a year later, Dell Books did an 800,000-copy first printing of its mass-market paperback edition when it used the book as a "lead" in one of its months of promotion. Nan Salerno and Rosamond Vanderburgh appeared on some radio and TV shows, did some bookstore appearances and some lectures, and each got a good deal of local publicity. While neither all of Prentice-Hall's 20,000 + hardcovers nor Dell's 800,000 paperbacks were sold, and the book did not become a best-seller, a good time was had by all.

Nan Salerno wrote a second novel published by Prentice-Hall and is at work on additional novels. Professor Vanderburgh was able to take much-desired time off for some research.

What can a hopeful beginning novelist learn from Nan Salerno's and Rosamond Vanderburgh's experiences with *Shaman's Daughter*? Here are some of the main points I see:

A writer and an expert can collaborate successfully to create a work of fiction.

The key to a successful collaboration is to draw an agreement that carefully defines the duties, responsibilities and rewards of each partner—and to stick to it.

When marketing the manuscript that results from the collaboration, it is better to designate one of the collaborators to represent the partnership in dealing with a publisher, though each partner should of course have the right to approve or veto any deal made.

Don't give up hope if an agent fails to sell your work. Keep trying on your own, or with another agent, or through a friend.

When your editor offers suggestions about your work, regard her as a friend and collaborator, not as a know-it-all critic.

Look around you to see if any of your acquaintances has good contacts or is a natural putter-together of people—and ask that person to read your work and help you find a publisher.

Sometimes things turn out all right! And all because two children met at story hour. And then . . . and then . . . and then . . .

13.

Genre Novelists

1. AN INTELLECTUAL WRITES A ROMANCE

Russell Kirk
author of the gothic romance, *Old House of Fear*

The publication of Russell Kirk's first novel, *Old House of Fear*, and its critical and commercial success opened a dam that produced a flood of mass-market gothic novels that continues into the present day.

The novel was published by Fleet Publishing Corporation, a small publisher in New York. It had been acquired by Robert Hunter, an editor of conservative leanings, and when Hunter left Fleet, I inherited it. My editing consisted of the remark, "The beginning is a little slow," and Russell Kirk reworked it. We published a small hardcover edition with a terrible dust jacket and sent out more than three hundred review copies. This review mailing, plus inclusion of the book in some announcement ads aimed at the book trade, was its only initial promotion.

A flood of rave reviews followed. Some quotes from them were put on the jacket of the second edition:

> *"We follow him with dazed and delighted attention from the first muffled cry to the final midnight scream."*
>
> The New Yorker

> *"Lovingly and thrillingly executed."*
>
> The New York Times Book Review

> *"It is terrifying, ingeniously constructed, and truly Gothic."*
>
> National Review

> *"No one need be either a cold-out addict of whodunits or an antiquarian to become utterly absorbed in what I confidently assert is the most exciting, thrilling, blood-curdling adventure mystery of the year*—Old House of Fear.*"*
>
> Richmond Times-Dispatch

Around 10,000 hardcover copies were sold, and Avon issued a succession of a dozen large paperback printings for about ten years after. The American Library Association chose *Old House of Fear* as one of the half-dozen best books for young adults. Detective Book Club used it as a selection. Gollancz published a British edition, and the whole novel was read serially over the BBC. Het Spectrum published a Dutch edition. And Fleet republished a more attractive hardcover edition two years later, which was reviewed by *The Wall Street Journal* and some other places that had missed it the first time around.

A memorandum about the book Russell Kirk prepared for me records, in the same third-person fashion he later used for his memoirs, "He intended—and in the judgment of reviewers, achieved—a *tour de force*, deliberately reviving a mode of fiction nearly forgotten, the gothic romance. His success was promptly followed by what Nathaniel Hawthorne (another strong influence upon Kirk) called 'a damned mob of scribbling women,' imitating him. One publisher suggested that Kirk write for his firm another gothic novel—but ascribe it to a feminine pseudonym, most of the readers of such books being women who identify themselves as much with the presumed authoress as with the romance's heroine. Kirk declined this offer, but suggested to his fiancée, the beautiful Annette, that she write such a romance, with his assistance; she too declined."

Though other historians might have other comments on the reasons for the success of the gothic novel in American paperback publishing, I believe Kirk has a good point. When *Old House of Fear* was published, it was classified as a mystery novel, as the "gothic" category didn't exist. Russell Kirk, by writing a good novel, unleashed an industry.

A gothic novel has come to be defined as a work much like Russell Kirk's: An attractive young woman is somehow confined in an old house and is menaced there by an awful and interesting villain with sleazy confederates. An admirable hero, who gets involved because of some respectable business mission, rescues her, but not before many terrifying complications. The villain gets his just desserts. The attraction of the novels lies in the delicious thrills produced by the menacing machinations of the ingenious and clever villains.

Originally no sex scenes were included in this genre. As an editor told John M. Kimbro, the "Katheryn Kimbrough" who wrote *The House on Windswept Ridge*, the heroine needs to be "squeaky clean." In his next gothic, Kimbro had his heroine take a bath, and afterward, she says, "I feel squeaky clean." Eventually sex crept in, and today, some gothics include sex scenes.

How did Russell Kirk, influential conservative thinker and old-fashioned man of letters, come to write a "gothic romance"? He wrote of his intellectual development:

> Mine was not an Enlightened mind, I was now aware: It was a Gothic mind, medieval in its temper and structure. I did not love cold harmony and perfect regularity of organization; what I sought was variety, mystery, tradition, the venerable, the awful. I despised sophisters and calculators; I was groping for faith, honor, and prescriptive loyalties. I would have given any number of neo-classical pediments for one poor battered gargoyle.

He said he was influenced in his romance by Walter Scott and Robert Louis Stevenson—though he did not take any particular books of theirs as models. His wide reading of nineteenth-century ghostly tales also was reflected in *Old House of Fear*. Although some reviewers tried to find political motives in the novel, he said he only intended to "arouse dreadful joy; the few political references were meant simply to amuse the reader."

The novel was written mainly for Kirk's own amusement, and for his "kith and kin." He wrote the book at night while living in an old hotel. The source came from Kirk's experiences during visits to Scotland. The setting, the island of Carnglass, is a composite of two islands in the Inner Hebrides. Various episodes and scenes "reflect Scottish castles the author knew well, among them the Fife houses of Dellie and Earlshall." Years later, wandering in the big island of Mull, Kirk visited Duart Castle and "found it amazingly like *Old House of Fear*. Even the guide at Duart, a beautiful red-haired girl, small and charming, was astoundingly like the Mary of the romance!"

Russell Kirk's other books of fiction, interspersed in a long list of nonfiction works, include a collection of ghost stories, *The Surly Sullen Bell*, *A Creature of the Twilight* and *Lord of the Hollow Dark*. Though the supernatural was an element of most of his fiction, he followed the gothic tradition of having apparently supernatural happenings turn out, in the end, to have been natural events— thereby safely returning the reader from his "bucket seat of suspense" back to the ordinary world at the end of the story.

What can you learn from Russell Kirk's adventure in writing a first-rate suspense novel "in unblushing line of direct descent from *The Castle of Otranto*," and thereby spawning a new literary industry? Mostly, I think, that a "genre" novel can be, with labor and love, as good as any other novel, even in the view of the most exacting critics.

Kirk's remarks about his fiction writing methods, taken from his nonfictional *Decadence and Renewal in the Higher Learning*, offer insight into an important power a writer needs to write effective novels, namely, the development of pictorial imagery:

> When I write fiction, I do not commence with a well-concerted formal plot. Rather, there occur in my imagination certain images, little scenes, snatches of conversation, strong lines of prose. I patch together these fragments, retaining and embellishing the sound images, discarding the unsound, finding a continuity to join them. Presently I have a coherent narration, with some point to it. Unless one has this sort of pictorial imagery—Walter Scott had it to a high degree— he will never become a writer of good fiction, whatever may be said of expository prose.

2. TWO FANTASY NOVELISTS

Karen Brush
author of *The Pig, the Prince and the Unicorn*
Niel Hancock
author of *Circle of Light*

John Douglas
Senior Editor
Avon Books
(address)

Dear Mr. Douglas:

As arranged by telephone today, here is *QUADROPED* later published as *The Pig, the Prince and the Unicorn*, a fantasy novel by Karen Brush. This is her first novel, and this is its first submission.

Ms. Brush is a recent graduate of Yale and is entering Columbia this fall to take an advanced degree in anthropology. She lives in New York, and is from here also. I didn't meet her until after reading the manuscript (she came recommended by another client), but I found her pleasant and amusing to talk to and be with. She has led an adventuresome life with much travel and sport, and knows a lot about geology, skin diving and animals.

Probably the beginning could stand a little speeding up, but otherwise I found the novel a really good read, and hope you will too.

Sincerely yours,

Oscar Collier

In writing the submission letter above to an editor I knew only slightly, but had previously queried by phone, I tried to engage his interest by stating facts: I reminded him he had asked to see the novel; it was the first submission of a first novel, giving him a chance to discover a new writer. After first making it clear I liked her novel, I painted her as a pleasant person to meet, adventuresome and, hence, possibly creative. By saying she came from another client, I was pointing out she had at least a tenuous connection to professional writing. As she was well educated, her novel would probably be written correctly and typed clearly. And while he might have to do a modest amount of editorial work, I tried to lead him into reading the whole novel by saying I found it enjoyable. This remark also assured him that I had done my agent's work of screening out an unsuitable submission. Since I had already described it by phone, I didn't go into the contents, preferring to let the novel speak for itself.

About nine months later, after receiving a few quick and quiet reminder calls and a couple of brief, newsy letters from me about Karen Brush's activities, John Douglas said he was going to recommend *Quadroped* for publication. Later he said he had authority to make a formal offer, and after getting some sales projections, did so. Karen Brush accepted.

I hadn't pushed John Douglas, because I felt, from our phone conversations, that he liked the work, so I left the timing of an offer up to him. Karen Brush had been just as discreet in her few phone calls to me, inquiring about what was happening.

The idea of writing *Quadroped*, which is well described in her query letter that follows, came to Karen Brush when she was a freshman at Yale. She started to write it in the first person, as narrated by one of the older characters, but quickly abandoned that approach "because it was hard to speak in the voice of an older man." She switched to the third person, and the reader always sees events by staying close to the novel's hero, Quadroped, a young and small white pig who lives in a magical world. She finally finished it as a senior "in a writing seminar taught by Francine DuPlessix Gray, who urged me to submit it for publication."

Quadroped is about 85,000 words long, but Karen Brush says, "I wrote it about two hundred times its final length in trying to get it right." She says she did not study books about how to write a novel until after she was finished; her approach was "just to write it."

As a young person, she "lived on Tolkien, C.S. Lewis, Lloyd Alexander's *Book of Three* and, of course, Lang's fairy tales. Also, *The Wizard of Oz*." She could find no better books of fantasy than these!

After she finished her fantasy novel, she had not the slightest idea of what to do next. She inquired of her parents about their circle of friends, and though several of them had published "books on sailing up the Amazon and exploration," none had published a fantasy novel. Her teacher, Francine DuPlessix Gray, a distinguished author, referred Brush to her teacher's own agent, but Gray's agent said she had never sold a fantasy novel, and so didn't have anything to offer. Finally, Brush's father came up with the name of Palm Beach attorney and author Carole Criswell, whom I knew, and Criswell gave her my name.

Since one of my clients was a successful fantasy writer, and I enjoy reading fantasy and science fiction novels, I was quite willing to read *Quadroped* after she telephoned me and described it. With it she sent the following submission letter (together with a handwritten note reminding me of our telephone conversation and Carole Criswell's referral), which, except for its length, is a model letter of its type:

Mr. Oscar Collier
Collier Associates
(address)

Dear Mr. Collier:

A thousand years ago the Black Unicorn of Ravenor was imprisoned in Chaos, and a terrible war was resolved. Every hundred years the gateway to Chaos begins to open. It must be locked or the Black Unicorn will escape and the war begin again. The Gate has begun to open . . . and the Key is lost. Heroes from both armies are searching for it.

Quadroped is the unlikely young hero of this story. He is a small white pig upon whose head the Key is accidentally dropped. As the unwilling Key Bearer, Quadro finds himself struggling for survival as the malevolent Warlords of Ravenor attempt to seize the Key before he can lock the Gate.

Through a series of encounters with the extraordinary leaders of both lands, and their humorous sidekicks, Quadroped demonstrates his innocent ability to always land on his feet and to make friends of his enemies. As his journey progresses, Quadro realizes that his problems cannot be solved by locking the Gate. Deprived of its king, the land of Ravenor is dying. Quadroped must choose either to free the Black Unicorn, plunging his homeland into war, or to lock the Gate and allow Ravenor to die. How Quadroped, universally scorned and scolded by his heroic companions, manages to resolve this monumental conflict without sacrificing either side, is the exciting climax of this tale.

Quadroped is a humorous fantasy that maintains a steady counterpoint between magic, science, and ordinary common sense. Its strong visual descriptions make it an ideal subject for illustration or animation. The novel was completed for a writing seminar taught by Francine DuPlessix Gray, who urged me to submit the piece for publication.

I am a cum laude graduate of Yale University with my B.S. in Geology and a strong background in English. I will enter the Ph.D. program in Anthropology at Columbia University in September. I have travelled extensively and my experiences form the background for *Quadruped*. I have explored caves in Australia, studied volcanoes in Iceland, gone on safari in Africa, and gone hot-air ballooning in France. I am a certified SCUBA diver and have made several night dives and participated in two underwater excavations. I have published poetry in *The Poet, Backpacker Magazine, American Poetry Anthology, Yale Alumni Magazine*, and *Poetry Press*.

Sincerely,

Karen A. Brush

I read the novel soon after it arrived, and called with an offer to represent her. She accepted, took a copy of my form of agreement to study, and later rewrote it to exclude her children's books and short stories (which I don't handle ordinarily). Meanwhile, John Douglas's name came to mind, because I had seen references to him in writer's newsletters, and I called him and described the novel. He asked to see it, and we were on our way.

The Avon contract, which arrived about a month after we had made an oral agreement by phone, called for a $2,500 advance against royalties, payable half on signing and half on Avon's acceptance of a final manuscript—John Douglas had some editorial comments and suggestions for revisions. Karen Brush was somewhat disturbed that the contract provided "The Publisher is authorized, at its sole discretion, to make any editorial changes, deletions, abridgment and condensation whatsoever in the text of said Work...." I was able to say truthfully to her that I had encountered no editorial problems with Avon on books placed with them, but I brought this up with John Douglas, and he agreed that we could insert "in consultation with the Author" in this provision, which reassured her.

Karen Brush wrote a sequel novel about her character Quadroped called *The Demon Pig*, also published by Avon, and John Douglas moved to HarperCollins.

By way of contrast, here are some brief notes on the experiences of Niel Hancock, author of thirteen published fantasy novels. Niel Hancock, who sometimes calls himself T.H.E. Otter, made over thirty submissions of his unfinished four-volume first novel,

Circle of Light, all of them to editors of juvenile books. He had turned to writing the fantasy after first doing a good deal of other kinds of writing, which he had discarded. Finally, a junior editor of juvenile books at Atheneum Publishers who liked his novel (and signed her letters to him "Toad") wrote him and said, "This is not a juvenile—you should get an agent and try adult publishers." She recommended James Seligmann, whom she had met through his submissions to her. Seligmann passed the submission to me. Fantasy is not one of his favorite kinds of reading, but he knows I enjoy it.

I happily offered to represent "Otter," who is a truly cheerful, sunny man. Since he had been practically everywhere with his manuscript, I submitted it to one of the few publishers he had never approached: Patrick O'Connor, then editor in chief of Popular Library.

O'Connor later told me, "I saw its commercial potential." His judgment proved correct, and Niel Hancock stayed with Popular Library and its present owner, Warner Books, where Patrick O'Connor was again his editor until his retirement to become a ski instructor. Popular Library paid a $15,000 advance for the four-volume novel. Hancock's subsequent novels about "Atlanton Earth" followed there, and at Warner Books. They were attractively packaged as mass-market books, distributed practically everywhere, and more than a million copies sold in the United States. They were published in Japan and Germany as well.

Why did it take Niel Hancock more than thirty submissions to find a sympathetic editor who referred him to an agent, and take me *one* submission to place his first quartet of books? The answer lies simply in his original belief that the books were juveniles, which, to me, they weren't. Is there any way he could have avoided this travail? And is there a lesson for you, a beginning novelist, in his story? Probably one way he could have told that the novels were not necessarily juvenile books was from their length—they are longer than most juveniles. When you are trying to break into a particular field, it is important to look at the length of the majority of the books published in that field or genre, and make your first effort no longer than average.

But by persistence Niel Hancock was able to get published anyway, and for a number of years, he was able to live and travel on his royalties.

3. WRITING NOVELS AS A NEW CAREER

Anna Lee Waldo
author of the 1,359-page novel *Sacajawea*

How did Anna Lee Waldo, a chemist by training and teacher in mid-western colleges, mother of five children and heretofore author mainly of chemistry articles, come to write a best-seller?

About her choice of subject, she said, "It has always been with me. When we were children, one of the games we played was 'Sacajawea.'" Sacajawea was the Native American woman who guided the epic Lewis and Clark expedition across western North America.

Anna Lee Waldo was born and spent her childhood in Whitefish, Montana, west of Glacier National Park, and this small town is served by the Great Northern Railroad, where Waldo's father worked. She graduated from Montana State University at Bozeman and then traveled east to the University of Maryland, where she received an M.S. in organic chemistry, and married Willis Waldo, an inorganic chemist.

She worked first as a chemist for Monsanto, and later did research in leukemia at the Miami Valley Hospital in Dayton, Ohio. Eventually she turned to teaching chemistry at St. Louis Community College-Meramec.

Not until her fifth child was born did she decide to write her novel. "My husband, Bill, had great empathy," she recalled. "He never complained about my dislike for housework, about my papers on the floor, and he never picks them up."

The research for the novel became a family project. She, her husband and children traveled over the Lewis and Clark expedition route three times. Besides the travel, Waldo's research took her to libraries, history societies and people who were experts in Native American lore. "I wrote to universities all over the country—even in Germany. That's where Sacajawea's first-born son spent at least three years," she told an interviewer in *Publishers Weekly*.

The research and writing took roughly ten years. She told me it was her "third or fourth draft I submitted to Avon." As the draft she sent to Avon was two thousand pages long, and was rewritten three or four times, that means she typed more than seven thousand pages—two million words—before she had her final manuscript.

When she finished the novel, she sent off query letters to hardcover publishers, "starting with *A* and continuing to *Z*. I sent queries one at a time. They wrote back letters showing they weren't interested. None invited me to submit."

Finally, Waldo decided to submit it to paperback publishers and composed a fresh query letter. Starting again with *A*, she queried Avon first. She got no farther down the alphabet. Nancy Coffey at Avon replied to her query and asked to see the manuscript. Waldo packed the manuscript into a 2×3-foot clothing box and sent it off.

"I know I sound cocky," she later said, "but I never once felt that the book wouldn't be published. There was more than a four-year delay after Avon bought it. I knew they couldn't *lose* the manuscript—it was too big."

Avon asked Anna Lee Waldo to make a publicity tour to promote the book. The publicity tour started in St. Louis, where on May 4, 1979, Mayor Conway proclaimed "Sacajawea Day" and presented Anna Lee Waldo with a parchment scroll memorializing the event. In the afternoon, several radio stations and the local KSD-TV interviewed her. She was relieved, because the questions were easy: "How long did it take to write your book?" "Why did you write this book?" "What did your family say?"

Waldo toured Chicago, Seattle, Portland, San Francisco. Then in Los Angeles, as had happened in St. Louis, Mayor Bradley proclaimed "Sacajawea Day," and in the council chambers of City Hall, spoke of how he, a black person himself, could identify with the black character in her novel, Ben York.

She continued on to Salt Lake City, then Albuquerque, Oklahoma City, Denver, Omaha, Kansas City, Chicago again. "Bookstores now generally had *Sacajawea* in stock, and it appeared to be selling well. I began to feel important. People said nice things about the book. Before calling it a day, my contact suggested I go to the Marshall Fields Department Store. Their book department did not have *Sacajawea*. In fact, the personnel had not heard of it. That brought me back to reality where I belonged, and my head shrank to normal quickly."

After Dallas and Ft. Worth, three weeks of traveling were over, and she was home with her family. Before she was settled back into her old routine, Avon called again and persuaded her to do another tour "along the Lewis and Clark trail. The tour would not only include plane travel, but also automobile travel, and there won't be a contact person in every city," the Avon representative said. "We would like to send your husband with you so he can see about car rentals and keep the media interviews lined up."

But her travels still weren't over; afterward, Avon called and asked Waldo to go to Toronto, to the Canadian Booksellers Convention, where she signed and put a feather in at least a hundred books. "*Sacajawea* was advertised as the number one best-seller in Canada. I was impressed." Eventually many more publicity appearances followed.

The book proved to be an enduring favorite—it was, just as Avon says on the jacket of the 1984 edition, "eight months on *The New York Times* Best-Seller List."

Waldo told me in the fall of 1996 that *Sacajawea* is still selling briskly, and she estimates that some two and a half million copies have been sold.

In addition, Avon made agreements with foreign publishers that have resulted in French, German and Dutch editions. After Avon failed for several years to make a dramatic rights sale, she persuaded them to return those rights to her, and she has optioned them to Greystone Productions for a theatrical film.

Meanwhile, Anna Lee Waldo was working on a new manuscript, which she called *Prairie*. It was, again, a historical novel set in the West. She asked me to handle it as her agent, and the reader can probably guess who contracted for it: Nancy Coffey, then editor in chief of Berkley Books. It also became a best-seller.

"Like everything Anna Lee writes," Nancy Coffey told me during our talks about the manuscript, "it's a magical book."

So Waldo's advice to other writers has the power of experience behind it:

> Never give up. If you feel strongly about your writing, someone will like it and publish it. Take a chance. Get it all out. Don't talk about it too much—your idea can wear thin. Put it all on paper. Don't depend on critics. Your novel must have conflict—man against nature, man against man. Your protagonist must survive conflict.

4. LOVE FOR SALE—WRITING ROMANCES

Susan Johnson
author of *Sweet Love, Survive*
Joan Wolf
author of *Portrait of Love*

Lola Smith
writing as Cleo Chadwick, author of *The Scarlet Spinster*

A wide range of difference exists in the way romance writers handle sex. Here are two samples; the first is much more explicit.

> Apollo ran his hands leisurely up her naked back and smiled knowingly, his pleasure infinitely enhanced by hers, pleasantly envisioning many more panting orgasmic cries before he brought himself to climax . . . His hands glided to her narrow waist, lean fingers splayed over her reed-slim slenderness and gently rounded hips. He filled her still, his hardness undiminished; she was impaled on him like a willing sacrifice, her ivory arms, pale against the dark silk of his robe twined around his neck, her head nestled into the hollow of his shoulder. The hands lying on her hips tightened and . . .
>
> from *Sweet Love, Survive*
> Susan Johnson

> His shoulders came away from the door in a kind of lunge and then he was across the room and holding her in his arms. Isabel closed her eyes and stopped thinking. Her whole life seemed to have narrowed down to this room, this man, this moment. His mouth was hard on hers, his hands moving possessively over her breasts, her waist, her hips. She felt his desire, felt also the unnamable, irresistible force in him that called out so strongly to something in her. Her head was pressed back against his shoulder and his lips left her mouth and moved, searingly, to her exposed throat.
>
> "Isabel," he muttered. "God. Isabel." And suddenly she was swept by fire. Her whole body shuddered and she clung to him fiercely. They almost didn't make it to the bedroom.
>
> "Would you like to go down to look at the beach?" he asked softly a very long time later.
>
> from *Portrait of Love*
> Joan Wolf

Writers have often asked me, "Should I include explicit sex scenes? Are they necessary to sell a novel?" As an agent, I don't feel this question has any one answer. I can't tell a writer what is morally or commercially correct; I am not a legislator or moral leader, and I see all kinds of novels succeed. So my reply is only, "If you want to, or your subject demands it, go ahead. But you don't have to include explicit sex scenes in order to succeed. Don't *force* yourself to write them."

The comments of two successful writers of historical and contemporary romances, Susan Johnson and Joan Wolf, whose love scenes you just read, may be helpful to a writer trying to decide this matter.

Susan Johnson is a former librarian and now a full-time novelist whose historical romances were published first by Playboy Press and its successor, Berkley Publishing Corporation, and now by Bantam and Doubleday. Her agent is Mel Berger of William Morris Agency, and her Bantam editor is Beth deGuzman. One of her latest novels is *Wicked*. Johnson writes novels that contain delightfully detailed and erotic sex scenes. She says, "My first story dealt with the mutual attraction of a hero and heroine in terms of realistic human sexuality. There's very little sex in romance writing today. The greatest number of romances published are what are termed 'sweet' romances. Then there are the romances labeled 'sensual' and lastly a very small number of 'sexy' romances. Sexy romances aren't easy to write.

"Many writers are uncomfortable writing about sex; others aren't capable of writing a sexy love scene. One sees many love scenes which are awkwardly embarrassing to read. And then, there are the writers who feel they must do the obligatory sex scene so an attempt is made. Both of these last two categories are the greatest turn-off in the world.

"I doubt you'll get too many openly to admit it, with all the 'good girl'-'bad girl' conditioning in our culture, but whatever degree of sensuality readers prefer, they *are* looking for 'amour.' Romances offer a delightful fantasy, removed from mundane reality, where one can immerse oneself in the adventures of an intrepid heroine, a dashing hero. It's sheer entertainment. My characters delight in life, feel each day is to be lived."

Joan Wolf, award-winning author of contemporary romances, historical romances and a prehistory series, published by New American Library, when I last spoke to her, was just starting a big new contract with Warner with publication of her romance *The Deception* in 1997. She resists including explicit sex scenes in her novels. She says, "I don't like to write about explicit sex, so I don't do it in my novels, and they succeed anyway."

Wolf believes women readers want to read about intense relationships, and many writers are deceived into thinking that the only way intense relationships can be described is through sex scenes. She thinks it is not necessary to describe sex in detail in order to show a powerful interrelationship between a man and a woman. Emotion is what romance readers are seeking, she believes, and so long as you provide it in your novels, you don't need to describe sex acts.

To generalize from what these writers are saying, they agree that you should write about what you consider most important, and what you can write about naturally and well. This may mean explicit sex scenes, or it may instead mean intense emotional scenes without a great deal of explicit description. So I would add to my answer above the following caveat: "Only write explicit sex scenes if you believe you can write them well."

Because contemporary romances are very popular, and can be seen by the score in bookstores, newsstands, supermarkets, drugstores and discount stores such as Kmart and Wal-Mart, many would-be novelists think they might as well join the herd, and write a romance. Actually, this kind of book is just as hard to write as any other novel, and today, maybe harder. Let's look at the career of Lola Smith, who writes Regency romances under the pen name "Cleo Chadwick."

Regencies narrowly deal with a particular period of English history—1800 to 1820, when King George III ruled and his son George, nicknamed "Prinny," served as regent during his father's bouts of madness. This was the period of the Napoleonic Wars. Today's Regency writers more or less follow two writers as their guides: Jane Austen, who wrote in the Regency period, and Georgette Heyer, who started writing in the Austen tradition some half century ago and died in recent years.

Kate Duffy, who had been editor of several paperback lines, explains this kind of book as a "comedy of manners." The motives of the characters and plots and twists, she says, turn on the social mores of the period and not on outside forces as they would in a standard romance. Humor, including arch humor, is also more a part of a Regency story than other romance types. She cited the work of Arthur Gladstone, who wrote some forty Regency romances under the feminine names he used in memory of his first wife—Margaret SeBastion and Maggie Gladstone. Kate Duffy put many of Gladstone's books under contract because, "He made me laugh out loud with his wit and humor."

Lola Smith, in her guise of Cleo Chadwick, is continuing in the

Jane Austen-Georgette Heyer tradition and won an award with one of her novels. She was a serious history student and the wife of a foreign service officer. Stationed on and off in Guatemala, Micronesia, Dominican Republic and Ecuador, she had time on her hands and decided to use it to write a history of American agriculture, a project that she placed for a $6,000 advance with Doubleday.

But writing a serious history wasn't as much fun as she thought it should be. It was gruelling work, and so, to relax, she joined a group of acquaintances who were studying novels. Smith happened to pick a Regency book to analyze and report on.

"It was amusing and well written," she recalls, "and it had a whiff of Jane Austen to it. I thought, *I can write one of these.* And so when I wanted relief from technical writing, I wrote a few scenes of the novel, which I called *Love Longing.*

When she was done, she found the name of an agent in an ad in the WIN (Washington Independent Writers) newsletter. The agent immediately said yes and just as immediately Zebra agreed to publish it if Smith would agree to "a few minor changes."

What were those *minor* changes, my coauthor, Frances Spatz Leighton, wanted to know. Leighton and Smith are both members of the same writers club, The Writers' League of Washington, where the interview took place.

Lola Smith chuckled as she said, "They wanted me to rewrite a scene in which the hero's arousal was described using the word 'erection' and another in which the heroine's nipples 'hardened.' " She added, "That's a laugh these days when some romance novels border on the pornographic, and even Regencies, in which it's required that sexual mores more or less be accurate to time and Jane Austen, are allowed a little sex."

Smith also learned another thing: Regency publishers pick their own titles. Thus her *Love Longing,* by Lola Smith, metamorphized into *The Scarlet Spinster,* by Cleo Chadwick. And a final thing learned was that romance publishers do not generally give good advances. She received $1,500, but she didn't care. She was writing what she liked and having fun.

And that agricultural history she had labored so hard over? The editor who had ordered the book, and highly praised what she had written so far, resigned; the new editor it was assigned to had no interest in it, and it never saw the light of day.

But *The Scarlet Spinster,* published in 1988, turned out to be such a success it was reprinted in 1992 and was still earning royalties in the late 1990s. Lola Smith was in Guatemala when it was accepted in 1987, and she got right to work on her second Regency, which she had been picking at for some time.

"What I did not know," she told Leighton, "is that romance novels do not permit adultery—even when justified—wife beaters or heroines older than heros. That novel, which included all of the above, was refused by all the romance publishers, so I put it on the shelf and went on to my next plot."

Let's take a quick look at the plot of *The Scarlet Spinster* to see how it fits into the rules and atmosphere of a Regency: The heroine is past marriageable age—horrors! she's twenty-four—and desperate to be married. Finally a gentleman agrees to enter into a marriage of convenience. They get engaged but the cold relationship heats up when another woman enters the picture.

Lola Smith received $3,000 in advance for her second Regency novel—double her first advance. *Midsummer Night's Kiss* was published in 1991 and received the *Romantic Times Magazine* Reviewer's Choice Award for the best Regency Intrigue of the Year.

And what was the intrigue? A well-bred young woman of a large family works hard to help her impoverished widowed mother keep up appearances. Things are looking up when an aristocratic young man takes an interest in her and is looked at as a godsend to renew their fortune, squandered by a profligate father. But it turns out that he has only pretended to be interested in the poor girl and is actually investigating her family in tracking down a spy.

The plot of Lola Smith's third Cleo Chadwick Regency—*A Lakeside Season*—is indeed amusing in view of today's standards: A nobleman falls in love with a banker's daughter and she with him, but her father is bent on breaking them up. Because if the marquis comes into the family banking business, he will have to change his name and take his wife's last name, and the father is sure the young marquis's proud family will not let him do that. The girl's father is not about to permit the name of his bank to be changed to accommodate the nobleman's family name.

Some consider Lola Smith's third Regency her best. But tired of the constraint, Smith at this writing is trying her hand at a straight murder mystery "without a hint of a romance novel about it." But she also has an order for another Regency.

Not every potential romance writer is as brimming with ideas and scenes as Lola Smith. So if you want to write romances, but don't have a lot of explicit ideas, you might try writing to the romance book publishers to ask for their "tip sheets," which tell what they are looking for currently and offer writing guidelines. For most writers, it would be a waste of time to enter this field without following this procedure, because the needs of publishers are constantly changing and evolving.

Another way to learn what is happening in the romance field is to go to large chain bookstores, such as B. Dalton or Borders, look at their stock and ask to see their lists of good sellers in this genre.

Harlequin-Silhouette is the main publisher of such novels, but any paperback publisher might like to see a good romance at the right time. It's up to you to follow this quickly changing field, or find an agent who is interested in romances.

As I mentioned in an earlier chapter, you don't have to have an agent if you are a romance author, as publishers will deal with you directly. But if you prefer to try to get an agent for your first romance, more than a hundred are listed in *Literary Agents of North America* under the heading of "Romances, Women's."

An agent who represents twenty-five romance writers—about a quarter of her clients—is Meredith Bernstein, who has had her own agency in New York for fifteen years. She sees the genre as "being in a holding pattern."

One of her clients is Janis Reams Hudson, president of Romance Writers of America, a national membership organization based in Houston that promotes romance writing as a serious book form. RWA, founded in 1980 with forty members, has grown to eight thousand members, the largest organization in the world of writers devoted to a particular genre. You might want to take a look at their book, *Writing Romances: A Handbook by the Romance Writers of America*, published by Writer's Digest Books.

Janis Reams Hudson told me that the market for romances is highly cyclic—after booms in the early 1980s and early 1990s, the market tightened, she said. This doesn't mean romances aren't being published by the carload, but just that it's harder for a first-time author to get started.

As a romance author, Janis Reams Hudson's first novel was *Foster Love*, published with editor Kate Duffy, at Meteor. After Meteor closed down, Hudson moved to Zebra (and Kate Duffy did too) with a western historical, *Warrior's Song*. A new trend she sees is romance series featuring heroines and heros with children, including single mothers and stepchildren.

Don't panic if you have trouble placing a romance novel and

someone says he doesn't want them any more. As Erich Segal, author of *Love Story*, remarked in *The New York Times Book Review*, writing about ancient Greek romances, "One respected scholar of the second century A.D. pronounced with certainty that the genre 'would never last.' He was wrong by at least 1,800 years." So if you want to write a romance, be assured that the genre itself will still exist when you do so.

14.

From Businessman to Novelist

B.H. Friedman
author of *Circles* and Founding Member of the Fiction Collective

Friedman, B(ernard) H(arper), writer; b. N.Y.C., July 27, 1926; s. Leonard and Madeline (Uris) F.; m. Abby Noselson, Mar. 6, 1948; children: Jackson, Daisy. B.A., Cornell U., 1948. With Cross & Brown Co., 1949–50; v.p., dir. Uris Bldgs. Corp., N.Y.C., 1950–63; lcctr. creative writing Cornell U., 1966–67; staff cons., dir. Fine Arts Work Center, Province-town, Mass., 1968–82; founding mem. Fiction Collective, 1973–; Adv. council Cornell U. Coll. Arts and Scis., 1968–83, Herbert F. Johnson Mus., 1972–87; author: (novels) Circles, 1962 (reprinted as I Need to Love, 1963), Yarborough, 1964, Whispers, 1972, Museum, 1974, Almost A Life, 1975, The Polygamist, 1982; (monographs) (with Barbara Guest) Robert

Goodnough, 1962, Lee Krasner, 1965, Alfonso Ossorio, 1973, Salvatore Scarpitta, 1977, Myron Stout, 1980, David Porter, 1983, Michael Lekakis, 1987; (story) Coming Close, 1982, Between the Flags, 1990; (biographies) Jackson Pollock: Energy Made Visible, 1972, Gertrude Vanderbilt Whitney, 1978; (plays) In Search of Luigi Pirandello, 1983, The Critic, 1986, Beauty Business, 1987, The Kleptomaniac, 1987, Tony's Case, 1991, Open End, 1993; editor: School of New York, 1959; adv. bd.: Cornell Rev., 1977–79; contbr. articles to mags., anthologies and reference vols. in U.S., Eng., Japan. Trustee Am. Fedn. Arts, 1958–64, Whitney Mus. Am. Art, 1961-, Broida Mus., 1983–86. Served with USNR, 1944–46. Recipient awards for short stories, including Nelson Algren award, 1983. Mem. P.E.N., Authors Guild, Dramatists Guild. Club: Century Assn. (N.Y.C.).

—from *Who's Who in America*

One of the most enduring myths in the lore of American artistic life is that an unbridgeable dividing line exists between business and the arts, including literature. B.H. Friedman has succeeded at both, but the power of the myth's possible truth is such that he finally had to succeed at them one at a time—first in business, then as a writer.

When Bob Friedman decided at thirty-six to abandon his career as a real estate executive at Uris Buildings Corp. (one of the major owners, builders and lessors of real estate in New York City) in favor of writing, his uncle, head of the company, and mentor of Friedman's business career, was not pleased. As Friedman wrote of it later, his uncle said: "Everything in your life has shaped you for the position you have and the higher one you will have. In writing, what hope of success is there? In five years or ten, you'll surely regret your decision. . . ."

I did not meet Friedman until he had written his first book and was struggling to place it. I was not then a literary agent but an editor at a publishing house, as you shall see. But I came to have a special interest in this unusual man and have kept track of him through the years.

His *Coming Close*, written in 1982, answered many of my questions about the man and his thinking, particularly his anxiety about his career change: "I make nervous little jokes to my wife, no one else, about going private."

The tension of doing business by day and writing by night and on weekends is expressed in this passage: "My career in real estate is, in itself, its extra-literary self, a way of attacking my writing. Years ago my uncle said perhaps I should consider writing under a pseudonym. I wish I could do business under a pseudonym."

Now, more than thirty-five years have passed. B.H. Friedman is author of six novels, several plays, a number of nonfiction books, many magazine articles and other writing, and he doesn't regret his decision.

How did Friedman, son of a New York shoe wholesaler, heir apparent to a substantial portion of New York—a man who, as the character in Freud's joke says, had "a great future behind him"— become a novelist? After years of casual acquaintance, study of his work and several interviews of him, I have a few answers to this question. One of them reminds me of an old New York tale.

A tourist asked a savvy New Yorker, "How do you get to Carnegie Hall?"

The New Yorker pondered a moment, then replied, "Practice, practice, practice!"

Another answer is that Friedman showed iron determination and persistence in the face of discouragement and rejection. This chapter is the story of that practice and determination, and its result.

Friedman aims at the big leagues in writing: *Coming Close* is sprinkled with such names as Shakespeare, Aristotle, Shelley, Keats, Byron, Rimbaud, Proust, Eliot, Pound, Stevens, Poe, Joyce, Woolf, Yeats, Powell and Céline. He says the writers who influenced him were Henry James, Evelyn Waugh, Ernest Hemingway and Marcel Proust.

His interest in contemporary and twentieth-century art helped shape his style, and he says his interest in jazz has, too. But probably the greatest influence on his writing is the discipline and orderliness he learned in business—how to manage his time.

He says he writes every morning immediately after breakfast, "fully rested, with more time than I need, more blank pages than I can fill. There is no help, as in business, from outside. By lunch I have produced all I can, typically no more than I did in the same number of hours during the years I wrote nights and weekends." But, in fact, he still uses a secretary to copy his handwritten material, and maintains his writing studio with the neatness of a well-organized office.

He suggests in *Whispers* the key difference between working at home and going to an office: "At home there's always the possibility the decision may be important. At business the important thing is to decide."

After service in the Navy during World War II and graduating from Cornell in 1948, B.H. Friedman came back to New York and took a job managing a building in Greenwich Village. He met a few people in the literary world and began to write. He became a client of Mavis McIntosh, a well-known literary agent of that period, and after a couple of years, she wrote him a "Dear Bob" letter, saying that while she liked his writing she was not able to do much with it. He continued to write, and after joining Uris Buildings, began to work uptown. Near his office at 575 Madison Avenue were many art galleries, and he stopped in to see their exhibitions. One of them was the Curt Valentin Gallery. He struck up a friendship with Valentin, a distinguished dealer in modern art. Valentin undertook to help in Friedman's art education, talking to him, lending him books and discussing what painting and modern art was all about.

Friedman found Valentin, whom he described in a statement published in *Library Journal* as "a character whose business was based on taste," so fascinating that he continued to think of him after Valentin's death.

A year later, "another close friend died, Jackson Pollock. He had, in his work, overthrown everything in painting that had previously been considered good taste (i.e., accepted art). In the two types—not the two particular individuals—I saw an aesthetic conflict, and later, as my ideas became clearer, a conflict between generations. This I tried to dramatize by placing a woman between the two points of view: thus the eternal triangle. My characters began to develop their own wills. The book does not end as I originally planned it to, which was to have the younger generation destroy the elder. The characters, as I have indicated, took over. The destruction of one generation by another became also the creation of one generation by another: reciprocity: beat *and* anti-beat. . . ."

So B.H. Friedman started composition of *Circles*, which became his first published novel, with its main character—and built from there. Since his character was a man of taste, how did he define him? One original and interesting way was to explicitly name the services and products his central character, Henry Lobelle, used—he flies Air France, he smokes Gitanes in France, Camels in the United States. His shoes are made by Oliver Moore, a British bootmaker in New York. His English bag by Peal was bought at Brooks

Brothers in New York. He imports three Picassos, two Braques, two Matisses, two Klees, a Mondrian, a De Staël, a Giacometti sculpture and two by Arp. He buys a Lalique ring to give as a present. He lives on Sutton Place. He drinks Pouilly-Fuissé. He brushes his teeth with a hard Kent toothbrush. He reads *New Art*. He has lemon peel in his martinis. All of these identifications come very soon in *Circles*, starting on the first page of the novel in its published version.

Later, Lobelle is shown at work, using his impeccable taste: "He lent his taste to the public at 50 to 100%. . . . He had watched a generation shift from jewelry to art: from pearls to Picassos, he had said, from diamonds to Dufys, from rubies to Roualts, from emeralds to Ensors. Lobelle could shift easily from jewels to furs: from mink to Matisse, from sable to Soutine, from beaver to Braque, from leopard to Léger, from ermine to Epstein . . . And from furs to securities: from Monsanto to Mondrian, from Alcoa to Arp, from Merck to Miró, from Kennecott to Klee, from Chrysler to Calder. . . ."

Actually, when I met B.H. Friedman, a lean, tall man, he himself had the clean-cut quality of a Léger painting. But in spite of his store of knowledge and discernment of quality, before Friedman could get his novel to its final salable form, he had to undergo a long apprenticeship: *Circles* was the *fifth* novel he wrote—the others, he told me, are still in the drawer. His first draft of *Circles* was about an art dealer getting involved with a woman artist who wants a show in his gallery. The dealer resists because the show would compromise his taste. The result, Friedman recalls, was too lopsided. Finally, in his third draft, he came up with the manuscript that was the one I saw. But the road that led him to me was indeed a long circle.

While writing *Circles*, B.H. Friedman began to use the contacts he had made as a vice-president of Uris Buildings and as manager of 575 Madison Avenue. He submitted the novel to Doubleday through George Hecht, who negotiated Doubleday's lease in the building. It was rejected. Another tenant was Avon Books, then a smaller mass-market paperback firm than it is today. At Avon, he met Charles R. Byrne, editor in chief, and others with the company at the time, and showed them *Circles* in its various stages. One of them introduced him to Bonnie Golightly, a writer and former owner of the Park Bookshop on Washington Square. Bonnie Golightly strongly recommended some changes, especially that he abandon his choice of writing the novel entirely in the present tense. He remembers her saying, "You'll never sell it that way. It sounds like stage directions." He took her advice (an excellent suggestion and a crucial decision, in my opinion) and switched to a more conventional way of handling the tenses.

When Charles Byrne left Avon to become editor in chief of Macfadden-Bartel Books, a large mass-market paperback publisher of that time, he telephoned me one day at Fleet Publishing Corp., a small general trade hardcover publisher, where I was editor and assistant to the president, to ask if I would read the manuscript.

Byrne said he wanted to reprint the book in paperback and would prefer to see it in hardcover first, so it could get some reviews. As Charles Byrne was the editor who had successfully reprinted the first novels of Nelson Algren, *Never Come Morning*, and Edmund Schidell, *Scratch the Surface*, I immediately agreed. When he added that he would offer $2,000 for a license to reprint the book in paperback after one year ($2,000 was a very satisfactory price for reprint rights to a first novel in 1962), I was doubly interested.

I loved the manuscript from first reading, because I knew its setting and background world, the art scenes of New York City and East Hampton, an art-literary-publishing-society resort near the eastern end of Long Island. I had tried my hand as a professional artist in this area. I believed that Friedman had done a brilliant job of depicting the art and literary scene. The novel reminded me of such works as *The Rock Pool*, by Cyril Connolly, *South Wind*, by Norman Douglas, *Crome Yellow*, the first novel of Aldous Huxley, and some of the works of Evelyn Waugh, Mary McCarthy and Nathanael West. I also believed that enough people would find this scene of interest to make publishing the novel worthwhile, because it not only appealed as swift-paced, somewhat sensational, sexy fiction, but also had the nonfiction appeal of offering information and opinion about the modern art world.

Though *Circles* had plenty of sexual action in it, the descriptions were discreet and never pornographically explicit or exploitative—they were an integral and necessary part of the plot. I liked the pop-art-like method of depicting Henry Lobelle's character partly by describing the expensive products he used.

But best of all, it had a subsidiary rights deal built in. As Bill Adler says in *Inside Publishing*, "Publishers are nice people, but in the final analysis they are only concerned with the bottom line— profit and loss."

Fleet made a contract with Friedman, who had no agent, paid him a $2,000 advance royalty and simultaneously made a contract with Macfadden-Bartel Books licensing paperback rights to them for $2,000.

Before describing the editing of *Circles*, the following is a description of the manuscript we received so you will understand what changes were made.

Part One of the book deals with Amy, the lead female character, in July 1961, and introduces Spike Ross, a young modern American painter who finishes his paintings by shooting through them with a machine gun. Spike and Amy make love. We go with them to the exotic and rich East Hampton party scene and meet a Bentley-driving art collector. They attend a nude bathing party at midnight. Spike, angry with Amy and jealous of the art collector, dumps his machine gun in the ocean.

Part Two, August 1961, introduces Henry Lobelle, worldly fifty-five-year-old dealer in twentieth-century European art. He returns from Europe to plan his first autumn exhibition, the work of "Foro," an Italian painter whose work consists of neatly painted circles. Lobelle is reunited with Amy, who has been his mistress, and they spend the night together. The second night, they go to a jazz club, and Spike Ross is there. Amy introduces them. Lobelle dislikes Spike and his brash American friends, but Amy invites them to Lobelle's gallery opening of the Foro show. Amy and Lobelle go to bed together again that night, but Amy thinks of Spike afterward.

Part Three describes a day in the life of Lobelle in his gallery. In contrast to Spike and his wild ways, Lobelle is completely organized—his life is built around good taste. He has even picked members of his staff as decorative elements. To me, part three is the best part of *Circles*.

Part Four is the opening of the Foro show. After it is well underway, Spike and his friends arrive. Amy is not yet there. Spike is antagonistic and gets into a scuffle with the art collector introduced in part one. As Spike is being escorted out, he swings at Lobelle and Lobelle pushes him away. He falls against a marble version of "Bird in Flight" by Brancusi, causing it to break in many pieces. Amy arrives just then. Spike asks her to leave with him. She declines, but says she will meet him later. After the show, Amy defends Spike without attacking Lobelle. She leaves alone, goes to a bar, has some drinks, realizes she has had too much and abruptly leaves to vomit, as the novel ends.

I gave the manuscript to a bright young editor, Marcia Prince (who later, under her married name, Marcia Freedman, became a member of the Knesset in Israel). She suggested a few minor changes and one major one: switch part one and part two, thus starting the novel with Lobelle returning from France, and turning the whole of the East Hampton scene with Spike and Amy into a long flashback. Friedman accepted this recommendation. The resulting novel has balance: The new arrangement is: (1) Lobelle and Amy, (2) Spike and Amy, (3) Lobelle in his gallery and (4) Lobelle, Spike and Amy brought together for the climax, which ends with them all apart.

The effect of this change is that Lobelle more thoroughly dominates the novel than before. This did not please Charles Byrne, who reprinted the novel a year later for the paperback mass-market under the title *I Need to Love* (a new title supplied by Friedman) with a beautiful seminude illustration of Amy on the cover. Bryne had been attracted to the novel for the paperback market primarily because of its sensational original opening of Spike painting with a machine gun, smoking pot and making love to the waiting Amy, and going on to what turned out to be a rather wild party.

So Friedman's career was possibly inalterably bent toward hardcover publication and more literary novels by his acceptance of a young editor's ideas on form, probably gained during her studies at Bennington.

How did the public receive *Circles*, and what did the publisher and author do to push it? Of its twenty-five or more newspaper and magazine reviews, eleven were quite positive. Fortunately for Friedman and his publisher, among newspapers, *The New York Times Book Review* and the book section of the *Los Angeles Times* published the most positive reviews, and most of the negative ones were in smaller provincial papers. But the situation was not quite as good among larger magazines: Though Friedman himself received nearly a full-page mini-profile in *The New Yorker* that was very positive, Dorothy Parker blasted the book briefly in *Esquire*, and it was roasted for several pages in *Art News* in a review-article written by May Natalie Tabak.

Publicity, in addition to *The New Yorker* piece, included "items" in nationally syndicated gossip columns, saying that the novel was causing talk in East Hampton and New York. The previously cited *Library Journal* statement by Friedman appeared in its regular roundup of statements by first novelists. Friedman was also interviewed on several radio shows.

Advertisements consisted of inclusion of the book in the publisher's catalog, sent to bookstores, libraries and reviewers; a flyer sent to major bookstores quoting favorable reviews; inclusion of a brief description and photo of the book in the publisher's announcement ads in trade and library publications; and some small ads, some of *Circles* alone and some of *Circles* together with other books of the publisher in *The New York Times* and New York *Herald Tribune*, Sunday and Saturday. One ad featured a longish letter from James Michener praising the book.

The fashionable Kootz Gallery of modern art in New York gave, in cooperation with the publisher, a well-attended reception to introduce the book, followed by a large party in the Friedmans' attractive New York brownstone.

Actually, the novel's publication *did* generate a lot of talk, and much of the talk was by influential tastemakers. While the talk was not all positive, B.H. Friedman was well launched into his career as a novelist.

Martin Levin, in *The New York Times Book Review*, concluded his review of *Circles* by writing, ". . . all of the conflicting currents in this intriguing, original book come together in one edifying explosion."

Ruth B. Solner, in the *Los Angeles Times*, January 24, 1962, wrote, "Contrast between middle age and youth is the real theme, well-handled by means of phrasing and rephrasing the sophisticated dialogue.

"The pace is fast as a young widow tries to lose the image of her late husband in her choice between a dynamic young painter and a worldly, successful middle-aged gallery owner who thinks in terms of 'generations.' Peopled with art critics, buyers, hangers-on, a painter and a socialite sculptor, the novel builds to an exciting climax right out of 'La Dolce Vita.' "

Though *Circles* played well to most of the more sophisticated book critics in the largest cities, and with a select few out-of-towners, it also had to run the gauntlet of provincial and more conservative reviewers.

H.E. Radaty in the Ft. Wayne, Indiana, *News Sentinel* said, "If you deleted the martinis, the sex, the pot (marijuana), the sex, the cocktail parties, and the sex, there would be little left in this novel."

The hardcover edition of *Circles* sold somewhere between 3,600 and 3,700 copies, and the later paperback had a first printing of 110,000 copies. Friedman's entire earnings from *Circles* to date was the original advance of $2,000.

He went on to sell a second novel, *Yarborough*, to World. He then began to use literary agent Gunther Stuhlmann. Through editor Betty Prashker, then at Doubleday, he contracted, for $45,000, to write a biography of Gertrude Vanderbilt Whitney. (His numerous other nonfiction works are detailed in the *Who's Who* biography above.)

At about the same time, Friedman and other published writers joined together to form the Fiction Collective, a cooperative group that published the works of its members. The small publisher Ithaca House had already published his prose-poetry novel, *Whispers*, and Fiction Collective published a very fine short novel called *Museum*. Both of these went into second printings, and Viking published his *Almost a Life*.

In 1981, Little, Brown published his novel *The Polygamist*, which sold 7,500 copies in two printings, received much critical acclaim and was optioned for the movies for a high sum. His novel *Whispers* has been adapted as a play; and a short story collection, *Between the Flags*, was published in 1990 by Fiction Collective. He has also written a number of plays, of which the most recent, "Heart of a Boy," was produced in 1993 at the Art Barge in East Hampton. He and producer Nick Benderoth have written a screenplay based on it. His most recent novel, *When Everyone Hated the Jews*, is set in the period of the great American Depression of the 1930s, and is with Gunther Stuhlmann, still his agent

Asked to describe his position in American letters, B.H. Friedman said he felt he was a serious and comparatively significant author of his generation—a characterization I consider reasonable, since most of his books were reviewed in publications like *The New York Times Book Review* and *The New Yorker*.

As advice to first novelists, Bob Friedman cited points he made to students when he taught writing at Cornell University. He advised them to learn by writing, and assigned one thousand words a week for the fifteen weeks of the course—less than a page a day, but enough to build momentum. He sees writing as a reinforcement of ambition and as an activity that strengthens a writer's direction.

Fiction to him is a rearrangement of experience; he believes that even Shakespeare drew from his own experience to depict such emotions as ambition in his characters. The novel is best explained by its root meaning—"new." A novel presents experience in a new way. Originality is being yourself—getting your own voice on a page.

In *Coming Close*, he writes, "I am full of ideas about moving as a metaphor for life, for writing itself. I see it, like writing, as a rearrangement of experience. Each carton is packed with three-dimensional experience, ready to be opened, dusted, replaced, reseen."

Beginning writers of fiction should publish as much as they can in literary magazines, he advises, and portions of his own works have appeared in *Noble Savage*, *QRL*, and elsewhere. I agree with this observation—book editors read such magazines, and the editors of literary magazines can be important nurturers of talent.

I asked him whether his remark in *Coming Close*, "When I write my anger is dissipated," represented his motivation for writing; he replied that the remark had meaning only in context. His actual motivation for writing, he said, is joy.

What lessons can an aspiring first novelist learn from B.H. Friedman's career? As I see it, even four or five unpublished novels are not too much practice if you are determined to become a writer of quality. Don't be afraid to imitate first-rate writers whose work you admire. But then try to develop your own voice—originality is being yourself. And most important to the theme of this chapter, just because you are a success in business does not mean you cannot become a writer and a good one. In the course of business life, be alert to those you meet—one of these contacts may offer entry to a publisher—after all, paper salespeople, printers, lawyers, stock and real estate brokers are everywhere, and they may be doing business with book publishers. Seek advice from experienced writers, and take it if you can. Persist in the face of rejections. Consider editorial suggestions carefully, as taking them may affect your whole career. Write to dissipate anger if necessary, but if possible, write to express joy.

15.

Chasing a $50,000 Advance

Ellen Recknor
author of *Me and the Boys*

Her first publisher was *Dog World*. She had been drawing and painting animals since childhood, and her portrait of a cocker spaniel appeared in that magazine when she was fifteen. In a very natural way, she developed a career of painting portraits of show dogs and fancy horses, and selling her wildlife paintings in art galleries. Her ambition was to paint portraits of the most famous animals, like Derby winners.

But during a period after a stock market crash, when the owners of Arabian horses were short of cash and she was short of commissions, Ellen Recknor found herself reading an article in a popular national magazine about a romance novelist who had got an advance of $50,000 for a first novel. With the story was an excerpt of the novel. The oft-said but rarely acted on thought, *Why, I could write better than that,* flashed into her mind.

Suddenly feeling a desperate need of $50,000, she borrowed a friend's computer and set to work—and finished her first novel in six weeks, the longest the friend could spare the computer. She confidently sent a query to New American Library, one of the publishers mentioned in the magazine article. When NAL answered her query after a few weeks with a request to read the manuscript, off it went.

Six months later, she called them, and was told she would have an answer in just six weeks more. Apparently a first reading had gone well, and the novel was with its second reader. After nine months, she called again, and was told that her editor had just left the company to become a legal secretary. Though the second reading was positive also, one of the last acts of her editor before leaving was dictating a letter of rejection. At that point, Ellen Recknor decided she needed an agent.

As she had read the first edition of this book on how to write and sell your first novel, she called its author, me, a literary agent, and I asked her to send her novel along to my then new office in Ohio. I liked it, and she asked me to sell it quick, so I sent it to Wendy McCurdy at Zebra, an editor I knew and liked.

Zebra, the main imprint of Kensington Publishing Corporation, has always occupied a special place in my categorization of book publishers. I remembered when Walter Zacharius and Roberta Grossman, its founders, came by the offices of Collier Associates in the mid-1970s, and pitched us for submissions by telling of their plans to begin publishing mass-market paperbacks. We tried them out with some works of good quality we had not been able to place elsewhere, and they bought and published them. Though their contract was not attractive, their advances modest and in early years of their operations, royalty reports often slow in arriving, most of the books earned more than the advances and kept on earning for several years.

I was pleased to think that I was getting some neglected good works finally published and, at the same time, helping a useful publisher survive, because I only sent them manuscripts that, in my opinion as a former book editor, would make it in the marketplace— even though sometimes editors at larger publishers had not agreed.

Wendy McCurdy and Zebra made an offer, and within a year, Recknor's novel, originally called *The Voice of the Turtle* was published by Zebra as *Wild Captive Fire*. As it happened, its length, 107,000 words, was just right for Zebra's Heartfire line, so the title needed the word "Fire" in it. Though the advance was nowhere near $50,000, she stuck with Zebra for eight novels and a novella.

After her first novel, Recknor's other books for Zebra were sold first on the basis of a synopsis and sample chapter, then just a synopsis and, finally, in the case of multibook contracts, sometimes just a book title or one-line description, such as "new historical romance set in the West." Because her mother had some reservations about the respectability of romance novels, Recknor published them under pen names—Caitlin Adams Bryan, Phoebe FitzJames and Ellen Archer—and constructed fanciful biographies for these pseudonyms. For example, inside the back cover of her romance *Renegade's Angel*, the author's bio reads, "Phoebe FitzJames is an avid horsewoman, gardener and amateur photographer. She and her musicologist husband, J. David, live in a restored 19th century Minnesota farmhouse with their two small sons, three pharaoh hounds, and a scarlet macaw."

What is her real author's biography? In a later book, published under her own name, it appears as, "A native of Iowa, Ellen Recknor moved to Arizona in 1977. Today she resides in Scottsdale with seven reasonably placid cats, two enthusiastic teenaged whippets, and a kindly but vigilant greyhound, Dash Hammett Recknor, whose hobbies include barking at imaginary monsters in the air-conditioning ducts." She also told me that she had attended, for one semester, the School of Associated Arts, in St. Paul, and for another semester, Drake University. With her earnings as a writer, she has been able to buy her own house and install a swimming pool.

But from my Olympian position as her agent, I have come to see Ellen Recknor's life and career not as a miserable grubbing for sufficient money for existence and some comfort, but rather as a superb example of what the contemporary psychologist Mihaly Csikszentmihalyi calls "flow" in action. She *enjoys* solving her problems by writing novels. When she has a financial or career disappointment, she sits down at her trusty computer and writes some more, and remains reasonably happy and cheerful.

When she writes, she uses the computer's marvelous capabilities fully. She rearranges sentences and phrases and words as she goes along, keeping up to five pages in her head at once, darting with the computer's ability to cut and paste here and there until all the words and thoughts are in places satisfactory to her. The result is that she doesn't have to write second or additional drafts; she just has to proof the manuscript carefully at the end to make sure there is no leftover undeleted material. In other words, because her work has flow, she enjoys it, so is able to get a lot done.

At Zebra, a succession of editors—Wendy McCurdy (who moved on to Dell), Beth Liebermann (who left to go to Dove on the West Coast), Sarah Gallick (herself author of best-sellers under the name "Nellie Bly"), and finally, Ann Lafarge—made sure Ellen Recknor's novels hewed to Zebra's guidelines. Most of her books for Zebra are what is now called "women's westerns," that is, action adventure romances set mainly in the Old West, starring energetic, colorful heroines with tough exteriors and tender hearts. Some of them have been published in foreign paperback editions also.

One, however, is a lively contemporary novel, *Taboo*, by "Ellen Archer," set in the art world, featuring a romance between a mature, psychically scarred and reclusive woman artist and a young art dealer. It is something of a stylistic tour de force in that the story is told in two first persons, with alternate chapters in the voices of the heroine, Sally, and the young dealer, Alex. *Taboo* was later published in England in hardcover.

With remarkable energy, she also managed to write two finished novels on speculation. One of these, after some near misses at hardcover publishers, was happily and enthusiastically bought by Gary Goldstein at Berkley, and was published, atypically, under its original title, *Me and the Boys*, practically exactly as written, and under her real name, Ellen Recknor.

Me and the Boys is a funny picaresque western adventure novel, written in the first person, in which a young woman recounts how she managed to cope with practically every misfortune and problem a girl could have in the not always golden Old West—a sort of longer and more detailed *True Grit*. It was a finalist in the Spur Award and got good quotes and reviews, such as "Exciting, fabulous read," *Roundup Magazine*; "A rollicking road story," *Minneapolis Star Tribune*; "An irresistible reading experience," Susan Wiggs, author of *Vows Made in Wine*; and "better than Belle Star or Annie Oakley," Anna Lee Waldo.

I hopefully sent it off to a West Coast coagent, who put it in the hands of various producers. At each producing organization, someone would call Recknor, rave about the novel and say, "You're going to be rich beyond your wildest dreams!" and then nothing more would happen. Our experiences with this novel and the movie industry certainly illustrate the maxim, "Don't celebrate a movie sale until you have deposited the check and it clears at the bank."

During the period when we were first trying for a movie sale, to give my coagent, Toni Lopopolo, something more to say, and because I genuinely admired the novel, I nominated it for a Pulitzer Prize. Most people don't realize that anyone can nominate a work published during a particular year for the Pulitzer Prize, and that it costs very little, with minimal paperwork. Thus my coagent was able to say, truthfully, that *Me and the Boys* was "Nominated for the Pulitzer Prize!"

To justify my action, I wrote a strong letter to the prize committee, saying that it seemed to me that a lot of good work was being written by paperback original authors, but that critics and prize juries usually neglected to write about and examine works published in that medium. Here was a chance to rectify the situation. Alas, when the prizes were announced a few months later, *Me and the Boys* was not among the winners, nor was any other paperback original work. But I was not dissatisfied with my effort, because the submission required a photo of the author, and thus I was finally able to learn what Recknor, previously just a voice on the phone, looked like.

Meanwhile, when not using one of her computers for writing novels, Ellen Recknor began to communicate with other writers by modem, visiting writing boards first on Fidonet, then Genie, and finally America Online (AOL).

Though she has been in contact with thousands of people online, she estimates that she has developed friendships with around two hundred of them, of whom 90 percent are writers, and most of the others are fans of her books who somehow found her e-mail address. So her modem has greatly enriched her life and advanced her career through exchanges of information with other writers, of whom many are published and some well known.

An example of the sort of help she has received online: When she tried to write a synopsis of *Leaving Missouri*, her 1997 Berkley 140,000-word historical lead title, for a movie agent to use, she was only able to compress it into thirteen pages. My heart sank when I heard by phone from her that the synopsis was thirteen pages. But fortunately, before I was forced to do my duty and explain tactfully that, even after all her labor, it was too long, she posted a notice on Genie's Screenwriting board bemoaning all she had had to leave out, and asked for help.

A professional screenwriter who uses the online identity "Max" took pity on her and responded that *nobody* in the movie business would read a thirteen-page synopsis. She had better reduce it to one or two pages—and put a one-, or at most, two-line capsule summary at the top as well, as a hooking lead. This was really valuable advice! Max said, "It'll break your heart, but you've got to do it." She did it. However, Recknor confessed to me that she had cheated a little, by making her page margins narrower than usual, seven-tenths of an inch rather than her usual full one inch, so she could get a few more words in.

To drive home to you, the reader who may one day want to sell your first novel for a movie, the importance of using a very short synopsis for such submissions, I will confess that, though I am a fan of Recknor's work, *until I read her succinct short synopsis*, I did not truly believe that there could be a movie in this long, elaborately plotted novel.

The brief synopsis stripped away the wonderful settings, the powerful characterizations, the marvelous and fascinating subplots, and left only the bare story line—and thus, finally, I was able to make the imaginative jump from one medium to another, not distracted by the readability of the novel. And though I had realized the novel was startling, and broke taboos, I had not realized how attractive it might be to moviemakers seeking to find new ground to appeal to audiences, sated with sensationalism, until I saw it in this stark new form. (I hope I've motivated you to buy and read the book!)

As of my interview with her, after ten years in the writing business, Ellen Recknor has sixteen novels published or under contract for publication and has now quite a genre spread: women's westerns, a modern romance, ghostwritten men's westerns and mysteries in a western setting. Her work has been published abroad as well as in the United States. Her novel *Leaving Missouri* made it to the Number 31 position on the Ingram Best Seller List. While nothing has as yet appeared in dramatic form, agents and producers have taken it seriously. Upon my partial retirement, she decided not to switch to the agency's new manager and now is going strong as ever with a new agent, and a new publisher, Avon, still chasing that $50,000 advance.

16.

Conversations With Five New Novelists

Every year some of the first novels published stand out, and win or get nominated for awards, receive wide critical coverage, or simply generate a lot of attention through their originality. Writer's Digest Books, publisher of this and other trade and reference books on writing, arranges for members of its staff to interview some of these new writers. I have selected five of these interview-profiles with first novelists of note for you to read and study in this chapter, because their comments illustrate in an informal, conversational tone many of the points about writing and publishing your first novel which we have emphasized in earlier chapters. Here you will see their struggles to get started, their rearrangements of their lives to create time to work, how they motivated themselves to continue to completion of their novels, how they studied the works of other writers, and their strategies to find an agent or, lacking an agent, to find a publisher themselves.

Angie Ray
author of *Ghostly Enchantment*, Harper Monogram

"I've always liked to write, but I never really intended to write a book," says Angie Ray, author of the RITA Award-winning *Ghostly Enchantment*. "It seemed impossible." Ray's attitude changed when a friend talked her into taking a fiction writing class at a local college. "The class was taught by Elizabeth George, who is a mystery writer, and our first assignment was to turn in a ten-page outline of our book. I had to do something, and that's how I started."

Although the class was taught by a mystery writer, it led Ray in another direction. "The teacher told us that we should choose to write something that we love, and for me that was romance. There was no question; I've always loved romance." Ray adds that it was more the *bad* romances that made her want to write than the good ones, because she thought she could write a better book.

She soon discovered that writing a better book was a lot harder than it looked, when she began work on *Ghostly Enchantment*. "I got the idea from a trivia column in the newspaper," Ray says. "There was a small article about how in the 1700s, I believe, a witness was once allowed to testify that a ghost had given him information about a murder. From that, I started wondering, what if a man were falsely convicted based on such unfair and ridiculous testimony. And wouldn't it be ironic if he was a ghost, and had come back." This provided Ray with her alpha (or "macho") hero, with whom her heroine would become fascinated. Then she added Bernard, the in-sect-studying beta (or "nice-guy") hero, who is the heroine's fiancé. "I used point of view to manipulate the reader," she says, explaining that she switched points of view several times and used it to intro-duce the main characters. "One of the trickiest things was that I had the heroine falling in love with the ghost and then I had to have her turn around and fall in love with Bernard. And the way I did that was through point of view." Although switching points of view often confuses and alienates readers, Ray's execution worked well. "Most people don't even notice it, but it is something that I did deliberately."

Ghostly Enchantment is set in 1847 England, and Ray spent a lot of time at university libraries researching the period and even visited the country. "There are different levels of research," she says. "There's researching the time period and there's researching insects. I had to do research on clothes and travel and eating and that kind of thing." She writes as much of the story as she can before hitting the books in order to figure out just what she needs to look up.

When she had finished writing the book, Ray sent three chapters and a synopsis to several publishers, noting in her cover letter that it was a multiple submission. Harper asked to see the complete manuscript for their Monogram imprint, so she sent it with a cover letter. "I had won a couple of contests, including the Golden Heart, and I had met an editor from Harper at one of the local romance writer's meetings, so I had something to put in my cover letter to spark their attention." The publisher called within two weeks to buy the book.

While Ray's manuscript sold on its own merits, her story exemplifies the bonuses of networking. Had she not joined that local writer's group, she may not have met the Harper editor. And had she not joined Romance Writers of America, she wouldn't have been able to win the Golden Heart Award, given annually by RWA for the best manuscript by an unpublished writer. In addition, Ray goes to a weekly critique group and participates online in Genie's Romance Exchange almost every day. "I think it's important for people to realize that writing is not something you study for four years and then you know everything," Ray says. "It's a constant ongoing process of learning. And the business side of it is a whole other aspect that you have to keep up with and try to figure out." It's not easy, she adds, but it's made easier if you join RWA and take advantage of the vast network of romance writers.

"You have to be willing to learn," Ray says. "And you have to finish the book. Someone, I can't recall who, said that if you finish the book, your chances increase 95 percent of getting published. The most important thing is that you have to be willing to really work at it."

Jonathan Lethem
author of *Gun, With Occasional Music*, Harcourt Brace

"I'm not certain everything I write is science fiction," says Jonathan Lethem, author of *Gun, With Occasional Music*. "I know that everything I write has other influences mixed in and that comes from my mixed reading habits growing up. When I was discovering fiction for adults, I was voraciously reading tons and tons of sf, tons and tons of hard-boiled mysteries and all sorts of literary fiction all at the same time. I never made hard distinctions between these categories; for me, it was all stuff I liked. The only thing I was certain of was that the stuff I liked best and that excited me the most, was the weirdest."

His affinity for the literature of the strange has had a definite impact on his work. *Gun, With Occasional Music*, for example, is set in a world filled with bio-engineered talking kangaroos, hyper-intelligent children known as "babyheads" and legal drugs such as Forgetall. Lethem's hero is a hard-boiled private eye who must solve a murder mystery before his karma runs out and he's literally "put on ice"—in cryogenic suspension.

Nominated for a Nebula Award in 1994, *Gun* received much critical acclaim in the speculative fiction field. "In a funny way," Lethem says, "it was a book that I wrote because there was a lot of talk in sf at that point about hard-boiled detective fiction. William Gibson had just been a huge success with *Neuromancer* and people were talking about what Gibson might have imported from Raymond Chandler. I felt there was a deep intrinsic quality in the classic hard-boiled voice that hadn't been imported yet, or had been imported in very goofball, satirical ways." Lethem says he became excited with the idea of applying the classic detective voice to a science fiction scenario. "Chandler's detective is already a man out of time. He's a tarnished knight from an earlier era walking around in what's essentially a dystopian future. The contemporary California that Chandler was writing about struck him as an amoral society, so his detective was a throwback. I took something that was under the surface of Chandler's works and made it extremely literal. Almost comically literal. I took a Chandleresque detective and put him in an out-an-out Orwellian dystopia. And that's what I do in general. Many of my ideas have to do with taking things that are already lurking under the surface of things and making them comically literal."

Lethem hesitates to call his work science fiction, however, because it is not based much in real science. "I tend to think that if I were writing in another language and being translated into English, my work might be regarded as magic realism. It certainly isn't very scientific in the classic sf sense. I draw my metaphors, my bizarre imagery and my pool of iconography and motifs very much from American SF and from living in a technological society. I am writing more in reaction to other science fiction than I am writing in reaction to scientific developments in the real world. I bought the ticket for a while that I was supposed to keep up with contemporary science and supposed to write things that were in some way made a nod to scientific accuracy. But as my real interest in writing emerged and clarified, that became a sillier and sillier mismatch for me. It didn't really have anything to do with what I wanted to do."

Lethem does research, but it is not usually in the sense one thinks of as research. "I deliberately provoke responses in myself with film and fiction influences. I reread novels and I review movies, sometimes obsessively, to catch narrative flavors that I'm looking to reproduce. Apart from few token investigations into bits and pieces of nonfiction information that I need, almost all of my research is reading other novelists and viewing films. For example, I have a book in progress right now that's a response in many ways to John Ford, the American filmmaker, and his westerns. Specifically *The Searchers* and *The Man Who Shot Liberty Valance*. I'm two-thirds of the way through this book and I've already watched *The Searchers* seven or eight times, and I wouldn't be surprised if I'll have seen it twelve or fifteen times in a two-year period before I'm finished."

Lethem says he is very conscious of his influences, even if the reader is not. His second book, *Amnesia Moon*, he says was influenced by Philip K. Dick, Steve Erikson, Jack Kerouac, R. Crumb and J.G. Ballard. Other reviewers have compared Lethem's work to that of Harlan Ellison and Jim Thompson, which Lethem finds complimentary, but somewhat inaccurate. "It may not be inaccurate from a reader's perspective, but those are not people I was holding consciously in mind or that I see traces of in the book myself, in terms of my own influences." But Lethem does agree with another reviewer, who says *Amnesia Moon* smacks of Dr. Seuss and says Dr. Seuss is even more of an influence on his third book, *As She Climbed Across the Table*.

Beside a few side jobs—teaching a writing class once a week and "doing a cyber-journalism gig" for *HotWired* (an online version of *Wired* magazine)—Lethem writes full time. "I try to look at it as very much a regular job, and I get up early every morning and get right to it. It always seems to me that the best energy is available first thing in the morning. It's not impossible to write later in the day, but it often seems to me there's this natural progression where other events begin to trickle in. The phone begins to ring, the mail comes and your mind begins to connect to the shallower stratum of activity. Most often I'm writing real first-draft material in the morning and doing other author-related activities in the afternoon. And, of course, the phone often becomes a big part of my work day, and I'm starting to start to talk to people and by the end of the day I'm impatient to see some people and have a life. Every day is a sort of progression from the solitary, Zen-like workspace into the world of people."

Part of that world of people includes Lethem's writers group. "The main purpose of the writers group is that it's just one of the things I do that cuts the isolation of the writer's profession. We're a social gathering, we're a sewing circle, and that part of our function is more important to me ultimately than the feedback on my manuscripts. I could revise my work on my own and generally get the results that I wanted, but it's very important to find ways to see other people, especially when you're writing full time and you're not in any other kind of workplace environment." Lethem says he attends sf conventions for the same reason.

Lethem says that, looking back, he wishes he had valued his earlier writing days a bit more. "It took me a long time to break in and all the time I was obsessed with breaking in. After I did, I realized that I was looking back nostalgically at the relation I had to my writing when there wasn't any audience and there wasn't any editor, when it was just me and my burning ambition and the blank page. There was something pure and wonderful about that time, and it will never be exactly like that again. It doesn't mean that I would ever want to give up the rewards that have come from finding an audience, but I wish I'd known to value that effort and that time for itself."

As a successful writer and a writing teacher, Lethem advises beginners to finish what they start and then move on. "I think you learn much more and you grow much more by writing another story than you do by revising the same one again and again and again. Sometimes I see young writers trying to perfect a given piece or wedded to a first novel and tenaciously revising it. Close the door on that project, put it out on the market and start another one. It's a little bit magical, but there are leaps you make just by moving on to the next project that you can never make no matter how hard you rework the one before."

Jeff Noon
author of *Vurt*, Crown Books

"It was like a release of energy from my head," says Jeff Noon, award-winning author of *Vurt*. "An explosion onto the screen. That's how *Vurt* came about, really." *Vurt* was an explosion in the field of speculative fiction, as well, earning Noon both the John W. Campbell Award for Best New Writer and the Arthur C. Clarke Award for Best Science Fiction Novel of 1994.

Vurt is the story of Scribble, a young Manchester man desperately trying to get his sister back from a virtual reality/alternate dimension called "the Vurt." The Vurt is accessed by feathers laced with nanotechnology programs, and Scribble's sister was lost when she and Scribble experimented with an illegal yellow feather. Now he must find another similar feather in order to get her back.

"It's actually a very simple story, if you look at it in its basics," Noon says. "It's got a lot to do with the Orpheus myth. It's a quest, it's a romance, it's a love story. It's all of that and it's also very weird on top of that. But underneath, at the core, you've got this very powerful, very old story which has been around since the Greeks started writing their plays."

It's no surprise that Noon's work is influenced by plays; he is a playwright himself. In 1984, he graduated college with a Bachelor's degree in painting and drama. "I decided to concentrate on one thing, and I chose playwriting because I was excited by it and I found it quite difficult. Music and painting seem to come easy to me, but writing I really found a challenge." Noon says he gave himself a year or two to see what developed from his playwriting, involving himself with the fringe theatre scene in Manchester. While he was doing this, he entered his play, *Woundings*, in a contest sponsored by the Royal Exchange Theatre, Manchester's largest theatre. It won, earning Noon the position of writer-in-residence at the Royal Exchange. "I survived on the money from that for about three years, during which time I started to write a second play and various other projects. And I didn't have any success at all. Nobody wanted it, and I started to feel despondent. I carried on and I kept writing, but I didn't have any success. So I ran out of money and I was on an unemployment benefit for a number of years, still writing, still trying to get people interested in putting the plays on."

With the money running out, Noon took a job at Waterstone's Book Shop in Manchester and found himself working with a friend from his fringe theater days. "We spent five years in the shop, plotting our escape and never quite managing it," Noon jokes. "And then one day, he came up to me and said, 'I'm going to start my own publishing company. Write me a novel.' I really hadn't thought about writing a novel before, but I went home that night and started writing." For Noon, it was a new experience in writing. "I used to plan my plays very, very carefully, but this time I didn't do anything. I just turned the computer on and wrote. And the first page of *Vurt* came out more or less as it is now." He enjoyed the process and let the story develop on its own as it went along. "I changed bits here and there to make sure it made some kind of sense, but I really wasn't too worried about that. I was just excited by the ideas and the style of the writing. It seemed like all the mad ideas that I hadn't been able to use in plays suddenly started coming out. The main idea I had in my head was to do something about virtual reality. By that time, virtual reality had more or less been done anyway. But I thought, 'I don't think it's been quite drained yet of ideas, so I'll have a go.' I made up the word 'vurt' because it was short for 'virtual reality.' I thought I would come up with a great name for it later on, but I didn't and it stuck."

Just as he didn't plan the writing of the book, he didn't really expect it to sell, either. "I'd been working in a book shop for five years, so I'd seen thousands and thousands of books come and vanish. So I had no illusions and I wasn't bothered if nobody bought it. If nobody reads it, fair enough, but it's there, I've done it and I can be proud of that. It's not that way with plays. Plays are blueprints; they don't exist until they've been put on."

Noon says it wasn't a conscious choice to write science fiction, and he really never read much sf growing up. He discovered J.G. Ballard's *The Atrocity Exhibition* when he was twenty, and quickly became "totally obsessed" by Ballard for years, reading everything that author had written. "The interesting thing about him is that he's been working for years, writing novels about Britain," Noon says. "But nobody reviewed them, none of the big papers touched them, didn't even know he existed. And then as soon as he wrote a realistic book about his childhood, *Empire of the Sun*, everyone discovered him. He's been writing these novels—brilliant books— for years! That's what happens to science fiction writers, you see. They get hidden."

Writing, Noon says, is a solitary occupation. "I think that my view on it is that writing is a lonely thing. And this can get you down. At the moment, it gets me down, because I've been two and a half years in my room, writing, and I want to get out again and work with people."

Noon's writing day typically begins at eleven in the morning and finishes about three in the afternoon, with occasional sessions at night. "Because I wrote *Vurt* while I was working at the bookshop,

I wrote it completely at night. So if I'm writing at night, I'll start again around eleven, and finish at two or three in the morning. I do my best work at night."

When he is writing, Noon says he must have his guard up against the "bad voice" of criticism. "There's two voices talking to you when you're a writer. One voice is the perfect reader. This reader is intelligent, he gets everything—every single idea, every single image, the lot. And he's saying to me, 'God, Jeff, this is great, I love this. Brilliant sentence! Yes!' Any other time, you've got this voice that's in the other ear saying, 'Oh, God, that is so boring. Why are you bothering? Why don't you get a real job?' So it's like this constant battle, and one day one voice is more powerful and the next day the other's more powerful. There's no way you can predict which it is. I think that when you get the bad voice, you just have to write a few sentences and wait. Just write crap and go back. You can always go back and change crap. As long as something's down on the paper, you can do something with it. But if you're just staring at the blank screen, nothing's going to happen."

One of the ways he combats the bad voice is to stay excited about what he is writing. "A novel is three hundred pages of manuscript, and that's a hell of a lot. That was the main fear I had, that it was going to be too long, that I was going to run out of energy. I think what you have to do is become excited by it. You have to actually want to write the next sentence because you can't stop writing. The way I do it is very scattershot; I'm just firing words down at the page and seeing what happens. If you do something like that, I think it's quite easy to keep the excitement going because you're not really sure what's going to come out next. Sometimes you write really embarrassing sentences, but they excite you because they're weird and strange."

"The other thing I'm doing is that I'm constantly thinking all the time, coming up with new ideas. Because when you reach page 100, say, of the manuscript, you're starting to think about what's going to happen on page 150, and then 200. And by the time you reach 200, you're thinking, 'Ah, now I've got to start thinking of an ending and it's got to be really good.' Once you come up with a great ending, you can move towards it. You've got to set yourself goals. By page 50, this has got to happen. And it's got to be something good, that you really want to get to, that you really want to enjoy writing."

Noon says he tries to keep one thing in mind while he writes.

"What I'm trying to do, basically, is amaze myself with what I'm coming up with. If I do that, then there's a chance that somebody else somewhere will be amazed as well. So the reaction I'm looking for most of all is 'How the hell did he come up with that?' "

Kathleen Cambor
author of *The Book of Mercy*, Farrar, Straus and Giroux

"I try to write before I do very much else in the morning and I often read poetry before I write," says Kathleen Cambor. "I find that if I read even the newspaper, my prose begins to sound like what I am reading. Where poetry is so much about the particulars of language, it helps me to let my ordinary life fall away and fall into a world of language again."

A Pittsburgh native who has lived in Houston since the early 1970s, Cambor returned to her childhood love of writing—she wrote a novel of the Nancy Drew variety at the age of eight—after beginning a career as a psychiatric nurse. "I became a nurse at my parent's insistence and, in many ways, it was the best thing that happened to me. It gave me an opportunity to understand and know things about the way people live in their hearts that I think I wouldn't have learned under any other circumstance." But with the birth of her second child came Cambor's increased desire to see if writing was a viable possibility.

After testing the waters in an undergraduate writing class, Cambor enrolled in the University of Houston's Graduate Writing Program in 1981. She then began to write *The Book of Mercy* as her master's thesis. By the time she received her degree, the manuscript was 600 pages long and she and her adviser, Donald Barthelme, were in the process of revising. However, when Barthelme died in 1989, Cambor lost the will to finish the revisions and put the manuscript away for about a year. She then turned her interest to writing short stories.

And, fortunately for Cambor, it was the publication of one of those short stories in a literary journal that got the attention of a New York agent. "She got in touch with me, told me how much she liked the story and wondered if I needed representation. I said I didn't think I was ready at that point, but she suggested we keep in touch." Cambor then contacted the agent when she felt *The Book of Mercy* was ready and asked if she wanted to see it. She did and the manuscript was sold in 3½ months to Farrar, Straus and Giroux. "When my agent originally agreed to represent the book, she thought it might take a year because it is a literary novel and that market had become more, not less, difficult. It was all very fortunate."

Published in June 1996, *The Book of Mercy* was very well received by reviewers and chosen by both Borders and Barnes & Noble for their special promotional programs—giving the book prominent display in all their stores nationwide. Cambor promoted the book by appearing at author signings in Houston, Austin, Dallas/Ft. Worth and Pittsburgh. The brisk sales required a second printing and hinted at the possibility of the need for a third. Also, the paperback rights were sold and it will appear in that format around the middle of 1997.

Now, with her foot in the door of a successful writing career and a new novel underway, Cambor's only regret is her lack of aggression when submitting earlier work. "I work hard, I care very deeply about what I am working on, but I probably did not submit things as much as I might have. I think it is very important to just keep your work out there to give people a chance to see it, even if you're being rejected. I would encourage other writers to write a lot and send it out and not be frightened by rejection."

And as an author who also does a lot of community-based teaching, Cambor does not hesitate to encourage others into a market that is already tight or worry about sharing her piece of success. "There is a lot of thinking right now that there is this tub of success and if you allow anyone to get to the trough there is going to be less for you. But I have always believed that good work finds its place, and when I teach I am always very happy to help students in any way I can—suggest markets, give them names of editors and publishers, photocopy pages, loan them books, even suggest how to go about finding an agent.

"And I really do believe that good work finds its place in the world, if you are persistent, thoughtful and careful. I'm not saying that every student should be told they are Thomas Hardy. But I think one never knows how far a student can progress and finding ways to be supportive and encouraging, especially when people are beginning to write, is extremely important. Writing is a question of practicing and getting better. There are so many stories of writers who were rejected over and over again who clearly made themselves writers by being persistent. You never know what can happen."

Jean Hegland
author of *Into the Forest*, Calyx Books

Even though Jean Hegland's first experience with the submission process left her with nearly fifty rejections for her creative nonfiction work (entitled *The Life Within: Celebration of a Pregnancy*) before it found a home at Humana Press in 1991, she has managed to maintain a realistic view of the process and to continue sending out her work. "Since then my essays and poems have been rejected by many journals and magazines, and accepted by a few. I try to think of submitting as a game of chance similar to playing the lottery. It's exciting to play and—who knows—I might win, but it's not wise to stake much on it."

With a similarly realistic attitude toward the writing process, this part-time creative writing teacher and full-time mother of three manages to squeeze her writing in during the baby's naps and after all the kids are in bed. "Of course, there are a million things that can threaten an ideal schedule, but, even so, I seem to be single-minded enough to manage ten to fifteen writing hours a week. It's not nearly as much time as I'd like, but it does add up." However, writing is not the only activity contained in this schedule and time must also be made for revision and marketing.

But Hegland begins her process with the basics—getting the word on the page. "I write wildly chaotic first drafts, allowing myself the freedom to write whichever parts of the story I've got in mind that seem most interesting, and I try not to worry about how those parts will be hooked together. I write notes to myself about what seem like significant insights about characters or plot or point of view. I leave blanks on the page when I can't immediately supply the right word or detail." Hegland continues working on a particular piece of the story until she loses her momentum or loses the "energy of discovery."

After getting all her ideas down, she then begins what most consider the tedious task of revising. But for Hegland, revising is the enabling factor for her writing. "If I couldn't revise, I don't believe I could ever write anything worth reading. Over the years I've come to rely more and more heavily on the opportunities offered by revision." Upon completing a first draft, Hegland then spends her time cutting, pasting, reshuffling current scenes and adding new ones. "Finally, once the characters seem clear and the structure sturdy, I get to do what I've been longing to do since I began—polish language, resort to the thesaurus and try to make each sentence as perfect as possible." But Hegland realizes that perfection is an unattainable goal. "Someone once said that no piece of writing is ever completed—it's just finally abandoned. I know something of mine is to the abandoning point when I seem to have reached the limits of my ability to improve it."

Hegland's novel *Into the Forest* took five years to write and went through at least twenty-five revisions before it was ready to be "abandoned." She then spent quite a bit of time looking for an agent willing to represent her and the book. "Although a number of agents flirted with me, no one ultimately proposed. Finally, I turned to the literary market guides and culled from them a list of presses I thought might be interested in *Into the Forest* and with whom I felt I'd like to work." So, Hegland sent a query letter, synopsis and sample of the novel to several dozen of the most promising presses. Calyx Books was the first to contact Hegland and express interest. "I'd just read an article about Calyx in *Poets and Writers*, so my concerns about whether or not it was the right press for my book were not as large as they might otherwise have been."

But by the time her manuscript was accepted, Hegland had already decided it was in need of further revision and, ultimately, Calyx agreed. So, she spent another six months working on the manuscript before sending Calyx the final draft. "That draft was edited by a team of marvelous editors who gave me many invaluable suggestions for yet a further series of revisions." *Into the Forest* was finally published in June 1996, two years after being accepted for publication by Calyx.

When contemplating the sale of her first work of fiction, Hegland has no regrets. "I don't think I could possibly be more pleased with the enthusiasm and attention Calyx has given my novel. The editors I worked with were superb, the book design and cover art are gorgeous and Calyx has proven to be very committed to promoting the book as aggressively as possible." In fact, the biggest challenge Hegland has had to face with the publication of her work is the need to divide her time between promoting her current novel and working on her next. "I'd like to think that the publication of *Into the Forest* will make the publication of my next novel easier, especially since the book seems to be doing well both critically and commercially, but, of course, that remains to be seen."

Even with the success of her first novel, Hegland tries to keep an unclouded view of what being published ultimately means.

"Publication is a wonderful way of validating what it is you do at your desk day after day. Being published helps you feel less crazy when you find you have to admit to the person sitting next to you that you are a writer, and being published can help you to feel more justified when you sneak away from all the rest of your obligations to write.

"But publication is also fluky and ephemeral. Manuscripts get rejected or accepted for a cluster of reasons, only some of which have to do with the ultimate worth of the writing. Books go out of print, and the remaining copies are subject to the normal ravages of time. Therefore, I think that it's important for all writers to remember that it's those hours spent at the desk, when we're engaged in the work and play of understanding what it means to be a human on Earth, awash in language and images and ideas and emotions, that is really what writing is all about. If writing itself isn't soul-satisfying, then publication will ultimately feel hollow; but if it is soul-satisfying, then publication will only be the icing on an already very rich cake."

17.

Final Checklist: Seven Do's and Seven Don'ts for First Novelists

Do study and master English grammar, usage and spelling before completing the final draft of your novel. If you lack these skills, do hire or beg the services of a literate professional writer, teacher or editor to correct your manuscript, then have it professionally typed.

Do read the works of well-known writers of the kind of novel you want to write.

Do carry a little note pad with you and write down comments you overhear that you may be able to use some day. Or ideas that might otherwise fade away.

Do make your first novel at least 50,000 words long (two hundred double-spaced pages of pica type, using a one-and-one-half-inch left margin and a one-inch margin on the other three sides). Try to avoid making it longer than 100,000 words (400 pages), unless it is a historical novel.

If you have a word processor, use a letter quality printer. Publishers don't like a dot-matrix printer. Do type with a new, black ribbon so your manuscript will be attractive and will photocopy well.

Do submit a perfect, plain-paper photocopy of your manuscript, and, no matter what anyone else tells you, retain the original so you can make more copies. That way, you always have a perfect copy yourself. The only alternative is a letter quality computer printout—one for submitting, and one *already printed* for yourself.

Do put your name, address and phone number on the title page and cover letter for every submission, whether query or manuscript.

Don't use clichés, stereotypes or commonplaces.

Don't use anachronisms in a historical novel or any novel: Jesus Christ probably never said, "Gee whiz!"

Don't plagiarize. If you want to borrow or adapt someone else's plot or characters, borrow from classic writers whose work is out of copyright. But even then, don't copy them exactly; editors are readers.

Don't submit your book without an invitation—send a query first.

Don't call your novel a "fiction novel" or "fictional novel." Those expressions are redundant. Just call it a novel.

Don't expect a reply to your submission or query unless you enclosed a self-addressed, stamped envelope, an "SASE."

Don't stop with one submission. Submit, submit, submit!

FURTHER READING AND REFERENCES

Theory, How-to Surveys

Allott, Miriam Farris. *Novelists on the Novel*. New York: Columbia University Press, 1959.

Applebaum, Judith. *How to Get Happily Published: A Complete and Candid Guide*. 4th ed. New York: HarperCollins Publishers, Inc., 1992.

Balkin, Richard. *A Writer's Guide to Book Publishing*. Ed. Nick Bakalar and Richard Balkin. New York: Plume Books, 1994.

Csikszentmihalyi, Mihaly. *Flow: The Psychology of Optimal Experience*. New York: HarperCollins Publishers, Inc., 1991.

Curtis, Richard. *How to Be Your Own Literary Agent: The Business of Getting Your Book Published*. Boston: Houghton Mifflin Co., 1984.

Forster, E.M. *Aspects of the Novel*. Orlando: Harcourt, Brace and Co., 1956.

Gardner, John. *The Art of Fiction: Notes on Craft for Young Writers*. New York: Alfred A. Knopf Inc., 1984.

Gross, Gerald, ed. *Editors on Editing: What Writers Should Know About What Editors Do*. New York: Grove/Atlantic, Inc., 1993.

Hale, Nancy. *The Realities of Fiction: A Book About Writing*. Boston: Little, Brown and Co., 1962.

James, Henry. *The Art of the Novel*. New York: Charles Scribner's Sons, 1934.

Romance Writers of America Staff. *Writing Romances: A Handbook by the Romance Writers of America*. Ed. Rita Gallagher and Rita Clay Estrada. Cincinnati: Writer's Digest Books, 1996.

Science Fiction Writers of America Staff. *Writing and Selling Science Fiction*. Cincinnati: Writer's Digest Books, 1982.

Sloane, William. *The Craft of Writing*. Ed. Julia H. Sloane. New York: W.W. Norton and Co., 1983.

Winn, Dilys. *Murder Ink: Revived, Revised, Still Unrepentant*. New York: Workman Publishing Co., Inc., 1984.

Style Guides

Chicago Editorial Staff. *The Chicago Manual of Style: The Essential Guide for Authors, Editors, and Publishers*. 14th Ed. Chicago: University of Chicago Press, 1993.

Fowler, H.W. *The New Fowler's Modern English Usage*. 3rd ed. New York: Oxford University Press, Inc., n.d.

Strunk, William, Jr., and E.B. White. *The Elements of Style With Index.* 3rd ed. New York: Macmillan Publishing Co., Inc., 1979.

Reference

Dictionary of American Slang. 2nd ed. New York: T.Y. Crowell, 1975.

The New American Roget's College Thesaurus in Dictionary Form. Rev. ed. New York: New American Library, 1978.

Oxford English Dictionary. 2nd ed. New York: Oxford University Press, Inc., 1989.

Partridge, Eric. *Dictionary of Slang and Unconventional English.* 8th ed. New York: Macmillan Publishing Co., 1984.

Rawson, Hugh. *Dictionary of Euphemisms and Other Doubletalk.* Rev. ed. New York: Crown Publishing, Inc., 1995.

Roget's International Thesaurus. 5th ed. New York: HarperCollins Publishers, Inc., 1992.

Webster's Third New International Dictionary of the English Language, Unabridged. Springfield, Mass.: G&C Merriam Co., 1961.

Wentworth, Harold, and Stuart B. Flexnor, eds.

Directories

Bowker, R.R. *Literary Market Place.* Annual. New Providence, N.J.: R.R. Bowker, 1996.

Fulton, Len, ed. *International Directory of Little Magazines and Small Presses.* 32nd ed. Paradise, Calif.: Dustbooks, 1996.

Guide to Literary Agents. Cincinnati: Writer's Digest Books, 1996.

"Literary Agents." *Manhattan Yellow Pages.* Annual. New York: NYNEX Information Resources Co., 1996.

Literary Agents of North America. 5th ed. New York: Author Aid/Research Associates International, 1995.

Novel and Short Story Writer's Market. Annual. Cincinnati: Writer's Digest Books, 1996.

The Writer's Handbook. Annual. Boston: The Writer, Inc., 1996.

Writer's Market. Annual. Cincinnati: Writer's Digest Books, 1997.

Contracts and the Law

Bunnin, Brad. *The Writer's Legal Companion.* Reading, Mass.: Addison-Wesley Publishing Co., Inc., 1988.

Kirsch, Jonathan. *Kirsch's Handbook of Publishing Law for*

Authors, Publishers, Editors, and Agents. Venice, Calif.: Acrobat Books, 1995.

Self-Publishing

Henderson, Bill, ed. *The Publish-It-Yourself Handbook*. 3rd ed. Yonkers, N.Y.: Pushcart Press, 1987.

Ross, Tom, and Marilyn Ross. *Complete Guide to Self-Publishing: Everything You Need to Know to Write, Publish, Promote and Sell Your Own Book*. 3rd ed. Cincinnati: Writer's Digest Books, 1994.

Magazines

Publishers Weekly. Weekly. New York: R.R. Bowker.

The Writer. Monthly. Boston: The Writer, Inc.

Writer's Digest. Monthly. Cincinnati: F&W Publications.

Acknowledgments

Oscar Collier wishes to thank the following writers for their help or permission to quote their work: Christopher Britton, Karen Brush, Clyde Burleson, B.H. Friedman, Arthur Gladstone, Bonnie Golightly, Niel Hancock, Joseph Hansen, Janis Reams Hudson, Susan Johnson, John Kimbro, Russell Kirk, Steven Linakis, Mark McShane, Robert Oliphant, G.J.A. O'Toole, Ellen Recknor, Nan F. Salerno, Rosamond M. Vanderburgh, Anna Lee Waldo and Joan Wolf; and the following editors, agents, publishers and others connected with book publishing for information, opinions and anecdotes; Richard Balkin, John Beaudouin, Mel Berger, Knox Burger, Lisl Cade, Catherine Carpenter, his daughter Lisa Collier Cool, Richard Curtis, John Douglas, Kate Duffy, Donald I. Fine, Arnold Goodman, Phyllis Grann, Robert Loomis, Leona Nevler, Patrick O'Connor, Hugh Rawson, James F. Seligmann, James O. Wade, Harriet Wasserman, George Witte, Ann Hukill Yeager and Genevieve Young; and his granddaughters Miriam Fitting, whose essay on using the computer cast light on a difficult subject, and Rachel Fitting, a bookseller who has helped assure the book's distribution. He wishes particularly to thank the professionals whose encouragement and assistance made completion and publication of this work possible: William Brohaugh, editorial director of Writer's Digest Books, who suggested this revision; manuscript editor Roseann Biederman; Mert Ransdell, who sold Italian and French language editions; and Carol Cartaino, freelance editor and his partner, whose encouragement, tolerance of his delays, and editorial input from his first handwritten outline to final printout were essential; and his coauthor, Frances Spatz Leighton, who brought professional zest to its research, writing and revision. Frances Spatz Leighton wishes to thank The Library of Congress with its many specialists in each field and its excellent Information Service; George Mason Library of Virginia—especially Alice Mihos; Martin Luther King Library of Washington, DC—especially Nineta Rozen and Marian Holt of the History and Biography Division; the Chevy Chase Library of Washington, DC—especially Adel Klalathari; Ellis Amburn, James M. Cain, Tom Clancy, Joan Collins, Inga Dean, Joyce Engelson,

James Michener, Robert Skimin, Lola Smith and Gene Winick. And for much sharing of anecdotes and help with research: Vicki Flick of Putnam; Dick Duane, Robert Thixton and Jean Free of Jay Garon-Brooke Associates; Tracy Kellum of Dell; Aileen Boyle of HarperCollins; Ellen Archer of Doubleday; Suzanne Williams of Pocket Books; Eleanor Smith, researcher-writer of Virginia; and Shirley Gould, researcher-editor of Washington, DC.

Index